D0211146

The Fight of Their Lives

ALSO BY JOHN ROSENGREN

Hank Greenberg: The Hero of Heroes

Hammerin' Hank, George Almighty and the Say Hey Kid: The Year that Changed Baseball Forever

Alone in the Trenches: My Life as a Gay Man in the NFL by Esera Tuaolo with John Rosengren

Blades of Glory: The True Story of a Young Team Bred to Win

The Fight of Their Lives

How Juan Marichal and John Roseboro Turned Baseball's Ugliest Brawl into a Story of Forgiveness and Redemption

John Rosengren

LYONS PRESS
Guilford, Connecticut
An imprint of Globe Pequot Press

Lyons Press is an imprint of Globe Pequot Press.

Project editor: Meredith Dias
Layout: Justin Marciano

Library of Congress Cataloging-in-Publication Data is available on file.

ISBN 978-0-7627-8712-8

Printed in the United States of America

10 9 8 7 6 5 4 3 2 1

To my teammates
Alison, Brendan, and Maria

Contents

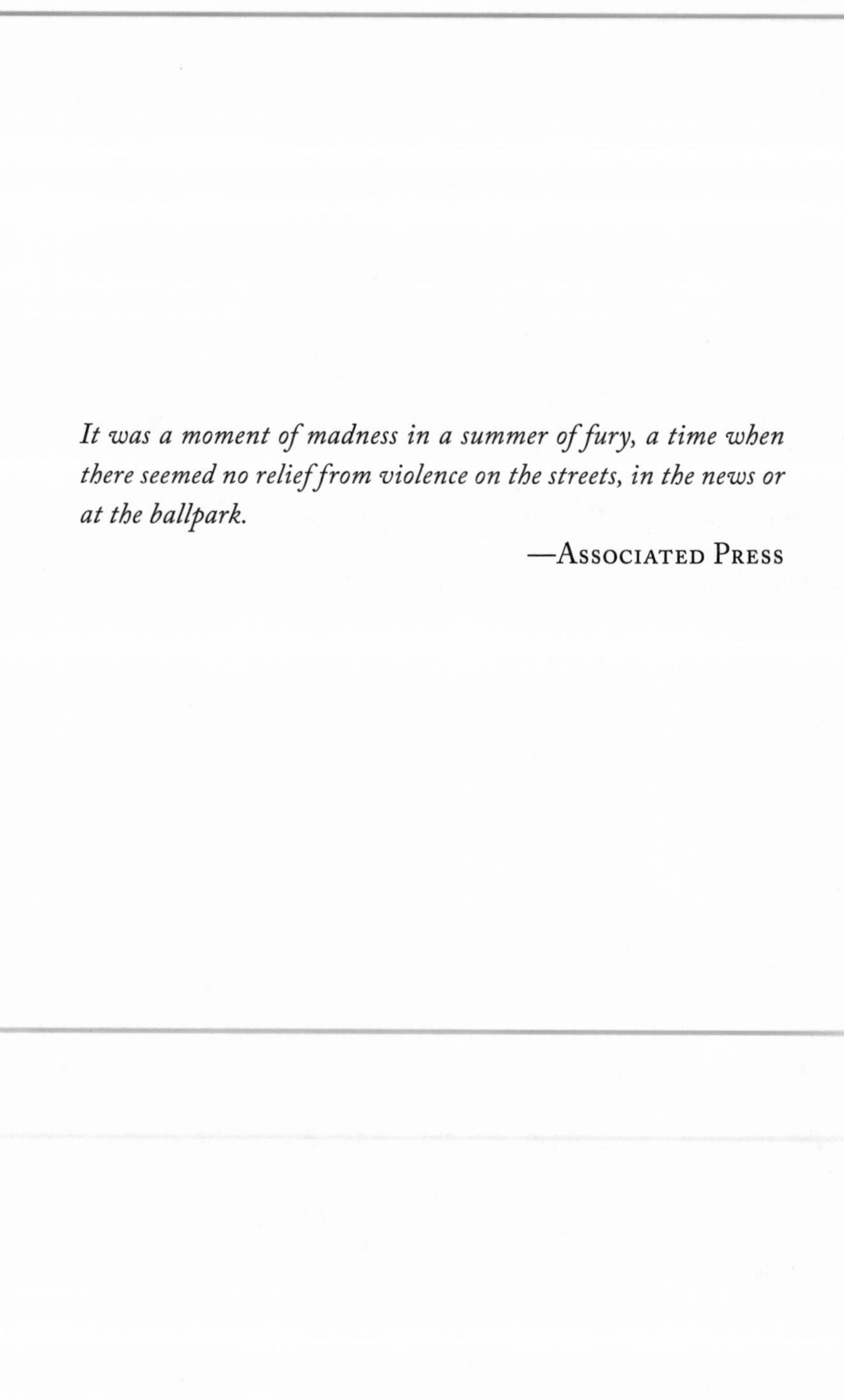

It was a moment of madness in a summer of fury, a time when there seemed no relief from violence on the streets, in the news or at the ballpark.

—Associated Press

PROLOGUE

A Moment of Madness

More than a million people were watching on television, but none of them saw it happen. Those who were there couldn't believe what they'd just witnessed before the benches emptied into a brawl. Had the batter just clubbed the catcher in the head with his bat?

KTTV had four cameras positioned around Candlestick Park for its Channel 11 broadcast of the Sunday afternoon game back to the Los Angeles area. After the pitch came in, viewers saw the standard shot of the pitcher—in this case, Sandy Koufax—from the camera trained on the mound.

That's when it happened. A different camera quickly picked up the scuffle, which had shifted to the grass in front of the plate: Television viewers see number 27 swinging his bat wildly, the catcher pumping his fists, the batting helmet bouncing to the side, the catcher's mask torn off. Other players rush in, Koufax off the mound, the on-deck hitter with a bat, the coach from third. The plate umpire moves in. The catcher stumbles to his left.

He has blood on his head.

The fans can't see this from the stands. They are too far away. They are still in shock. But the players rushing in see the blood smeared down the left side of the catcher's face and think he has lost his eye.

The ump pulls down the mad batter. Others swarm in. Some swinging. The man on his back kicks his spikes.

The battle at Candlestick meshes and crushes for 14 full minutes. All the while and long afterward leaving those who saw it and those who didn't to wonder, what happened to start this madness?

CHAPTER ONE

El Rey de Ponche

CONTRARY TO YOUR FIRST IMPRESSION OF A MAN WHO CLUBBED ANOTHER over the head with a baseball bat, Juan Marichal was a man of deep faith who read his Bible daily and carried a picture of Blessed Martin the peacemaker in his pocket. His cheerful disposition and easy smile earned him the nickname "Laughing Boy." He doted on his daughters. He was not the violent sort. Yet violence—and its aftermath—shadowed his life.

Juan Antonio Marichal Sanchez was born on a farm in the Dominican Republic on October 20, 1937, two weeks after the Parsley Massacre, when the Dominican dictator Rafael Trujillo ordered his soldiers to slay the Haitians on the border 20 miles south of Juan's birthplace, ostensibly for stealing fruit and cattle. The massacre more closely resembled an ethnic cleansing. For five days in early October, Trujillo's butchers hacked the foreigners with their machetes and shot them dead. They dumped the 15,000 or so bodies of men, women, and children in the Massacre River, which separates the two nations of the Caribbean island. Such was the world Juan was born into.

Rum killed Juan's father when the boy was three years old. Francisco Marichal left his young son without any memory of him. Natividad Marichal took her husband's death hard. She wore black for 11 years and never remarried. Rooted in her deep Catholic faith, the widow raised her four children on the 60-acre family farm in Laguna Verde where they kept horses and goats. She taught the children—Maria Altagracia, Gonzalo, Rafael, and Juan—to work. Juan did his chores faithfully in the morning and evening, when he and Rafael, four years older, herded the goats into their pens and fed them. They lived in a simple three-bedroom house with palm-bark walls and a roof thatched with banana leaves that sometimes leaked when it rained. The house had no electricity or running water. They used a *letrina,* or outhouse, in the back.

Juan wanted nothing more than to play baseball. He and the other boys climbed *guacima* trees to pluck branches that they let dry in the sun before whittling them into bats. They fashioned gloves by folding burlap over a piece of cardboard and sewing it in place with fishing line. For *pelotas* they collected golf balls from a course run by the United Fruit Company, rolled one of their mother's or sister's nylon stockings around the ball, and paid the village shoemaker a couple of pesos to cover it in leather. Some days after doing his morning chores Juan set off on the 8-kilometer walk to school but wound up in a field playing ball instead, much to his mother's dismay. A shortstop who loved to hit, Juan tormented Natividad with his talk that he was going to grow up to be a baseball player. "You'll hear me on the radio one day," he told her frequently.

Those were the visions of nearly every boy in the Dominican, where *beisbol* has long been the national obsession, regarded more as religion than sport. "In the Dominican Republic, baseball has a place all out of proportion to the normal one of sport in society," sociology professor Alan Klein writes in *Sugarball: The American Game, the Dominican Dream.* "There is nothing comparable to it in the United States, nothing as central, as dearly held as baseball is for Dominicans." In a country where the people have endured the occupations of the Spanish, French, and Americans and where many live in poverty, the game of baseball bonds communities with its shared suffering and inherent promise. "Through it the village experiences moments of happiness, when its team realizes its desire and wins or passing moments of dejection if defeat becomes a rout . . . but above all, the village experiences the hope that always prevails in baseball of coming from behind or winning the next game," Dr. Tirso Velez explains in *Nota Acerca del Beisbol.*

Juan listened to ball games at home on his battery-powered transistor radio. He dreamed of being one of the players on the national team, the pride of the Dominican Republic. One day, his older sister's husband took the 10-year-old Juan to see Bombo Ramos pitch for Los Caballeros of Monte Cristi. Ramos taunted batters, telling them a fastball was coming before blowing it by them. He had a distinctive windup, turning his back on batters, then wheeling with a sidearm release. Ramos made such a strong impression on Juan with his shutout that day that the boy decided to become a pitcher himself and began emulating Ramos's sidearm delivery. "That guy became my idol because of the way he pitched," Juan recounted years later.

Not long after Juan watched that game, on January 11, 1948, Ramos and the Dominican national team's plane crashed in bad weather near the Rio Verde. No one survived. A quickly assembled substitute team won the amateur world tournament in their memory, "fueling an emotional rebirth of the sport that has never subsided," Jim Kaplan observes in *The Greatest Game Ever Pitched: Juan Marichal, Warren Spahn, and the Pitching Duel of the Century.*

Juan had a life-altering brush with death himself the summer he was 10 years old. He fainted while goofing around with some other kids after eating a meal. He remained in a coma for days. The hospital staff puzzled over his condition. They could not revive him. After nine days a doctor told his family that if Juan did not regain consciousness soon—by midnight, the doctor somehow determined—the young boy would die. His uncles bathed him in very hot water and the family prayed. They believed God delivered Juan from death when he started speaking 15 minutes before midnight. His faith has remained firm ever since.

Juan's brother Gonzalo, seven years older, taught him to throw a curveball and a sinker. When Juan was 15 he dropped out of school and left home to live with Gonzalo in the capital, Ciudad Trujillo.* Gonzalo found work for Juan driving a rig in his fleet of dump trucks and a spot for him on the Esso Company baseball team. Juan returned to Laguna Verde in 1955 and played for the Monte Cristi Las Flores team sponsored by the Bermudez Rum Company. He helped the team win a tournament and was selected to represent the city on an all-star squad at the national amateur championship in the capital, where he pitched the team to victory.

Juan's ability to throw strikes and win ball games created a demand for his talents. A division of the United Fruit Company hired him for $12 a week supposedly to inspect banana shipments, mow grass, and water trees, but primarily to pitch. The 18-year-old Marichal, who had grown to 5-foot-11 and filled out to 180 pounds, led the Manzanilla-based United Fruit Company team to the national championship against the Dominican Aviacion (Air Force) team.

The Aviacion nine was the premier amateur team in the Dominican Republic and run by Ramfis Trujillo, the dictator's son and commander of the air force. El Jefe had appointed his son a colonel

* So named by the country's dictator. Before and after Trujillo's rule, the capital has been known as Santo Domingo.

at age four and a brigadier general at nine. Ramfis shared his father's sexual appetites and violent tendencies. While his father eliminated political opponents, the boy Ramfis blew away farm animals with a large-caliber pistol. Rafael preferred horse racing to baseball but well understood the latter's importance to the country. Ramfis's passions ran toward baseball and especially the Aviacion team he oversaw. The younger Trujillo was not pleased when Marichal stole the national championship for his United Fruit team with a 2–1 performance.

The following day at 8 a.m., an air force lieutenant arrived at the house where Marichal and his teammates were staying. The officer delivered a telegram—an order signed by Ramfis Trujillo for Marichal to report for duty with the air force immediately. Juan had no desire to join the military; he just wanted to play baseball. Shaken, he packed his clothes and went home to show the telegram to his mother. Doña Natividad said he was too young to become a soldier yet knew no one could refuse "an order from God." She paced the floor with worry for her baby. Later that afternoon, the same lieutenant arrived with another telegram repeating Trujillo's demand. "Son, you cannot say no to these people," Natividad told Juan. The next morning, he volunteered for service.

Marichal was commissioned to play baseball. His first assignment sent him to Mexico for a Caribbean tournament along with future major leaguers Manny Mota and Matty Alou. The airplane flight to the event was the new air force recruit's first. He won a game and saved another to put Aviacion in the championship against the home team. When the Dominican pitchers warmed up in the bullpen, Mexican fans flashed revolvers. Fans sitting on top of the dugout brandished knives. The umpire called Juan's pitches thrown over the middle of the plate balls. "We should have won that championship, but the umpires took it away from us," Marichal said. Never mind the loss; the Dominican team was relieved to escape Mexico without injury.

Ramfis Trujillo accepted that defeat but would not tolerate another. After the Aviacion team lost both games of a Sunday doubleheader to Juan's old United Fruit team in Manzanilla, the general jailed the entire ball club. He appointed a commission to investigate, certain that his players must have been drinking beforehand. Juan, who had pitched well in a 1–0 loss despite having a fever, blamed the loss on contaminated drinking water. Ramfis finally released the players after five days and a monetary fine equivalent to two dollars apiece. He fined the manager $50 and kept him in the clink for 10 days. "From then on, we were sure not to lose a doubleheader," Marichal said.

The air force team practiced daily and played games on Sundays. Marichal benefited from the tutelage of Francisco Pichardo, the team's trainer and one of the country's top baseball instructors. Viruta, as everyone called him, worked the players hard, having them sprint from foul line to foul line in the outfield and running them through calisthenics to increase their endurance. A former pitcher, Viruta preached control over velocity, the importance of being able to move pitches with precision. "I listened to everything he said and tried to pitch like he told me to—with attention above all else to control," Juan said. It paid off: During his 14 months in the military, Marichal lost only three games.

He was learning about baseball but still had lots to learn about life. Knowing rum had cut short his father's life and adhering to his mother's Catholicism, Juan didn't imbibe. The older players called him *cobarde,* coward, and *niño de faldas,* mama's boy. So he finally relented one night and drank with them. The next day, Viruta ran them hard in the hot sun "until most of those guys were puking their guts out," Marichal said. Viruta made his message clear before that Sunday's game. "*Mira,* Juan, stay with those guys and their habits, and you'll be one of them," the veteran trainer told the promising pitcher. "They have no future in baseball. You do. If you want to pitch in the major leagues, you can."

Scouts started to notice the hard-working kid with the sidearm delivery and excellent control. The Dodgers and Pirates tracked his progress. In 1957, after Juan struck out 16 in a game in Aruba, a Washington Senators scout talked to him but never followed up. Jose Seda, a professor at the University of Puerto Rico, scouted the Dominican Republic for the New York Yankees, who had a partnership with Los Tigres del Licey. Seda requested Ramfis Trujillo's permission to sign Marichal and second baseman Pedro Gonzalez. Trujillo had an allegiance to Los Leones del Escogido, Licey's crosstown rival.* He approved the signing of Gonzalez but refused to give Escogido's rival his top pitcher.

Horacio Martinez, who had played shortstop in the Negro Leagues and served as the New York Giants' bird dog, succeeded where the others failed. He had already signed Manny Mota, Felipe Alou, and Matty Alou to the Giants. The scouting report on Marichal read: "He is devout. He reads the Bible constantly. He has a beautiful delivery. No one taught him anything." Because the Giants had an arrangement with the Escogido team, Martinez was able to win General Trujillo's permission for Marichal to sign with them and then the Giants. On September 16, 1957, a Lincoln Continental chauffeured Juan and his brother Gonzalo, who had worked out details of the deal with Martinez, to the home of Francisco Martinez Alba, the Escogido team president and Ramfis Trujillo's brother-in-law, to sign his contract, which called for a $500 bonus.† That night, Juan was in the Escogido dugout to watch an exhibition against a team of barnstorming major leaguers led by Willie Mays, the first time Juan saw his future teammate play. He was delighted that his dream was about to be fulfilled. The next day, Juan told his mother the news and bought her some new clothes with his signing bonus.

---

* The Tigers and Lions are two of the oldest teams in the Dominican Republic, with a rivalry analogous to the Giants and Dodgers.

† By prearranged agreement, the Escogido team sold his contract to the San Francisco club for one dollar the next day, making Marichal a Giant.

When Marichal arrived in Sanford, Florida, for the Giants' spring training in March 1958, Alejandro Pompez, the team's director of Caribbean Basin scouting, surprised him. Pompez, a dark-skinned Cuban-American who used to barnstorm with the Cuban Stars, told the 20-year-old Marichal and fellow Dominicans Manny Mota, Matty Alou, Danilo Rivas, Julio Cesar Imbert, and Rene Marte that they might encounter difficulties with people in the United States who would not like them because of their dark skin. "Be careful," Pompez warned. And above all else, "Don't fall in love with a white girl."

Marichal did not grasp Pompez's meaning. He thought the old man was telling him "fairy stories" about this new land. In the Dominican Republic people were not divided into black and white categories; the stratification was more nuanced, with lighter shading more highly esteemed than darker. Ultimately, wealth determined one's place in the social hierarchy. "Although whiteness may be considered desirable [in Latin America], an individual's status is more clearly demarcated by class position," sociologist Harry Kitano explains. Though Juan was aware that discrimination existed, his experience growing up in the Dominican Republic did not prepare him for the way skin color could rule one's social life and crush one's career in the United States. He was shocked and discouraged that the team spontaneously segregated into groups of whites, blacks, and Latinos. "That really shocked me," Marichal said. "I felt like I was on another planet. I'd never experienced that."

Assigned to the Giants' Class D club in Michigan City, Indiana, Juan rode a Greyhound north with his new white teammates, though he sat in the back with three other Latinos and four blacks. The first time they stopped to eat, Marichal and the other dark-skinned players had to wait on the bus while the white players walked into the restaurant. Someone went in to order their food and then brought it outside, where they ate on the bus. The indignity startled and disturbed Juan. It was a long trip.

Even north of the Mason-Dixon Line, where Jim Crow laws weren't enforced, restaurants refused Juan and his Latin teammates service, and people sneered at them. In Michigan City the dark-skinned Latinos and African Americans could not stay in the same hotel with their teammates; they had to find boarding houses run by black families. That kind of humiliation defined the dark-skinned Latin ballplayer's experience in North America. On his first day in the United States, the Puerto Rican Orlando Cepeda was abandoned at the train station in Kokomo, Indiana. He started walking to where he thought the team might be staying. A policeman picked him up and dropped him off on a street corner in the town's colored neighborhood. Felix Delgado, also from Puerto Rico, was barred from using the stadium restroom, forced to urinate in a can on the team bus. Fellow Puerto Rican Felix Mantilla received death threats when he played for a Jacksonville, Florida, team in the Sally League. When the Giants assigned two dark-skinned players, Marichal's countryman and childhood friend Felipe Alou along with Ralph Terry from Harlem, to their Lake Charles, Louisiana, team in 1956, Louisiana governor Earl Long invoked a state mandate that barred competition between black and white players to run the two out of the league.

Vic Power (né Victor Pellot Pove), a dark-skinned infielder from Puerto Rico, had married a light-skinned Hispanic woman, but when he drove her around Kansas City—where he played for the Athletics in 1955—police regularly stopped him to question him about the white woman in the passenger seat. Another time, after Power bought a Coke at a gas station in Florida, the attendant boarded the team bus and demanded that Power return the bottle. Power complied with some choice words. A patrol car soon pulled over the bus, and the officer arrested Power for profanity. Power's teammates posted bail of $500 but warned him not to go back for the trial. "What kind of country is this?" Power asked. America's team gave him his answer. Power batted .330 and drove in 109 runs for the New York Yankees' AAA team in 1952, but the parent club did not promote him. The next year, Power won the American Association batting title with his .349 average but still didn't get called up. Knowing that Power's stylish play and his relationship with a white woman (whom he would soon marry) might ruffle the team's staid fan base, Yankees general manager George Weiss said Power wasn't the "right kind" of black man to integrate the Yankees. The team's traveling secretary Bill McCorry was more blunt: "No nigger will have a berth on any train I'm running." Yankee president Dan Topping tried to justify the team's decision by labeling Power a "poor fielder." Once Power finally did get a crack at the big leagues after the Yankees traded him to the Philadelphia Athletics in 1954, the infielder went on to win seven Gold Gloves, and he could have won more had the award been introduced prior to 1958. Baseball culture reflected American society's prejudice.

Minnie Miñoso had modeled a means of survival when he became the first dark-skinned Latino in the major leagues in 1949. "They used to call me terrible things," Miñoso said. "I had to listen and laugh, even though I was crying inside. But never did I let them see it bothered me." Marichal adopted the same attitude. "I took it because I wanted to be a baseball player," he said. "I promised my mother that I was going to be a baseball player. I didn't want to go back home and hear her say, 'You failed. Your dream didn't come true.'" So, like Jackie Robinson and Minnie Miñoso before him, Marichal learned to turn the other cheek and draw upon his competitive nature to survive as a ballplayer in a hostile environment.

In his debut for the Michigan City White Caps on May 5, 1958, Marichal had to deal with climate shock. Temperatures dropped below 40 degrees. He didn't do poorly for a young man used to the Caribbean sun, giving up eight hits and three earned runs while striking out six batters in seven and a third innings of a 10–6 loss, but he was more convincing five days later with a seven-hit, eleven-strikeout shutout over Dubuque. From late May through early August, Marichal was the hottest pitcher in professional baseball, posting a 17–2 record and a 1.43 ERA. During one stretch the sidearmer pitched nearly 40 consecutive innings without allowing an earned run. By the end of the season, he had tallied a league-record 24 complete games in 28 starts (demonstrating the durability that would mark his career), won 21 games, and recorded a 1.87 ERA. Employing the impeccable control that Viruta had emphasized, he averaged better than a strikeout an inning (246 in 245) and walked only 50 batters. His performance earned him the Midwest League's Most Valuable Player honors.

Unfortunately, the only time Marichal felt comfortable that summer was on the mound, particularly with two strikes on a batter. He did not know enough English to ask for a glass of water. In restaurants he glanced at other customers' plates for a dish that looked good and ordered by pointing to it. The inability to communicate made him feel disorientated and isolated in America. So did having to live in a boarding house in the colored neighborhood. He had brought with him a record player and some old 78s, which he listened to with the handful of other Latin White Caps such as Rene Marte, his battery mate, but after a while the merengue music made him too homesick. He gave away the records. At times the pain of being away from his family and his country became so strong that he considered giving up and going home. But he wanted his mother to hear his name on the radio, and he figured he could make more money for his family by staying with baseball. At the time, he was sending home a third of his $300 monthly wages to Doña Natividad. He prayed for the strength to persevere.

Juan survived his first summer away from home and returned to play winter ball for Los Leones del Escogido, the team that Ramfis Trujillo favored, and went 8–3. The following spring, the Giants promoted him to their Class A team in Springfield, Massachusetts, which also meant a pay raise to $450 a month. With only eight teams in the National League at the time, the competition was strong at the Class A level. Marichal rose to the challenge under the tutelage of Springfield manager Andy Gilbert, who had collected one hit in the major leagues in a very brief career as a Red Sox center fielder. It also helped to have Manny Mota and Matty Alou on the team. The three Dominicans shared an apartment in Springfield.

Even in the Northeast, Juan had to endure the ignorance underlying the prejudice in America and its national pastime. When Dewey Griggs, the Milwaukee Braves scout who had signed Hank Aaron, watched Marichal pitch in Springfield that summer, he was impressed by the young pitcher's performance, noting he "should go all the way." He also wrote on his scouting report that Marichal was "colored," and "Cuban or Puerto Rican." Juan ran to the mound to start each inning and battled batters, yet Griggs recorded as a weakness "possibly too easy going," a perception perhaps derived from the stereotype of laid-back Latinos.

Gilbert employed economics to motivate his players. He fined batters for not moving along runners and pitchers for giving up hits on 0–2 counts. Marichal paid his share. To avoid being charged one dollar, he began a habit he carried into the majors of running to and from the mound. More significantly, Gilbert taught Juan the slider and changeup, which he added to his arsenal. He also worked on the 21-year-old's confidence. "I learned to have courage and not to fear any hitter," Juan said. "He always told me I could get anybody out."

Marichal turned in another MVP performance, finishing 23 of the 32 games he started, winning more games (18) than any other Eastern League pitcher, striking out four times as many batters as he walked (208 to 47) in 271 innings, and posting a 2.39 ERA. He won an additional two playoff games, as he had the year before. "He [Gilbert] taught me more about pitching than I had dreamed it was possible to learn," Juan said.

Gilbert's most significant influence transformed Juan's delivery into what became his signature windup. Toward the end of the season, the manager asked Juan why he threw sidearm. Marichal told him about Bombo Ramos. "You're too young to throw sidearm like that," Gilbert said. At first Juan was reluctant to change because he had been successful throwing sidearm, but Gilbert convinced him that throwing overhand would make him a "much, much better pitcher against left-handed batters." When Marichal first tried the new overhand delivery, his pitches came in high. "Kick higher with your leg," Gilbert instructed. "That will bring the ball down, because the body force will be coming down as you release it." Juan practiced the new motion dutifully, though he was not ready to use it in a game that season. "I had to make the change through repetition," he explained in his memoir *Juan Marichal: My Journey from the Dominican Republic to Cooperstown.* "But I fell in love with the style and saw that I could throw more pitches and thought I would be more effective."

He went home after the season and worked on the windup with the Escogido team. It did prove effective. Marichal won four, lost two, and earned the nickname El Rey de Ponche, "the King of the Strikeout." Back at spring training in 1960 with the Giants in Phoenix, the team had him throwing batting practice every day to hone his new overhand style. In the days before protective screens for BP pitchers, one of the hitters drilled a ball back up the middle that struck Juan in the right testicle.* He crumpled in pain. He spent the next three days in the hospital with a bag of ice tucked between his thighs. After nearly a week the Giants sent him back to

* That day, because of a rash on his groin, he was not wearing a protective cup. He also was not expecting to pitch batting practice, but when summoned to do so, he was too timid to request time to strap on his cup.

the minor league camp in Sanford, Florida, but he could not pitch for a month.

The Giants eventually assigned Marichal to their AAA Tacoma team in the Pacific Coast League, where he was paid $700 a month. At first Tacoma manager John Davis complained that Marichal was inadvertently tipping off pitches, but the director of player development, Hall of Fame pitcher Carl Hubbell, told Davis, "Leave him alone until he gets to the big leagues."

Meanwhile, the racist attitudes Marichal had encountered in Sanford, Michigan City, and elsewhere softened on the Pacific Coast. "It was so different," he writes in *My Journey*. "Those people in Tacoma cared about you as a human being."

The Tacoma press nicknamed him "Laughing Boy" because it seemed he was always smiling, never complaining. Despite jumping two levels, from Single- to Triple-A ball, Marichal continued his winning ways in the Pacific Coast League. On July 10, 1960, Marichal beat the Sacramento Bees, a victory that improved his record to 11–5 with a 3.11 ERA. He had completed 11 of his 18 starts, struck out 121 batters while walking only 34 in 139 innings, and earned a spot in the AAA All-Star Game. He was excited to appear in the game and to receive the expensive watch given to each player. But around midnight in Sacramento, the Giants called. In his first major move as the Giants manager, Tom Sheehan, who had replaced Bill Rigney, summoned Marichal to join the team's starting rotation. Though disappointed that he wouldn't get his watch, Juan was delighted to be promoted to the big leagues. The next day, the team's trainer drove him from Sacramento to San Francisco.

In two and a half seasons of minor league ball, Marichal had struck out 575 batters and garnered a winning percentage of .658 (with a 50–26 record) and an ERA of 2.35. More significantly, he had demonstrated the control that would make him legendary. Over 655 innings he had walked only 131 batters, an average of 1.80 bases on balls per nine-inning game. It remains rare to find major league pitchers with that kind of control, let alone a young minor league pitcher.

Felipe Alou, Marichal's childhood friend, and Orlando Cepeda, who in 1958 became the first Latin American player to win Rookie of the Year honors, welcomed Marichal in *español* when he entered the Giants clubhouse for the first time. They shook his hand and brought him over to meet Willie Mays, whom Marichal had first seen play three years earlier on the day he had signed his professional contract. "I thought I was in heaven because I dreamed for so many years to be in the major leagues, and I was shaking the hand of the best player in the game," Marichal recalled. "I thought it was God in front of me." He wrote home to his mother about all of the players he had met, mentioning each by name. "I felt so beautiful and happy because I proved to her that I was going to be a baseball player," he said. Now all he had to do was prove himself fit to fulfill the dream.

Alou, Cepeda, and Marichal were part of the new wave of dark-skinned Latin Americans playing baseball in the United States. As a boy who idolized Tetelo Vargas, the Dominican Republic's best ballplayer of the 1930s, Marichal had not thought it possible for someone like himself to play in the major leagues because Vargas—nicknamed "the Dominican Deer" for his fantastic speed (legend had it he once beat Jesse Owens in a sprint) and a great hitter with a golden arm who starred for teams in the Dominican, Puerto Rico, Mexico, Venezuela, Cuba, Colombia, Canada, and the Negro Leagues—was unable to crack the color barrier in the United States. The major leagues' unwritten segregation policy blocked others, like the truly multitooled Cuban Martin Dihigo, who threw no-hitters in Mexico, Puerto Rico, and Venezuela and won three home run titles playing for the Homestead Grays in the United States, and his countryman Jose Mendez, who pitched the Kansas City Monarchs to three straight World's Colored Championships (1923–25). "We can't help thinking what a sensation Mendez would be if it was not for his color," Cincinnati baseball writer W. A. Phelon observed in 1908. "But, alas, that is a handicap he can't outgrow."

Not long after Phelon's observation about Mendez's "handicap," the Cincinnati ball club tested the limits of the color spectrum with two Cuban players, outfielders Armando Marsans and Rafael Almeida. Their signing in April 1911 was met with the headline Baseball to Lower Color Line? Reds Signing Two Cuban Players Is Step toward Letting in the Negro. In response to complaints about the two men's darker complexions, the Reds management issued a press release that described Marsans and Almeida as "two of the purest bars of Castilian soap ever floated to these shores." Fellow Cuban Dolf Luque, who broke in with the Boston Braves in 1914 and led the National League with victories (27), winning percentage (.771), ERA (1.93), and shutouts (six) for the Reds in 1923, was called a "Cuban nigger."

In 1947 Jackie Robinson not only integrated major league baseball for African Americans but opened the door for dark-skinned Latinos. Saturnino Orestes Armas "Minnie" Miñoso Arrieta was the first black Latin player to follow in Robinson's footsteps when the Cuban leftfielder debuted for the Indians in 1949. His early success (by 1951 he was an All-Star) inspired teams to scout for prospects in Latin America and laid the pipeline to the major leagues. Prior to 1950 only 54 Latin players had graced the major leagues' fields, dating back to the Cuban Esteban Bellan with the Troy Haymakers in 1871; in the '50s 69 Latinos joined the ranks. Orlando Cepeda, the Puerto Rican who joined the Giants in 1958, said Miñoso was "to Latin ballplayers what Jackie is to black ballplayers. Minnie is the one who made it possible for all us Latins."

Juan Marichal took note, especially when Ozzie Virgil debuted with the Giants in 1956, becoming the first Dominican to make a big league team. Until Virgil's breakthrough, Juan had dreamed of pitching for his national team, the highest honor he thought he could achieve. Now, he was about to realize the new, bigger dream. He finally had his chance.

CHAPTER TWO

My Own Little Bailiwick

Coming up Interstate 71, about an hour and a half from Columbus, Ohio, you see a sign off exit 186 that welcomes visitors to "the world headquarters of nice people." That sign wasn't there when John Roseboro Jr. grew up in Ashland, in the 1930s and '40s, but the nice people were. His family was one of only a handful of colored families in the city of 11,141 residents, yet Ashland was relatively free of the racial prejudice that haunted other areas of the country. "The Klan had been in Ashland, but since there weren't any blacks, they had to pick on the Catholics and Jews," said Joe Mason, a longtime resident who grew up with Roseboro. "The Klan had disappeared in that area by the 1930s." Niceness didn't necessarily translate into cultural sensitivity.

The other kids liked Johnny, though he was afraid they wouldn't. He wet the bed until the third grade and slouched in shame at school, afraid he smelled bad. He did the things the other boys did: took swimming lessons at the Y, learned to tie knots in the Boy Scouts, built tree forts in the woods near his house, rode his bike around town, and played pickup ball. He made several friends but remained shy and happy by himself. Though he felt accepted by them—"It didn't seem to matter that my friends were white and I was black," he wrote in his autobiography, *Glory Days with the Dodgers*—there were painful reminders that his skin color marked him as different. Like the time his Boy Scout troop pedaled their bikes to a camp miles outside of town and the camp director turned away Roseboro. Johnny had to pedal back by himself. When his scoutmaster found out, he pulled the entire troop out of the camp, but the situation made young John acutely aware of his otherness.

This was the 1940s in America, a time when Negroes were expected to be deferential, even in northern cities like Ashland. John Roseboro Sr. had arrived in 1928. He had played ball for the Homestead Grays in the Negro Leagues and with the Havana Giants in Cuba but abruptly given up baseball when his mother died—his father had already passed away when he was four years old. He felt shaken to be orphaned at 23. He went north to follow a lead on a chauffeur job for a man named Ezra Spreng, who had married into one of Ashland's prominent families. "It was five months before I saw another colored man," he said. After Mr. Spreng died, John Sr. found work driving Maurice Topping, owner of a Ford dealership. That's when he discovered Geraldine Lowery, a pretty black girl whom he often saw sitting on her front porch when he drove by. He soon made her acquaintance, and they became friendly. Her parents objected, thinking their light-skinned daughter could do better than to court a dark-skinned chauffeur almost twice her age. When Geraldine got pregnant, she and John Sr. eloped to West Virginia to marry. John Jr. arrived less than four months later on May 13, 1933. His mother was 15.

John Sr. worked at Topping Bros. Ford and later at Hoover Chrysler Garage fixing and washing cars to support his family, which soon included another boy, Jim, born 18 months after John Jr. Geraldine washed and ironed other people's clothes. "Nigger's work in a white town, I guess," Roseboro wrote in *Glory Days,* "but it never seemed like that because it wasn't a bigoted town." When Johnny reached high school, his mother took a job at J. C. Penney, becoming the first African American to work at one of Ashland's downtown department stores. "She was a lovely lady," said Betty Plank, another longtime white resident of Ashland. "There wouldn't have been anyone in town having a problem with her waiting on them at J. C. Penney."

John Sr.'s second home was the pool hall, where he went before work to eat breakfast, where he sometimes ate lunch, and where he hung out after having dinner at home. He didn't drink there; he shot pool, which gave him an outlet for his competitive obsession. An excellent player, he hardly lost. When he did, he wasn't happy. "If he got beat, he didn't like it," said Ted Jacobs, who grew up in Ashland and played baseball with John Jr. "He played to win, like the kid [Johnny]. That's how the kid got it."

The father also bought his son a baseball glove at a discount store and played catch with him in the backyard. Johnny and his younger brother played pickup ball on bumpy pastures with hardened cow chips for bases. The boys wrapped bats with black friction tape to make them last longer. Johnny used his $2.98 glove until it no longer fit on his hand. He and Jim also played softball at Brookside Park and in the schoolyard, with John trying every position and batting from both sides. He awed the other kids with some of his long home runs. But he didn't dream about playing professional baseball. He wanted to be a police officer. Or an FBI agent. Law enforcement fascinated him. It wasn't until high school that Johnny got serious about baseball.

Nice as the people of Ashland were in those days, they did not invite the Roseboro family to Sunday dinner or summer picnics.

Sundays, the family often drove 16 miles to New London—which had a black community large enough for the town to segregate its churches and movie theaters—to attend church services and visit Geraldine's relatives. Johnny wasn't into church. He preferred going to movies at the Palace Theater on Ashland's Main Street and eating 12-cent hamburgers from Peppy John's across the street. He liked shooting pool, like his dad, and playing table tennis. He learned to play cards from his relatives in New London and applied that knowledge to win money off the guys back in Ashland. Cards continued to be a source of entertainment and income for him later as a professional ballplayer.

But girls posed a problem for a black teenager in Ashland. More than 15 years before Sidney Poitier announced himself for dinner, Johnny didn't dare test the nice people's tolerance for interracial dating. "Even if there really wasn't any bigotry in that school, I was still a black cat in a world full of white girls, and I didn't have the guts to go after any of them," he wrote. When the phys ed class had a session of square dancing, Johnny begged the teacher to let him shoot baskets in the gym that period. "Looking back, I think of that as a turning point in my life," Johnny wrote. "It may seem like a little thing, but I think if I'd gone and learned to dance and forced myself to socialize with those girls, I wouldn't have become so withdrawn and shy and might have developed more personality and learned how to handle those situations. . . . I'm still haunted by the social failures of my youth."

Jim, two years behind him in school, was the extrovert to Johnny's introvert. An excellent athlete who went on to play football at Ohio State on a scholarship, Jim ran for senior class president and won with 257 of the 260 votes. Jim was the guy joking around with classmates in the locker room while Johnny sat by himself in the YMCA lobby, feet propped on a chair, staring out the window. "I didn't fit in the black community," Johnny said. "I didn't fit in the white community. So I decided to fit in my own little bailiwick and the hell with the rest of them."

John Sr. sometimes drove his boys out to nearby Mansfield to watch the semipro Negro teams play baseball. Other times he took them to Cleveland, 70 miles north, or the boys went with youth groups to watch the Negro League's Cleveland Buckeyes or the Indians at Municipal Stadium. The Indians of the late 1940s had strong teams with Bob Lemon, Bob Feller, Mike Garcia, and Early Wynn, but Johnny chose for his hero Larry Doby, who integrated the American League three months after Jackie Robinson's debut with the Dodgers. Johnny also admired catcher Jim Hegan, whose smooth, effortless style he later tried to copy.

But football was Ohio's state sport, so Johnny went out for the football team in high school and promptly broke his right leg when he tried to hurdle a pileup in an end run and came down wrong. The injury kept him out of basketball, but he did make the varsity baseball team in the spring and played football again the following fall. Blessed with natural speed, he became one of the best halfbacks in the school's history, racking up touchdowns and admirers in two years those Friday nights. He was named the team's Most Valuable Player his senior year when his nine touchdowns made him the A's leading scorer. In the team's yearbook photo, Johnny and Jim are the only two black faces—30 years had passed since the first black student, their uncle, had graduated from Ashland High—yet Johnny boosted his social stock among the white students with his athletic achievements. "Football for me was my first taste of being an all-star, a trophy winner, a hero, someone who stood out, and I really liked it," Johnny wrote. "Who wouldn't?"

His sophomore year, Johnny also had gone out for baseball. The coach, Bud Plank, a short, wiry man with a deep appreciation for the game's essentials, molded Johnny into the player he would become. "When I got to high school, I really got into baseball," Roseboro wrote. "Bud Plank liked me and helped me. He taught me more about fundamental baseball than anyone else did. He may have been a little old school, but I think he knew more about fundamental baseball than anyone I ran into in the big leagues until I coached for Ted Williams."

Johnny liked playing the outfield. He was fast, so he could get to fly balls, and he had a strong arm. But he tried out for catcher because the varsity didn't have one, and he figured he would get the chance to play at that position. He needed help from Coach Plank with the adjustment but didn't flinch at balls thrown in the dirt or plays at the plate. And while Roseboro pitched some, too, he made his biggest contribution with his bat. His junior year, he hit .588. The next year, he batted .530 and was named the team's MVP. He was perhaps best remembered for his speed on the base paths—and his reckless disregard for the fundamentalist coach's signals. More than 60 years after Roseboro graduated, Plank's widow enjoyed telling the story of Johnny missing Plank's sign from the bench canceling the steal sign. Johnny stole second. Then he missed another sign and stole third before missing yet another sign and stealing home. "But Bud couldn't chastise him because he was safe each time," Betty Plank said with a laugh. "That happened more than once—John stealing bases without the sign."

At the time, baseball was a second-class sport in Ohio—Ashland had no organized summer league—so football seemed the natural sport for Johnny to pursue. He had the ability but not the grades to go Division I. He had considered school more a place for sports than studying, a place where he goofed off by surreptitiously pelting the printing class teacher with small pieces of type rather than applying himself. When he was about to graduate from Ashland High in 1951, his father asked him one day at the kitchen table, "What are you going to do?" All Johnny could answer was, "I don't know." Johnny's only option for postsecondary athletics, er, academics, came from Central State College, a small black college in Wilberforce, Ohio, about 130 miles south of Ashland, that offered him a football scholarship at the last minute.

The Central State team had better, older running backs, so Roseboro drifted among various positions until one day in practice he was slotted at defensive back. A wide receiver—who was interested in the same girl Johnny was—caught a pass, and Roseboro creamed him. Coach Country Lewis noticed. Johnny won a starting spot at linebacker. He learned how to crouch low and drive through opponents. Even though he weighed only 180 pounds, he hit much bigger players hard. "I wasn't afraid to hit someone before he hit me," Roseboro wrote. He drove his shoulder into the ball carrier, sometimes flipping him over his back. "It was something I was able to use years later as a catcher, blocking the plate."

Roseboro lettered for the football team, but by spring his nonexistent study habits sabotaged his chances with the baseball team. Though his 1.7 GPA rendered him academically ineligible for games, the sympathetic coach still let Johnny practice. One day, Cliff Alexander, a scout who covered the Ohio territory for the Dodgers, showed up at the practice field and invited Roseboro, who was tossing batting practice, for a tryout in Cincinnati, where Brooklyn was playing a weekend series. Johnny was stunned. He had no idea how the scout had heard about him, but he happily accepted the invitation.

Johnny put on the only suit he owned, a baggy brown tweed, and drove to Cincinnati with Alexander, who introduced him to Roy Campanella and Joe Black, the only other black ballplayers on the Dodgers in 1952 besides Jackie Robinson. Campanella and Black invited Roseboro, who had never stayed in a hotel, to have dinner with them in their room at the Netherlands Plaza. Already in awe, he nearly fainted when a uniformed waiter delivered a cartful of food. Johnny, who loved to eat, had never seen sour cream on a baked potato, and here was this spread of shrimp cocktail, steak, vegetables, strawberry shortcake, and baked potatoes oozing sour cream. After they had feasted, Roseboro was surprised when Campy simply signed the tab. "You don't have to pay for all this?" he asked.

"No, the club does."

This is the life for me, Johnny thought.

He put on a Dodgers uniform the next day for his tryout on Crosley Field, afraid he might blow his big chance for free food. Manager Charlie Dressen watched him take some swings, lay down a couple of bunts, and catch infield practice. Coach Jake Pitler yelled at him, "Throw the ball. Let it go." Roseboro did—over the second baseman's head and into the outfield. Johnny felt awful afterward, certain he had blown his chance. But Dressen must have spotted potential because the Dodgers offered Roseboro a $150 monthly contract with a $5,000 bonus. Johnny signed before they could reconsider. "Hell, I'd have signed for nothing," he wrote.

The Dodgers assigned the 19-year-old prospect to Sheboygan, their Class D club in the Wisconsin State League. Roseboro joined the team in June. He had left the shelter of Ashland still somewhat naive about the perils a black man faced in the world. Other than the Boy Scout camp, the worst discrimination he had suffered occurred in Cincinnati when he traveled there to play a semipro baseball game and was not allowed to eat with his white teammates in—of all places—a White Castle. His teammates had walked out with him. Before the civil rights movement gained momentum, he had not yet encountered the full force of racism as a young African American.

The Sheboygan Indians had several black players, but the town on Lake Michigan had only one black resident, a man who shined shoes. Roseboro wrote home asking his father to send a pair of clippers: "The peckers don't know how to cut a nigger's hair, so we'll cut our own." Johnny met a girl who lived around the corner from his boarding house, the first white girl he dated. They kissed on her porch swing, but he was scared to take her out in the town. Wisconsin proved a fairly tolerant place, though one day in Wausau a white fan behind home plate harassed Roseboro, calling him "chocolate drop" and "snowball." When Johnny turned to glare at him, the man shouted, "I'll come out and give it to you if you want, nigger!" Johnny decided to focus on the field.

In his first game behind the plate, a foul ball caught Roseboro on the index finger of his right hand and chipped a bone. A doctor fitted the finger with an aluminum splint. Joe Hauser, the Sheboygan manager, was a tough Milwaukee German who had been a minor league home run king. "What the hell is that?" he asked when he saw the splint.

"I busted my knuckle," Roseboro said. "I can't catch."

"Then you can play the outfield," Hauser said. "And take that goddamn cast off."

His finger throbbed, but Johnny taught himself to throw with three fingers. He bunted more often, able to get on base with his speed. When the finger healed, he caught a few more games but played most of the season in the outfield. His .365 average ranked him second best among Wisconsin State League hitters. Hauser skippered the team to the pennant, which gave Johnny his first ring, a happy souvenir of his debut season in pro ball.

Johnny arrived for spring training at Dodgertown, a converted barracks in Vero Beach, Florida, in 1953 unprepared for the crash course in segregation and prejudice the town would teach him. Even though the Dodgers had progressively signed Jackie Robinson and generally treated the African Americans on their team well, they still held spring training in Dixie, a hostile environment. The train took Roseboro past the tourist section of town, which featured golf courses, beachfront hotels, fine restaurants, and tourist shops. His traveling companion, Maury Wills, a fellow black ballplayer who had made the trip before, told Johnny that they weren't welcome in that area. At the train station the two players had to call the camp to ask for a lift because no taxi driver would give a black man a ride. When he wanted to see a Buck Jones western, Roseboro had to go to the impoverished town up the road because he wasn't welcome in the Vero Beach movie theaters. He discovered that blacks weren't welcome most places in Vero Beach, from the laundromat to the medical clinic. White guys picked fights with blacks they saw on the street. His awakening to racism in America was much like what Marichal and other Latin ballplayers experienced coming from an environment where they had not encountered that treatment. "All of a sudden the racial problem hit you right in the eye in Vero Beach," Johnny said. "What a shock that was. I knew right away that this wasn't a good place for me. I hated it."

But if you were a young African-American ballplayer who wanted to make it to the big leagues, you swallowed hard and took it. Roseboro was fighting for a place in the organization, not a seat at the lunch counter. He made it up a rung on the minor league ladder to the Dodgers' Class C team in Great Falls, Montana, as an outfielder. He lived with his black teammates in a boarding house in the town's colored section and took long bus rides to the other towns in the Pioneer League. In the outfield he showed a strong but erratic arm—most of his 23 errors those first two seasons were wild throws. He hit eight home runs and batted .310 in 82 games before Uncle Sam snagged him in late July. Roseboro finished the season at Fort Knox.

The army shaved his head, gave him a uniform that didn't fit, and treated him "like dirt." "I hated it," Roseboro wrote. "I was always worried I'd lose my temper and slug someone and spend six months in the stockade." He just wanted to serve his time and resume his baseball career. The United States was fighting a war in Korea, but Johnny drew the lucky straw with an assignment in Lapeim, Germany. His official duty was as a mortar man, but there was not much work. His schooling in the ways of the world continued. He lost his virginity in a Berlin brothel to a *fräulein* with a black mole on one of her enormous breasts. On the base he lost the money he made shooting pool in crooked card games. His most important duty was playing outfield for the division baseball team in games around

Germany. Midway through his second season, his hitch ended, and the Dodgers sent him to play for the Pueblo (Colorado) Dodgers, their Class A team in the Western League.

The Dodgers wanted Roseboro to catch again. That frustrated him. He had returned from Europe thinking of himself as a star outfielder. Plus, the Dodgers had a future Hall of Fame catcher in Roy Campanella. When a team official told him that Campy, then 33, was slowing down, Johnny thought he was being conned. While Campanella hit .318 with the parent club, Roseboro's worries *behind* the plate—learning to handle pitchers and block pitches—affected his production *at* the plate. His average dropped to .278, and his extra-base hits fell off. After 32 games the Dodgers demoted him to their Class B team in Cedar Rapids, Iowa. The reassignment discouraged him. So did his reaction to an incident in Salt Lake.

After a game Roseboro and three of his black teammates went out to dinner. Knowing the white restaurants would not serve them, they tried a Chinese place. They sat at a table, but no one greeted them. Finally, a Chinese man approached and said, "We wouldn't mind having you eat here, but our customers would." Angered, Roseboro thought, *What makes the Chinese think they're better than blacks? Or the whites think that?* He wanted to do something. Around the country, in Montgomery and Mississippi, African Americans were taking a stand. But he was at a loss. "I had the guts for a fistfight," he wrote. "But I didn't know what to do about the bigotry."

He had to contend with the bigotry in the Triple-I League, too. At one park when he swung his bat in the on-deck circle, a white fan yelled, "Hey, Sambo, out of the way." Roseboro glared at him. "Cool it, nigger, and move your ass," the white man said. "Or I'll come and kick it." Roseboro didn't move, but he didn't stand up for himself either. Each time something like that happened, he experienced a little death inside.

His immediate concern was molding himself into a catcher. He asked Ray Perry, the Cedar Rapids Raiders player-manager, for help.

Perry obliged. He had been a minor league star who likely would have made it to the majors if it hadn't been for World War II and a broken leg afterward. Perry reminded Roseboro of his high school coach Bud Plank, a master of the fundamentals. Perry had Johnny show up two hours before the other players and work with him on blocking pitches, fielding bunts, catching pop-ups, and throwing to the bases. Roseboro had been lazy about his training in the past, but he worked hard with Perry and was a fast learner. Perry knew when to chew out his catcher and when to put an arm around his shoulder. Over 55 games Roseboro's batting suffered—he hit only .235—but he gained more confidence in his defense.

With regard to his game off the field, Johnny had made some fumbling attempts at dating women but finally met someone he felt comfortable with on a visit to his brother, Jim, who was playing football at Ohio State. Jeri Fraime was quiet, tall, and pretty and enjoyed being around Johnny. His parents liked her, and her mom liked him (Jeri's parents were divorced). They went to Buckeye football games in the fall and wrote to one another when Roseboro headed south to play winter ball in Venezuela.

Buzzie Bavasi, the Dodgers general manager, wanted Roseboro to work on his catching skills with a team in the Gulf city of Maracaibo. The manager of the Venezuela team, Clay Bryant, who was working his way up the Dodgers coaching ranks, told Bavasi he didn't want an inexperienced catcher on his team. Bavasi read between the lines that Bryant didn't want a black player. The general manager told Bryant, "Either you take Roseboro or you come home." Bryant acquiesced and gave Roseboro a fair chance. Johnny didn't find out about Bryant's resistance until years later.

Playing in Venezuela was different than bivouacking on an American base in Germany; this meant immersing himself into a foreign culture where he did not speak the language or understand the customs. The music was different, the food was different, and the fans were different. They yelled at Roseboro and his teammates, cussed at them, and spat at them. Much like the Latin players who had headed north to play baseball in the United States, Roseboro felt alienated and often afraid in Venezuela.

Johnny sought out the company of other Americans, with whom he felt a comfortable familiarity, befriending his teammate, center fielder Don Demeter, and Earl Battey, who caught for the team across the bay. He won over Bryant, a tough man nicknamed "Tiger." For all of his prickliness, Bryant became another mentor to Roseboro as a former pitcher able to show him some useful aspects of the catching trade. Roseboro ended up leading the league in homers and stolen bases, unusual for a catcher but not surprising for Roseboro given his speed. When he returned to North America that spring, he made the leap to the Dodgers' Triple-A team in the International League, the Montreal Royals, for the 1956 season. He was 22 and moving up.

The white folks of Ashland embraced their native son's success. "Ashland can certainly be proud of the fact that young John has progressed as rapidly as he has," wrote an *Ashland Times-Gazette* staffer who hadn't even seen him play. "John still has his big days ahead of him. And we'll all be waiting for them anxiously and with anticipation."

When Montreal played in Columbus, which also had a team in the International League, Johnny spent time with Jeri, who lived there. One day when they were window shopping downtown, they paused outside a jewelry store. Soon they were inside looking at engagement rings. They set a date for August, when the Royals would be back for a weekend series. The night before his wedding day, a foul tip struck Roseboro in the family jewels. He crumpled to the ground. Once he was able to limp to the bench, his teammates couldn't stop laughing at the timing of the ill-placed injury. Same thing the next day in Columbus: His dad, brother, and buddies couldn't suppress their mirth at his swollen testicles on the day of his nuptials. The injury did spoil some of the wedding night festivities, despite his best efforts, which perhaps foreshadowed the future of the young newlyweds who did not know one another very well.

Johnny made a good impression in Montreal, catching 113 games for the Royals and putting up decent numbers at the plate, including a career-best 25 home runs. Manager Greg Mulleavy, a former infielder with a brief Major League Baseball résumé, had suggested Roseboro pull the ball to take advantage of Montreal's short right field fence. Johnny returned to Venezuela to play in the top-tier league based in Caracas. He lived in a hotel downtown and ate most of his meals there. He liked the seafood and was getting accustomed to picante dishes but was often bored and sometimes lonely when not at the ballpark. He took refuge in one of his favorite hangouts, the cinema, watching American movies or Spanish movies with English subtitles. His play that winter—solid behind the plate and batting .338 for the pennant winners—attracted attention and started the serious talk of him being the successor to the Dodgers' perennial All-Star backstop, Roy Campanella. "Roseboro is the number one prospect I've seen any place," said Mickey Owen, who managed a Puerto Rican team and saw Roseboro play that winter. "He can do all things big—run, hit, throw. Sure he can be another Campanella. He can do things Campanella can't do right now. He can run like an outfielder, and on top of everything else, he's a left-handed hitting catcher with power."

During the 1957 spring training, the Brooklyn brass fingered Roseboro as "Campanella's eventual successor." That sort of talk made Roseboro uneasy. How do you replace a three-time MVP? Campanella had raised expectations for Dodgers catchers. But Brooklyn manager Walt Alston kept Roseboro's ego from swelling when he sent him back to Montreal with the comment to the press, "He can run, he can throw, he could be a good hitter, but his catching could be better."

Mid-June, Brooklyn called. The parent club needed a replacement for the injured Gil Hodges at first base. Bavasi wanted Jim

Gentile, the Royals' power-hitting first baseman, but he was out on the town and couldn't be found, so the general manager promoted Roseboro, who had made a handful of starts at first for Montreal. Through 48 games Johnny was batting .273 with seven home runs, which on its own would not have been cause for the call-up, but Bavasi said he had planned to bring Roseboro to Brooklyn anyway, figuring he would learn more on the bench with Campanella and bullpen coach Joe Becker, a former catcher, working with him. "We feel that type of experience will come in handy," Bavasi said. "He could be our first-string catcher next year." *New York Daily News* columnist Dick Young commented on this succession strategy, "They plan to force feed him with savvy."

Johnny caught a flight to New York and arrived by cab at Ebbets Field but was afraid to walk into the clubhouse. He had to give himself a pep talk to open the door to the room where Campanella, Reese, Snider, Furillo, and the Dodgers' other stars were putting on their uniforms. Then he had to convince the attendant, who had no idea who this 24-year-old was, that he belonged there. Finally another clubhouse guy showed him to his locker with a uniform hanging in it. Roseboro pulled on the white jersey with the blue Dodgers script in a silent feeling of reverential respect. Several of the players he knew from Vero Beach nodded hello, but nobody greeted him warmly until manager Walt Alston came over and handed him a first baseman's mitt. *Shit*. They had converted him into a catcher and now they wanted him to make his debut that night at first base. He emptied his nerves in a bathroom stall.

Roseboro started slow. He bunted his way on base in his debut on June 14, 1957, but it took eight games and more than a month before he collected another hit. Ten days after filling in at first, he caught his first game and made an error. He appeared in only 35 games during his three and a half months with the club, eight of those as a pinch runner and only 19 behind the plate. He managed a mere 10 hits, though two were doubles and two homers. He was scared to catch Don Newcombe, a pitcher who was quick to air his anger. "If I made a mistake, I thought he'd have my ass," Roseboro wrote. Campanella calmed him, saying, "Son, Newk is the easiest guy in the world to work with. You just get behind the plate and put down whatever you want him to throw, and he'll bring it to you."

Campanella welcomed the rookie and became his mentor on and off the field. He tutored Roseboro in catching philosophy, the art of setting up hitters and outthinking them. They roomed together on the road. Campy taught Rosey how to treat fans, how to talk to the press, how to order in restaurants, how to shop for a big leaguer's wardrobe, and how to carry himself. He invited Jeri and Johnny to join him and his wife for weekend outings on his yacht up the Hudson and had them over for dinner. Johnny warmed instantly to Campanella's *bonhomie* and considered him, 12 years his senior, a second father.

Campanella had not had a good season the previous year. The summer of '57 confirmed his decline. The 35-year-old had started only 94 games behind the plate, and while he was still steady defensively, his offense had fallen off dramatically the past two years, in large part because his left hand was so mangled after a decade catching that he could barely grip the bat. Talk of Roseboro replacing him became more urgent, though Johnny didn't believe it. He had spent most of his time in the bullpen warming up pitchers and hardly looked like the heir apparent to the future Hall of Famer.

Roseboro had not played much during his rookie season, but an incident in a game he caught against Milwaukee showed that the young man from Ashland had the intestinal fortitude of a major leaguer. With two strikes on the Braves shortstop Johnny Logan, Roseboro set up inside and thumped his glove loudly behind Logan's ear, but called for a curve. When the pitch started inside, Logan backed out of the box, only to watch the ball break over the plate for a called third strike. Embarrassed, Logan turned on Roseboro and said, "What are you, one of those wise-ass rookies?" Logan had a reputation as a feisty player. That frightened Roseboro, but he didn't want to show it. He stood up, ripped off his mask, and glared at Logan. The plate ump pushed between them before they could fire their fists. Roseboro had made his point. He wouldn't back down, not even when scared.

Johnny and Jeri had found an apartment in Brooklyn's Bedford-Stuyvesant neighborhood, which was poor and black but not dangerous then. They liked the city life and enjoyed taking in the sights such as the Empire State Building and the Statue of Liberty. Best of all for Johnny was the chance to be part of the Dodgers tradition in Brooklyn. But before the season ended, Dodgers owner Walter O'Malley announced the team's move to Los Angeles along with the New York Giants' departure for San Francisco. Roseboro was there for the final game at Ebbets Field, when the Dodgers shut out the Pirates, organist Gladys Goodding played "Auld Lang Syne," and many fans wept. Johnny had been there long enough to know what a special place the ballpark and its fans were and was grateful to be part of it, though sorry to leave so soon.

He went to Los Angeles via Venezuela. He brought Jeri for another season in Caracas, which made it a working vacation. The team played three days, then had three days off. The young couple shopped, attended a bullfight, lounged on the beach, and traveled some. Johnny was playing well, but the political scene soured the vacation atmosphere. They heard rumblings of revolution, with discontent mounting toward the dictator Marcos Perez Jimenez. One night Roseboro's team played with tanks lined outside the stadium amid rumors that an uprising would take place at the ballpark. It didn't, but no one liked playing under those conditions. Johnny and Jeri decided to leave early and go home for Christmas. Just in time, in fact, because less than a month later a coup d'état ousted Perez. Roseboro's teammates in Caracas were pinned in their hotel by the gunfire in the streets outside.

Five days later, Roseboro learned worse news. On January 28, 1958, he was still in bed upstairs at his parents' house when his mother heard it on the radio and called up to him. "Roy Campanella crashed his car." He was badly hurt and taken to a hospital in New York. Johnny was shocked. He phoned the hospital but couldn't get through. The diagnosis eventually came out: Campanella was paralyzed from the neck down. He would never play baseball again. The news devastated Roseboro. He loved Campy almost as much as his own father. And now he had to do his job.

CHAPTER THREE

The Pride of the Dominican

After a week of throwing batting practice, Marichal made his first start for the Giants on July 19, 1960. Until his call-up, the only major league games he had watched had been on television. Now he had to perform in front of 13,279 fans at Candlestick Park on a cold and windy night, the type of weather he did not favor. Giants catcher Hobie Landrith ran through the Phillies lineup with him before the game, but Juan did not recognize any of the opposing hitters.

When he heard his own name announced throughout the cavernous stadium, Juan felt an unfamiliar chill of nerves that nearly paralyzed him. He threw his warm-up pitches uncertain that he would be able to pitch in that condition. But when the Phillies leadoff batter Ruben Amaro dug in, a calm settled on Marichal, and he struck out his man. He fanned the next batter as well. Through six innings Marichal modeled perfection, retiring the first 18 batters.

With one out in the seventh, an error by the Giants shortstop gave the Phillies their first baserunner and a walk gave them another. Juan still had a no-hitter with two outs in the eighth when pinch hitter Clay Dalrymple plopped a "dying quail" into center field for a single. Juan calmly retired the next four batters to finish the game with a 2–0 victory. The Candlestick crowd rose to its feet with applause when he walked off the field after the final out. His one-hit shutout marked one of the most impressive major league debuts ever seen. Serving up a mix of fastballs, curveballs, screwballs, and sliders with his overhand delivery, Marichal had walked just 1 batter and struck out 12. Phillies manager Gene Mauch praised the rookie: "He changed speeds tonight better than any pitcher I've seen this year."

Juan had not been thinking about his no-hitter. He just wanted to pitch the entire game to win it for the Giants and prove himself. His fine performance gave him the confidence he needed to stay in the big leagues. "It established me," he wrote in *My Journey*. "I knew then that I belonged with the Giants and that I wouldn't have to go back to the minor leagues."

The Giants recognized they had something special in Marichal, and so did others. The *New York Sun* headline the next day read Marichal May Turn Out to be the Miracle Giants Need (to revive their pennant hopes). Another paper said of the 22-year-old rookie with the baby face, "And a little child shall lead them." After his second game, a four-hit, 3–1 complete game win over the first-place Pirates, Smoky Burgess, Pittsburgh's All-Star catcher, described Marichal as a "guy who throws like he's thirty-one instead of twenty-one," and after Juan won his third start 3–2 in 10 innings over the second-place Braves, Hank Aaron said Marichal was "faster than Walter Johnson."

Juan's second start had been broadcast in the Dominican Republic over the Caribbean network, the first play-by-play sent out of the United States by Western Union. Finally, his mother heard the name of her son, the professional ballplayer, on the radio. Dominicans celebrated his success. So began a long devotion to Marichal.

But Juan discovered that making it in the big leagues required more than just good stuff and a competitive spirit. The newspaper reporters dwelled on his complexion, "skin color of a new penny"; referred to him with diminutive stereotypes, such as the "sunny señor" and "cool caballero"; and seemed to make a point of quoting him in his broken English and giving his accent phonetic spellings, the way they had with Pittsburgh Pirates star Roberto Clemente. The press's portrayal reflected the prevailing North American attitude of superiority and a ready willingness to lampoon Latin culture. Television audiences laughed at Ricky Ricardo's heavily accented malaprops on *I Love Lucy*, and newspaper cartoons poked fun at Hispanic pronunciations of English words.

The rise in the number of Latin major league ballplayers during the 1950s exposed inflated stereotypes and prejudices. While players like Marichal struggled to adapt to a foreign language, navigate the alien practice of Jim Crow segregation, comprehend different coaching styles, and discern the varied nuances of social interactions, they also faced scorn largely born of ignorance about cultures south of Texas at a time when Hispanics composed only about 3.25 percent of the US population. Cincinnati Reds pitcher and pioneering baseball memoirist Jim Brosnan displayed this ignorance and the patronizing attitude that often accompanied it in his account of the 1961 season with this comment: "Venezuelans, like most Latin Americans, seem to prefer vigorous, bloody revolutions to the dull peace and platitudes of U.S.–style democracy, but they do love baseball. Ergo, they can't be all bad." In his sweeping generalization he ignored the fact that the United States backed many of those "bloody revolutions" and exercised the grandiosity so often expressed toward Latin culture.

The larger numbers of dark-skinned Latinos playing in North America seemed to intensify the perceived threat they posed, ready to take roster spots that had been traditionally reserved for white American players; the resistance grew with their numbers. Latin players were thrown at, spat upon, and spiked on the field; in the clubhouse they were shunned and regarded with suspicion. "It's not shocking that there is an undercurrent of feeling in baseball for the growing roster of Spanish-speaking ballplayers," Leonard Shecter wrote in his *New York Post* column in June 1961. "What does bring you up sharply, though, is how ready to erupt these feelings are; that so many players speak as though all the cliché prejudices are accepted facts of life." He quoted one player from the Minnesota Twins, which had seven Latinos on its team, as saying, "You don't know what they hell they're saying, whether they're laughing at you or what. They're in America, let 'em talk American."

The prejudice could eclipse opportunity. Also, seeking a better life than their native poverty—common to many of the Latin prospects—and not understanding English exposed them to exploitation. When the major league teams swooped into places like the Dominican Republic to harvest talent in the '50s, "they never saw Latin American baseball as anything but a backwater and believed they were doing the poor people a favor by giving them an opportunity to play ball in the major leagues—an opportunity for which most North Americans would have given anything, and one that the Dominicans welcomed just as eagerly," Alan Klein writes in *Sugarball.* Joe Cambria, the Washington Senators' only official scout, who reportedly discovered 400 Cuban prospects, often signed them to blank contracts and filled in the salary amounts later. The prevailing belief among Latinos was that they were paid less than white American players of equal ability. "Baseball is a business, a 100 percent capitalist business, and if the opportunity is there for exploitation, there will be exploitation," said Felipe Alou, who played 17 years in the majors and managed in the bigs another 14.

Just like African-American ballplayers in the post–Jackie Robinson era, dark-skinned Latin players had to work harder than their

Caucasian counterparts to make teams and get the recognition they deserved. Roberto Clemente, who described his position in the United States as being a double minority, was discouraged that he got overlooked for his accomplishments, ranking only eighth in the MVP voting in 1960 after batting .314 for the season and helping his team win the World Series; he was overshadowed in the local papers by white teammates Dick Groat and Ralph Hoak. "Roberto was as valuable as either of them," said Bill Mazeroski, the Pirate who hit the home run that won the Series.

For the dark-skinned Latino, the prejudice carried a double edge: He was derided as an "idiot nigger," dismissed first for the color of his skin, then for his perceived stupidity if he didn't speak English and had difficulty reading foreign social cues. "While Latins and American blacks confront racism together, Latins alone deal with the additional trauma of acculturation," notes historian Samuel Regalado in *Viva Baseball! Latin Major Leaguers and Their Special Hunger.* In a variation on its exploitation, Major League Baseball seemed to regard the Latin players as nothing more than seasonal migrant workers. "The baseball establishment has always treated Latin Americans as strangers and has tried to keep them at arm's length," remarked Happy Chandler, who was the commissioner when Robinson debuted in 1947. That stance left the players resigned to a permanent status as outsiders. "One fact that Latins must never forget is that as ballplayers, we were, are, and always will be foreigners in America and cannot hope that we will ever be totally accepted," Alou said. Tony Oliva, a dark-skinned Cuban who would win three American League batting titles with the Twins from 1964 to1976, remarked, "We are like some stray dog."

Not surprisingly, Latin players were rarely able to cash in on endorsement deals. Baseball historian Jules Tygiel, author of *Baseball's Great Experiment: Jackie Robinson and His Legacy,* observed in 1996, "While it's probably not what it was years ago, the American players, both black and white, get more endorsements and the fans relate to them more than the Hispanic players." After he had established himself as one of the game's superstars but only managed to land a radio spot plugging apple juice, Marichal said in 1964, "I think there is a prejudice against those of us from other countries. It isn't a racial thing, so much. It is more that we are strange to you and even among those who are in the game, there is a feeling we are different. We do not get so many opportunities, I think, as we should."

When he did get the opportunities, the spots were more demeaning than lucrative, such as one promoting apple juice for a San Francisco company that made him sound like a Ricky Ricardo knockoff. "Where I come from, I do not know about apple juice," Marichal said on the radio. "No, it is strange to me. But here I learn to dreenk it and now I dreenk it every day. It makes me feel VERY good. My arm, it makes it stronger. Thees is what it do for me! I am glad to learn to dreenk apple juice."

Such were the pejorative attitudes of America and the conditions of Major League Baseball when Marichal made his debut in July 1960. He was confronted by the range of stereotypes about Latin players—that they didn't hustle, didn't mind losing, quit when behind, feigned injuries, and, perhaps most damaging, were hot-blooded, quick-tempered types prone to violence. The latter was an assumption built upon unfortunate occurrences, beginning with Dolf Luque in 1922. "The first great Latin pitcher, Dolf Luque of the Cincinnati Reds, had authored the lasting stereotype when he charged from the mound in 1922 to hit Casey Stengel on the New York Giants bench in the old Crosley Field," Peter C. Bjarkman writes in *The Elysian Fields Quarterly*. "It had taken a host of officers to subdue the enraged bat-wielding Luque once he charged back upon the diamond after an initial ejection from the field of play." That led many Americans to conclude, *That's just the way they are.*

Luque birthed a stereotype unfortunately reinforced by further incidents. The Giants' Puerto Rican pitcher Ruben Gomez gained notoriety as the "beanball king" of the 1950s. In a July 1956 game, Milwaukee Braves slugger Joe Adcock approached the mound after Gomez hit him on the wrist with a pitch. Gomez fired the ball at Adcock, then raced off the field with the slugger in pursuit. Gomez returned to the Giants dugout brandishing a switchblade or an ice pick, depending on who tells the story. Two years later, after Pirates manager Danny Murtaugh ordered his pitcher to throw at Gomez, the rookie Orlando Cepeda, Gomez's teammate and countryman, went after Murtaugh with a bat. In both situations, the players were stopped by teammates before they could strike their targets, but they inflicted a wound upon the image of the Latin ballplayer. "They call us hot-tempered and say that we don't play under control—that we are too emotional," Marichal later said. "But there are a lot of American players that do the same. It's part of the game. It's the excitement that makes you act like that."*

Juan started 11 games for the Giants that summer of 1960. After winning his first three games, he went 3–2 with a 2.66 ERA during the remainder of the season. He continued to pitch with remarkable control in his inaugural year, walking only 28 batters in 81.1 innings. He did not prove to be the miracle the Giants needed—the team finished 16 games back, in fifth place—but his success endeared him to the Dominicans who listened to his games broadcast over the radio. He returned to the Dominican Republic that fall a hero. In a place where baseball was a source of national pride, he had served his countrymen well. He was a popular starter for the Escogido *nueve* that winter.

After his call-up, Juan had experienced back pain that flared so severely at times he had to sleep on the floor. Giants manager

* In 1955 Gomez also had a fistfight with Willie Mays when they played winter ball in Puerto Rico. Before a game in San Juan, Mays decked Gomez with a right.

Tom Sheehan sent him to see specialists in several cities, but none was able to diagnosis the source of Marichal's pain. It eventually subsided, though it marked the beginning of a variety of strange ailments that would trouble Marichal throughout his career—and not all of his managers would be as sympathetic as Sheehan.

Marichal began the 1961 campaign as a regular in the Giants starting rotation. He did not dominate that season as he had the first three games the previous summer. The 23-year-old pitcher still had plenty to learn about pitching to hitters like Frank Robinson, Hank Aaron, and Roberto Clemente. He finished a third of his 27 starts, going 13–10 with a 3.89 ERA. He missed seven starts because his back again troubled him. His season ended on September 9, when the Dodgers' Duke Snider accidentally spiked him in the heel while Marichal was covering first base and nearly tore Juan's Achilles tendon. His heel felt strong enough to pitch again, but Alvin Dark, who took over as the Giants manager that season, decided to sit him with San Francisco out of the pennant race once again. "This gave Dark an excuse not only to keep me out for the rest of the year but to insist that I do no pitching in the Dominican winter league," Marichal wrote in his first memoir, *A Pitcher's Story*. Though Marichal was not one to speak out against his managers, he insinuated his frustration with Dark's mandate. Dark and Larry Jansen, the Giants pitching coach, thought pitching the previous winter had worn out Marichal and accounted for his modest performance in 1961. Marichal's relationship with Dark would be turbulent over the next three years.

During the '61 season Felipe Alou set up his brother Matty, Marichal, and Andre Rogers, a dark-skinned infielder from the Bahamas, in a boarding house next door to where Felipe stayed with his wife. They lived with Blanche Johnson and her husband. Blanche, a no-nonsense African-American woman, told the young men, who were to her the children she never had, "You want to make good in this country, you learn to speak English." She made them practice their pronunciation in the mornings, and when she caught Juan and

Matty speaking Spanish, she chased them with a dishtowel or mop. The two men grew fond of her and called her "Mama." Juan worked diligently with the English-Spanish dictionary Mama gave him and improved his English slowly.

Juan lived clean. He recited a Psalm at night and in the morning. He did not go out drinking or carousing with teammates. Instead, he sought out Catholic churches on the road to attend Sunday Mass. He went to bed early the night before he pitched. In San Francisco he sometimes ate meals next door prepared by Felipe's wife, Maria. They also found a restaurant on Fillmore Street that served a fish that they were able to order back home. Juan took comfort in the familiar food.

But he and his Dominican teammates had other preoccupations that season. Once outside of his home country, Juan had started hearing stories that challenged the national fable of Rafael Trujillo as the Dominican savior. Juan learned about Trujillo's secret police force that imprisoned, tortured, and killed political opponents and critics, stories that the Trujillo-controlled newspapers in the Dominican Republic did not tell about El Jefe.* "This was all completely new to me," Marichal wrote in *My Journey*. "We never talked about such things in the Dominican." The US government had backed Trujillo because of his anticommunist stance,† but President Dwight Eisenhower became disillusioned with Trujillo after he tried to bump off his critic, Venezuelan president Romulo Betancourt.‡ Eisenhower resolved to replace Trujillo with a more suitable puppet. That's where the CIA came in.

---

* *Time* magazine reported in 1965: "Thousands of political opponents died in his [Trujillo's] secret police dungeons, mysterious 'auto accidents' and 'suicides.' There were electric chairs for slow electrocution, another many-armed electrical device attached by tiny screws inserted into the skull, a rubber collar that could be tightened to sever a man's head, plus nail extractors, scissors for castration, leather-thronged whips and small rubber hammers. P.A. systems in the torture rooms carried every blood-curdling scream to other prisoners waiting their turn."

† Cordell Hall, US Secretary of State from 1933 to 1944, defended the United States' support of the tyrant: "He may be a son of a bitch, but he is our son of a bitch."

‡ The attempt on June 24, 1960, wounded but did not kill Betancourt.

The United States had actively protected its economic interests—primarily sugar, fruit, and coffee—on the island of Hispaniola throughout the 20th century. With US troops already occupying Haiti and the Dominican government floundering financially, President Woodrow Wilson sent in US Marines on May 16, 1916. They stayed eight years, establishing an administration that some Dominicans refused to serve in and guerillas resisted. By the time the marines left in 1924, Rafael Trujillo had risen to head the Guardia Nacional that the Americans had created. Within six years El Jefe seized control of the country. Thus began the Era of Trujillo, when the dictator constructed hospitals, housing, schools, airports, and roads; steered the country out of debt; expanded the middle class; and amassed one of the largest personal fortunes in the world (estimated at $800 million)* through nearly absolute control of the country's resources. Now in 1961 the CIA—which over the next several years would rub out Patrice Lumumba, prime minister of the Republic of the Congo; Abd al-Karim Qasim, prime minister of Iraq; and Ngo Dinh Diem, president of South Vietnam—set its sights on the Dominican Republic's undesirable dictator.

On May 30 the Giants played a doubleheader at Candlestick against the Cincinnati Reds. Marichal lost the second game after giving up five runs in four innings and being lifted for a pinch hitter. Afterward he heard the news: Trujillo had been assassinated. Late that evening, a group of men had ambushed El Jefe's chauffeured Chevrolet on the dark road to San Cristobal, where Trujillo kept his young mistress, and shot him dead in a gunfight with their M1 carbines supplied by the CIA. The United States had failed spectacularly six weeks earlier in the Bay of Pigs invasion of Cuba, but it had succeeded in its mission to take out Fidel Castro's neighbor.

The scramble for power in the aftermath of Trujillo's assassination plunged the country into a summer of uncertainty. Ramfis

---

* Dominican-born author Junot Díaz sarcastically credits Trujillo with "the creation of the first modern kleptocracy."

Trujillo, who had been living in Paris, returned to take charge and began executing rivals. Two of his uncles also returned from exile to challenge him. In November US President John Kennedy expressed his preference for the law professor Joaquín Balaguer to rule by sending naval ships loaded with 1,800 US Marines to cruise the Dominican coast. Ramfis fled and Balaguer, the figurehead president under El Jefe, assumed power. Throughout that summer of 1961, Juan tried to keep up with the situation by reading his country's newspapers at the Dominican consulate in San Francisco. Constantly worried about his family's safety, he still pitched every four days. Though not wanting to make excuses, his concerns kept him from performing at his best. "When you're doing a job like that, you want your mind to be clear, but sometimes it's impossible," he said.

Juan had another preoccupation that summer: Alma Rosa Carvajal. She lived next door to the Alous in Santo Domingo. Juan had met her two years earlier, when Alma was just 15, and been stirred by her beauty. Her father, Jose, a pensioned army officer, had been close to Trujillo. Jose had been shot in the leg while fighting in Trujillo's service and was good friends with El Jefe's cousin, Lieutenant General Jose Garcia Trujillo, the secretary of armed forces from 1955 to 1960. El General, as they called him, was a passionate baseball fan who followed the major leagues and Cuban *beisbol.* When Juan was back in town, El General used to invite him over to talk baseball. "I was nervous, a young kid talking to a general while he would sit back and drink vodka," Marichal remembered. But El General came to like Juan and so did Alma's parents, whom he called Papa Jose and Doña Polonia.

One day after Juan had come home following the 1961 season, he visited Alma and found her holding a baby. She told him that the baby was hers and that she was married. Juan felt immediately jealous. "No, you're not."

"What difference does it make to you?" she challenged him.

That's when he knew how much he loved her.

Not long afterward, El General spied the couple kissing in a car parked outside Alma's house. He summoned Juan and Alma to face her parents. Juan burned with embarrassment. Needlessly, it turned out. Papa Jose and Doña Polonia gave the couple their blessing to marry. "Now you can kiss her," El General said, smiling.

Juan left for spring training with plans to marry his sweetheart in October after the 1962 season ended. But the political situation worsened. A general strike forced Balaguer to share power with a Council of State that included two of Trujillo's assassins. Two weeks and two days later, air force general Pedro Rodriguez Echavarria toppled the Council in a coup d'état. But Rodriguez lacked sufficient support, including that of the United States, to stay in power, and the Council of State resumed functioning until a national election could be held. The turmoil rocked Alma's family because of its connection to Trujillo. Extremists threatened to bomb their house. Alma was afraid to go out into the street. Juan feared for her safety from afar in Arizona.

Finally, he could no longer bear his worry. He asked Alvin Dark for permission to leave spring training, so that he could return to marry Alma and bring her to safety in the United States. Dark asked why she couldn't come to the States to marry him. Marichal explained that she was still a minor, only 17. Dark consented, for which Marichal remained forever grateful, even in their strained days ahead. On March 5 Juan left spring training, and two days later a Catholic priest at the Church of San Juan Bosco in Santo Domingo pronounced Juan and Alma husband and wife. Under the headline Lovesick Marichal Leaves . . . to Marry, the *San Francisco Examiner* reported that it was "the first time anyone could recall a player leaving in the middle of camp and traveling 4,000 miles to get married." The American press underestimated the emotional severity of the political situation for Marichal and his country.

Two days after exchanging vows, Juan and his new bride returned to Phoenix. Once the season started, they shared a house in San

Francisco with Maria and Felipe Alou. In a magazine piece typical of the day, *Sport* reported an interview with Marichal: "'I ask maself that springtime how I can repay the Skeeper,' Juan was recalling not long ago. 'Then I have it! I pitch him one hellofa sonofabuck opening day game!'" Though Juan did not speak with that caricatured simplicity, he did pitch one helluva Opening Day game on April 10, given that honor as the Giants' top starter. He struck out Hank Aaron three times and shut out the Braves before 39,177 fans at Candlestick. He also singled, doubled, scored twice, and drove in two runs in the 6–0 victory.

Juan's success continued throughout the 1962 season. Pitching in front of a team loaded with talent—Willie Mays, Willie McCovey, and Orlando Cepeda (all future Hall of Famers), Jim Davenport and Felipe Alou (All-Stars in 1962)—Juan won 18 games, exactly half of his starts, and pitched 18 complete games. Now 24 years old, he began to fulfill the potential he had flashed in his first three games of 1960.

His success won him a berth on the National League squad for the 1962 All-Star Games.* Marichal earned the win in the first game with two shutout innings.† Being in the clubhouse with established greats like Clemente, Aaron, and Stan Musial thrilled him. He had arrived among the ranks of the game's elite players. "It made me so happy and proud to be one of the players selected to play in that All-Star Game," Juan said.

He was beginning to master the art of changing speeds and locations with his pitches. He had two different speeds for his fastball and two for his curve, which he mixed with his changeup, slider, and screwball. Sometimes he delivered the pitches overhand, sometimes sidearm. He did not rely on one pitch when in trouble but was willing to select from his vast assortment the right pitch for the

---

* From 1959 through 1962, Major League Baseball hosted two All-Star Games each year. In 1962 they played the first on July 10 at D. C. Stadium, the second on July 30 at Wrigley Field.

† That made him the first Latin American pitcher to win an All-Star Game.

situation in the location he thought best. He kept batters guessing and off-balance, never quite sure what to expect where. "That's what it's all about, going against the batter like a chess game," Marichal said. "The secret of pitching is not so much the *kind* of pitch as it is *moving* the ball. You should know *where* you want to pitch as much as *what* you want to."

Marichal was just as likely to deliver a pitch sidearm as he was overhand or three-quarters, but the pundits entertained themselves with descriptions of his high leg-kick motion. He thrust his left foot over his head, leaning back so that the knuckles of his hand holding the ball nearly scraped the dirt behind his right foot, and whirled to unleash his throw, looking like he might topple over with his follow-through. "When he winds up, it's like a helicopter getting ready for takeoff," Furman Bisher wrote in the *Atlanta Journal.* "When it is working right, the high kick, seen by the hitter, is something like a pinwheel viewed from the side," coauthor Charles Einstein wrote in Marichal's first autobiography. "First the leg comes over the top, then the glove, then the pitching hand, finally the ball." Sandy Grady of the *Philadelphia Evening Bulletin* wrote that Marichal "looks like a double-jointed drum majorette trying to pick up a dropped baton." Roger Angell, the *New Yorker*'s designated baseball scribe, wrote that Marichal looked "like some enormous and dangerous farm implement."

What mattered most was that the motion was effective and had made Juan a better pitcher, as Andy Gilbert had convinced him it would. "If his control wasn't great, the leg kick would have been useless," said Steve Stone, who would win the American League Cy Young Award in 1980. "It might have helped with his deception, but the overwhelming stuff and control were what set him apart."

Juan was also becoming more comfortable in the clubhouse. The young man who had been nicknamed "Laughing Boy" back in Tacoma had a penchant for practical jokes. He hid teammates' car keys or encouraged them to take a whiff of a new cologne that turned out to be a fluid with an awful stench. He playfully snapped a towel at teammates coming out of the shower. He also discovered that he could make the big man Willie McCovey jump like a startled cat with a well-placed firecracker under his chair.

On Opening Day of 1962, the Braves' Joe Torre hit a ball back up the middle that struck Marichal on the right leg. It hurt so badly that Juan couldn't put weight on it and had to alter his windup. But he stayed in the game to complete his shutout victory. Despite his willingness to play through pain—or maybe because of it—Marichal did not garner sympathy from Giants management, particularly Alvin Dark, for his ailments. When the team was in Pittsburgh, Juan's face became inflamed, so he went to a doctor who told him he had tonsillitis. After Juan explained that he had already had his tonsils removed years ago, the doctor responded that he couldn't treat him. Dark's cure was to have Marichal pitch in Pittsburgh and Milwaukee despite Juan feeling miserable. Back in San Francisco, a doctor properly diagnosed him with mumps and prescribed complete rest.

In early September Juan jammed his right foot covering first base and broke a bone. He had to be carried off the field and taken to the hospital. His foot swelled up, but X-rays did not show the fracture. Juan knew something was wrong. His foot throbbed, and even as it healed there was a rise on the instep.* He could not play for more than three weeks. On the final Saturday of the season, with the Giants in a tight pennant race, Dark called upon Marichal to start. Juan felt the manager was making him pitch when he wasn't healthy; Dark rationalized that the X-ray had shown no fracture. By the fifth inning it was clear the foot was not ready. Marichal had allowed four runs, and Dark pulled him. "He said very little,

* An X-ray four years and 96 victories later would finally reveal the break in his foot.

but the look in his eye told me that he thought I was trying to quit under pressure," Juan wrote in *A Pitcher's Story.* After the game the team's Latin players clustered around Juan's locker; they believed Dark could have caused Marichal permanent damage by making him pitch, and accused the manager with angry looks.

"I found Alvin Dark to be a hard man to understand because of the way he would change," Marichal wrote in *A Pitcher's Story.* "At times he was good-natured and understanding." Like when he let Juan leave spring training to marry Alma. "Then he would change." And become cold and rigid with his players, like he was earlier that summer when he thought his starters had gone soft, so he closed the bullpen and forced them to go the distance, with Marichal the first involuntary volunteer.

Dark had trouble dealing with his Latin players. A college football All-American at LSU, former National League shortstop for 14 seasons, and Christian from the Bible Belt state of Alabama, Dark was perhaps representative of many Americans who simply did not understand the vast differences between American and Latin cultures. He barred the Latinos from speaking Spanish in the clubhouse and dugout. Though other managers had done the same with the intent to overcome cultural divisions, the move was deeply resented by players who felt the policy stripped them of an integral part of their identity and imposed a false means of communication with one another, making the three Alou brothers, for example, speak to one another in English. "If I am going to talk to Felipe Alou, whom I have known most of my life from the Dominican, we are going to speak Spanish," Marichal wrote. "I think he [Dark] just felt we had too many Latins on the team and he felt left out when we were talking." Dark also banished music, an edict seemingly directed at Orlando Cepeda, the man they called "Cha Cha." Dark was prone to violent outbursts. After a loss that season in St. Louis when he didn't think Cepeda was hustling, the manager kicked over the clubhouse buffet table, which insulted the Latinos, who believed it was a sin to waste food when so many people went hungry. Felipe Alou picked up some of the food Dark had thrown on the floor, glaring at the manager in the eyes, and ate it, a gesture rife with symbolism.

The Giants lost the game in Houston that Marichal pitched on his bum foot but managed to defeat the Dodgers in a three-game playoff to capture the National League pennant. Juan pitched the deciding game, his foot still in pain, and gave up three runs in seven innings. The Giants rallied to win the game and the pennant even though they had trailed the Dodgers by four games with only seven left to play in the regular season. "It was God's will," Marichal said matter-of-factly.

The Giants had lost two of the first three World Series games to the Yankees when Marichal started Game Four in New York. Through four innings he had given up only two hits, struck out four (including Mickey Mantle twice), and not allowed a run. He felt strong, confident, detecting no serious trouble from his previously injured foot. He batted in the top of the fifth with runners on first and third, no outs. Juan got the bunt sign, but the first two pitches from Whitey Ford were balls. He had the fake bunt sign for the next three pitches, which ran the count to 3–2. Then Dark surprised Marichal by calling for a two-strike suicide squeeze, which Juan considered "a stupid play" in the situation. Juan knew he had to make contact, even when Ford's pitch veered inside and low. The ball struck the index finger of his right hand, his pitching hand, which immediately started to swell. The umpire called him out for fouling off a third-strike bunt. Juan protested that the ball had hit his finger first but lost the argument. He threw his helmet in frustration. The Yankee Stadium crowd booed, not understanding his anger. His finger throbbed with a blood blister that would eventually push off the nail. His World Series debut ended abruptly.

The Giants held on to win, and the Yankees took the fifth game before the Series returned to San Francisco, where it rained for four days. A reporter asked Dark about Juan's finger. "Marichal won't pitch again," Dark said. "I don't care how long it rains. Marichal won't pitch."

One writer commented, "I've never in my life heard a manager throw one of his players to the wolves the way Dark did with that crack."

Dark's crack stung Juan. It "left the impression with them [the reporters]—and me—that he thought I did not wish to pitch, and that with an attitude like that he didn't want me pitching," Marichal wrote in *A Pitcher's Story*. "It was not the first time, and it would not be the last, that he indicated this line of thinking about me." Juan had not expected to start again because the rain gave the team's two top starters, Billy Pierce and Jack Sanford, the rest they needed, but he would have pitched in relief if his finger allowed him to. Marichal chafed at the challenge to his competitive spirit—which simmered intensely—and the seeming condescension to the stereotype that Latins quit when behind.

The Yankees ended up winning in seven games. Juan figured that he would have another chance to play in the World Series with the great team that the Giants had. But that would not happen, making Dark's call for the suicide squeeze that ended with Marichal's bruised finger an even bigger disappointment, though Juan would not realize that until years later.

When Juan returned to the Dominican Republic, he found conditions still unsteady, the country under civilian junta rule with elections scheduled toward the end of the year. In November Juan, Felipe Alou, and Cardinals second baseman Julian Javier joined their country's team in a seven-game series against a Cuban All-Star squad in Santo Domingo. Ford Frick, Major League Baseball commissioner, had instituted a ban on players participating in such contests unless they had his permission, which he did not grant for the seven-game interisland series. Frick's stance smacked of the colonialist attitudes practiced by other US businesses involved in the islands. But Marichal didn't believe he needed the foreign commissioner's permission to represent his country. Besides, the Dominican's top players faced danger beyond that of disciplinary action from the league or even that of disappointing the ruling junta. "If we didn't play, there would have been a revolt right there on the spot, and we would have been the prime targets," Felipe Alou said.

Frick fined each of the players $250 and threatened by telegram to bar them from spring training if they didn't pay. Alou responded with an article in *Sport* magazine calling for a Major League Baseball representative for Latin players who could interpret the cultural and political nuances that the commissioner so obviously misunderstood. Frick did not take him up on the suggestion but instead locked him out of spring training until he paid his fine. Alou and Marichal—who had also stated he would not pay the fine on principle—now felt they had no option other than to comply if they wanted to play the '63 season in the United States.*

Juan reported to spring training shortly after Juan Bosch Ganio, a leftist scholar and author of short realistic fiction, assumed the Dominican office of the president he had won in the December election. But Bosch's insistence on the separation of church and state alienated the powerful Roman Catholic Church, and his policy on land reform threatened the elite class. He also aggravated the US government by awarding public contracts to Europeans. His tenure would not last through the Giants' baseball season; the right wing backed a military coup that deposed Bosch in September.

---

* Frick's successor, William Eckert, did appoint Bobby Maduro, former owner of the Havana Sugar Kings, as an ambassador for Latin players, but Maduro did little to improve conditions. By the 1970s the position was abolished.

Marichal held out for a higher contract until March 13, longer than any other Giant had until that point, finally signing for $24,000, and proved himself worth every penny. In the 1963 season Juan went from good to brilliant. He won 25 games, or 76 percent of his 33 decisions. He allowed only 2.41 earned runs per nine innings. He struck out 248 batters while walking only 61 in 321.1 innings, the best ratio in the majors. Certainly Marichal's numbers—like those of every pitcher—benefited from the expansion of the strike zone from the "top of the knees to the armpits" to the "bottom of the knees to top of the shoulder," a change that curbed home run output and stifled batting averages league-wide by 16 points. Regardless of the size of the strike zone, he pitched two of the most memorable games of his career that summer.

On June 15, before the Giants played the Houston Colt .45s at Candlestick Park, Juan told leftfielder Willie McCovey that he should play deeper than he normally did. Marichal planned to alter his windup because Houston had hit him pretty hard the last several times he faced them. McCovey thought Marichal was nuts to tinker with what had worked—Juan had won his last five starts—but did as he was told. It paid off in the seventh inning when Houston's cleanup hitter, Carl Warwick, lifted a long drive that McCovey managed to haul in at his limit beneath the left field screen. The catch kept Houston from recording its first hit. The game remained a scoreless tie and tense affair until the Giants scored a solitary run in the bottom of the eighth. Marichal had worked eight innings with no margin for error. Only four batters managed to hit balls out of the infield, and all were caught. Marichal walked two and struck out five but needed only 89 pitches to become the first Latino to pitch a no-hitter.

Juan saved his best game for 17 days later. In perhaps the greatest pitching duel ever, Marichal battled the Milwaukee Braves' future Hall of Famer Warren Spahn through 15 scoreless innings on July 2 at Candlestick. Dark had wanted to take Marichal out in the 9th, 12th, and 13th innings, but he insisted on staying. Marichal, then 25, pointed to the 42-year-old Spahn in the Braves dugout and told his manager, "I am not going to come out of this game as long as that old man is still pitching." Marichal was painting a masterpiece, despite throwing more than two games' worth of pitches, and he wanted to finish the job. His teammates left him alone on the bench, and he ran to and from the mound each inning. By the 16th Marichal and Spahn had been pitching four hours without either allowing a run. After Marichal set down the Braves, he told Willie Mays, "This is going to be the last inning for me." Mays responded, "Don't worry. I'm going to win this game for you." Sure enough, Mays knocked Spahn's first pitch in the bottom half of the 16th out of the park.

Marichal had pitched 16 innings, thrown 227 pitches, and shut out the Braves on eight hits. In these days of careful pitch counts and relief specialists, it is unlikely that anyone will ever better his remarkable performance. Sportswriter Jim Kaplan authored an entire book about the game, aptly entitling it *The Greatest Game Ever Pitched.* That's how good Juan was in 1963.

Juan seized whatever advantage he could over batters. He used the cold weather in Candlestick, when contact with the bat on the ball stung the hands, to gain an edge. "I liked it when a pitch hurt the batter's hands at the start of the game," he wrote in *My Journey.* "I tried to get their hands to sting right from the beginning. Then they wouldn't want to go back and hit."

He also knew the value of an inside pitch and did not hesitate to use it. "He could burn the letters off the chest of your uniform with 'message pitches' that didn't require translations," wrote Bob Stevens, the *San Francisco Chronicle*'s beat writer for the Giants.

The message sometimes sent was *Don't mess with my teammates.* In Marichal's next start after his 16-inning duel with Spahn, the Cardinals' Bob Gibson hit the Giants' rookie Jim Ray Hart with a pitch that sent Hart to the hospital with a broken shoulder blade. "He [Gibson] played fiercely," Marichal wrote in *My Journey*. "They called Gibson 'The Head Hunter' and he loved to be called that. He loved that name. He wasn't trying to hurt the batters, but he wanted to make them nervous. It was okay with him if they thought of him like that. That was to his advantage." That was the way it was done then, and Marichal understood it. So when Gibson took his turn at the plate, Marichal delivered a message close to Gibson's head. Plate umpire Al Barlick stepped in front of the plate and waved his finger to impose the requisite $50 fine for a deliberate beaning attempt. "He'll get it again!" Juan shouted. Dark and catcher Ed Bailey had to restrain Marichal to keep him from being ejected.

True, his competitive spirit could sometimes get the better of him. Another time, teammates had to hold him back when he wanted to charge Cincinnati pitcher Joe Nuxhall after he threw at a Giants batter.

But Juan also believed that the warnings and fines weren't always meted out fairly. Some umpires, he said, were prejudiced against Latin players. "They throw at Willie [Mays] all the time and then I let them know they have to stop it," he said. "Who gets fined? Me—not the guy who tried to hit Willie."

Marichal squared off against Sandy Koufax for the first time on May 11 in Los Angeles. In the past when the Giants had played the Dodgers, the San Francisco manager had always pitted his ace against Los Angeles' premier pitcher. In 1963 Marichal won that distinction. Koufax beat him 8–0 with a no-hitter. Two weeks later, Marichal beat Koufax 7–1 in the rematch in San Francisco, giving up only four hits. Still, as good as Juan was in 1963, Sandy was better. Both won 25 games and pitched no-hitters. Marichal lost eight games; Koufax lost only five. Koufax was the only pitcher in the majors to give up fewer than two runs a game (1.88 ERA); he fanned a major league–high 306 and walked only 58. He led the major leagues with 11 shutouts. He also won both of his starts in the

World Series to help the Dodgers take the championship. Koufax was voted the National League's Most Valuable Player and was also the unanimous choice for the Cy Young Award.*

After working 321 innings that summer, Juan was exhausted when he returned home to the Dominican Republic in October, less than a month after Bosch had been ousted in the coup. Marichal would have liked another off-season rest, but his status had grown so large coming off his incredible season that he couldn't refuse to play winter ball at home. He agreed to pitch again for Escogido.

When Los Leones traveled to Caracas for an inter-Caribbean series, Marichal heard that there were plans to kidnap him. He took the threat seriously because Venezuela had its own political turmoil at the time—the rise of communism in Cuba had shaken the region—and thugs had recently kidnapped a high-profile soccer player. The Venezuelan government assigned a permanent police escort that stayed with Marichal even when he did his business in the bathroom. But when he pitched he stood alone on the mound and flinched every time the home crowd fans let off a firecracker—which sounded to him like a pistol shot. The trip stressed him, which made what followed even more difficult.

Juan won seven games and lost only three, helping Los Leones make the playoffs, but along the way he grew frustrated with the Escogido owner, Maximo Hernandez Ortega, for trying to maximize his profits by cutting player salaries and skimping on expenses. When Juan wanted to take a hot shower after winning his seventh game and the water came out cold, he lost his temper and vented his frustration to Ortega. The owner either suspended him or Marichal quit—accounts vary—but the result was the same: Marichal did not pitch for Escogido in the postseason.

That enraged Escogido fans. They accused Marichal of shirking his duty to his country. *El Caribe,* the biggest newspaper in Santo

---

* Just one award was given to the best pitcher in the major leagues.

Domingo, called Juan a rat. People jeered at him on the street. They made intimidating comments to Alma in stores. They phoned the Marichals' home with threats to torture the pitcher. When Marichal attended a playoff game, some angry fanatics threw bottles at him and several threatened to kill him. A group of policemen had to escort Juan and Alma out of the ballpark. On New Year's Eve Juan had to protect himself with his fists when revelers-turned-rioters attacked him in a Santo Domingo nightclub. After fighting his way out of the club, he was jailed briefly on the charge of "street brawling," though ultimately acquitted. "I became worse hated than Trujillo in his worst days," Marichal said.

Frightened for his safety, he retreated to his family farm in Laguna Verde. Paranoid and nervous, unable to sleep, he jumped at any loud or sudden noise. He visited a doctor who suggested he would feel more serene in the United States. Back in San Francisco, Juan applied for residency papers so he could buy a house and not have to return to the Dominican Republic in the off-season. But the American press again misunderstood the cultural milieu that threatened Marichal. Prescott Sullivan, a columnist for the *San Francisco Examiner,* poked fun at him: "While Marichal might have chosen a more congenial form of exercise, it is gratifying to hear that he hasn't been idle. Juan, with a few more brawls under his belt, should report to spring training camp in Phoenix, Arizona, in prime condition."

The American press also misunderstood Marichal's application for residency papers at the US consulate and reported that he was seeking citizenship. Those reports further enraged the Dominicans. "If you ask many fans what they think of their one-time idol, they hiss that Marichal is contemptible, ungrateful, a man who has thrown them down and a disgrace to the patriotic creed of a proud people—a *trador* [traitor]," Al Stump wrote in *Sport* magazine. Despite the derision directed his way, Juan remained proud to be a Dominican. He was simply concerned for his safety and that of the young family he had started with Alma.

During this time Marichal's stress index multiplied while he negotiated his 1964 contract with the Giants. When holding out in 1963, he had asked for $30,000—a raise that would have doubled his salary from the previous season—but had settled for $24,000. After Marichal won 25 games, as many as Koufax, the team offered him a $6,000 raise. The increase still would have left Marichal underpaid—a condition common among Latin players—compared to Koufax (who earned $70,000 in 1964) and the other top pitchers (Don Drysdale, $70,000; Whitey Ford, $53,000; and Warren Spahn, $60,000). Marichal settled for $40,000 but thought his salary should be closer to that of his peers.

The Giants had traded Juan's good friend Felipe Alou after the 1963 season, perhaps for his defiance of Dark over the buffet table turnover. Juan missed him but still felt close to the other Latin players on the Giants, like the other two Alou brothers (Matty and Jesus), Jose Pagan, and Cepeda, who was like a brother to Juan. Even when Latin players didn't come from the same country, they felt a connection through their shared language and culture. "The Latin players had a special bond, a brotherhood," Marichal wrote in *My Journey*. "We were from the same part of the world with the same kind of climate. We spoke the same language. We had darker skin and we had experienced discrimination in the United States because of that." The fraternity extended to players on other teams. Marichal and his Latin teammates socialized with players like Roberto Clemente, Manny Sanguillen, Vic Davalillo, and Manny Mota when the Giants traveled and when opposing teams came to San Francisco. "We showed the visiting guys some hospitality because we knew it could be lonely on the road as a Latin person in another city," Marichal wrote.

The San Francisco organization had been progressive in signing Latin and African-American players. With Cepeda at first, Pagan at short, Jesus Alou in right field, Mays in center, and McCovey on first, more than half of the Giants' eight starting position players were minorities. Dark wrote their names onto the lineup card, but that didn't mean he treated them well. Cepeda thought that the tension Dark provoked on the team, which divided it into cliques of whites, blacks, and Latinos, cost the Giants a pennant or two during his tenure. That season of '64, Marichal had started strong, winning eight of his first nine starts, yet Dark, who never seemed to show much regard for his pitchers, told Juan to change the way he pitched to the Mets. Even though Marichal had never lost a game to the startup club, Dark thought the batters were getting used to him. "Pitch every hitter differently than you've been pitching him up till now," Dark said. "I'll call the pitches from the bench." Juan beat them despite Dark's intervention.

In July the Giants and Phillies were flip-flopping between first and second place in the National League when Dark lost his temper again, this time over a base-running gaffe involving Cepeda, Pagan, and Del Crandall, a white player, that almost resulted in a triple play. He told Stan Isaacs of *Newsday,* "We have trouble because we have so many Spanish-speaking and Negro players on the team. They are just not able to perform up to the white ball player when it comes to mental alertness. . . . You can't make most Negro and Spanish players have the pride in their team that you can get from white players. And they just aren't as sharp mentally. They aren't able to adjust to situations because they don't have that mental alertness. . . . One of the biggest things is that you can't make them subordinate themselves to the best interest of the team. You don't find pride in them that you get in the white player."

When Dark's comments ran in *Newsday* at the end of July, the Giants' black and Latin players met in Willie Mays's hotel room in Pittsburgh ready to mutiny. Mays talked them out of it. He figured Dark would be fired at the end of the season. Forcing the issue would make a martyr out of him for the bigots. Mays also reasoned that a managerial change at that point in the season could cost the team the pennant. He succeeded in quieting the rebellion. Dark, of course, claimed he had been misquoted. Perhaps more disturbing was the support he received. Giants owner Horace Stoneham defended him in public. So did commissioner Ford Frick. A *Sports Illustrated* editorial asserted, "He [Dark] has treated them [Negroes and Latin Americans] as individuals, not stereotypes. He has knit together a club that was chaotically divided, partly by racial and nationalist hostility, at the time he took control." That was certainly not the prevailing opinion on the team or among close observers, but the situation exposed the widespread tolerance for slandering minorities at the time.

To Stoneham's credit, he did fire Dark after the 1964 season, though it may have been as much for the team's collapse as for the manager's ugly opinions. After his public outburst, the Giants never regained first place and finished fourth. Marichal had another strong season—despite missing eight starts because of back spasms—going 21–8 with a 2.48 ERA and leading the majors with 22 complete games. After the winter of Dominican discontent the previous year, he had planned to stay in San Francisco with Alma and their two daughters at the house they had bought. But if he wanted to see his mother—who was afraid of flying and never traveled to the United States—and visit other family members, Juan knew he needed to go home. He also believed that there might be help for his back troubles in the Dominican Republic.

He made his annual pilgrimage to the Rio Sanate, said to have healing powers. Along the way he stopped at the Basílica Catedral Nuestra Señora de la Altagracia, where he prayed before the portrait of Our Lady of Altagracia, protector of the island and the Dominican faithful. At the river he swam in the cool water. He knew the stories of others who claimed the waters had cured their ailments, and Juan desired the same for his troubled back.

Once home in the Dominican, he felt pressured to pitch again for Escogido. His acceptance seemed to heal some of the bitter sentiment directed his way a year earlier. Record crowds packed the stadiums for his pair of starts in late December, including one against the rival Los Tigres del Licey. "His appearance, like that of a typical national hero, attracted widespread attention," a newspaper reported.

But the political climate remained tense. The ruling triumvirate still struggled for support, and unrest grumbled from within the military and among loyalists for Juan Bosch, the scholar who had won the presidential election only to be thrown out of office by the military coup. Before Marichal left for the 1965 season, he heard the more ominous resonance of revolution in Santo Domingo's streets.

CHAPTER FOUR

Filling Campy's Shoes

ROSEBORO DID WELL DURING THE DODGERS 1958 SPRING TRAINING following Roy Campanella's career-ending injury, but he did not think he was in Vero Beach competing for the starting catcher position. Johnny had conceded that role to 10-year veteran Rube Walker. Dodgers manager Walt Alston eased the pressure by starting Walker on Opening Day. For the first month Alston alternated his catchers, but by mid-May Roseboro had won the job. Not through any sensational play but more due to the attrition of Walker's skills. Roseboro struggled to receive pitchers like Sandy Koufax, Johnny Podres, and Clem Labine, who threw a lot of low breaking balls. "Campy was an expert at blocking those wicked pitches in the dirt," a profile in the team guide observed. "But Roseboro reached for them like a lady warding off a mouse."

In their first season on the West Coast, the Dodgers did not adjust well to Los Angeles, finishing in seventh place (of eight teams), 21 games back. Pitching was problematic: Newcombe didn't last the season, and Koufax, Podres, and Don Drysdale all lost more games than they won. Los Angeles also had the lowest team batting average in the league, with Duke Snider the only Dodger hitting above .300. Many of the team's critics singled out the "catching problem." Roseboro caught 104 games, made eight errors, and batted .271 with a third of his hits for extra bases. It wasn't a poor debut season—he was even named to the National League All-Star team, though he didn't play—but it did not approach the standard by which he was inevitably measured. "You don't win a pennant when Roy Campanella sits in a wheelchair and Johnny Roseboro does the catching for you," Jimmy Cannon sniped in the *New York Journal-American.*

Johnny and Jeri bought a small house in Compton, just south of the Watts neighborhood. On his minimum Major League Baseball player salary of $7,500, they could afford only one car, an old Plymouth convertible, so Johnny commuted by streetcar to the Coliseum. He took a salesman job at a downtown clothing store to make some extra cash and indulge a haberdashery habit he had developed while in Montreal. Johnny prided himself on looking fine. Even though Jeri was the more sociable one, dancing at parties hosted by other players and their wives, Johnny was certain to look good when he did go out.

Campanella came to Dodgertown in the spring of 1959 as a special coach with a specific project: John Roseboro. Campy, in his wheelchair and a shiny Dodgers windbreaker, talked Rosey through his throws to second, quickening his release. They spent hours on the nuances of stopping low breaking balls. "When Campy got through working on Roseboro, John was digging in the dirt in the manner of a dog burying a bone," Bob Laughlin noted in the Dodgers' team guide. "These coaches threw pitches in the dirt to me until I had to learn how to catch them or become the biggest bruise in Florida," Johnny said. The tutoring sessions continued in the Dodgertown lobby after practice with the veteran instructing the younger man how to handle pitchers.

The lessons stuck. Roseboro called pitches confidently, and pitchers began to trust him. That season, he allowed only 17 steals and threw out 24 aspiring sack thieves, his 59 percent spoiler rate the best in the league. On August 31, 1959, he caught an 18-strikeout performance by Koufax. Johnny's 19 putouts (the catcher gets credit on a strikeout) set a major league record for most in a nine-inning game. His 848 putouts during the season exceeded Campanella's big league mark of 807 established six years earlier. With their catching problem seemingly solved, the Dodgers finished in a tie on top. Roseboro hit a two-run homer in the eighth inning of the final game to provide insurance and set up a best-of-three playoff with the Milwaukee Braves. He had fewer than 100 hits that season, batting only .232, but he delivered his biggest hit in the first playoff game, a sixth-inning, 375-foot home run that won the game for the Dodgers. "Roseboro finally looked like a fair facsimile of his famous predecessor in the gloom at Milwaukee yesterday," the UPI wire story ran. The home run won over Cannon. "The game belonged to Johnny Roseboro," the *Journal-American* critic wrote. "Not even Roy Campanella could do any better."

The Dodgers won the playoff to face the Chicago White Sox in the World Series. These were the "Go-Go Sox" that had raced to the Series on the speedy feet of Luis Aparicio, Nellie Fox, Jim Landis, and Jim Rivera. The press forecast that the Sox would steal the Series off the arm of the Dodgers' green catcher. Alston boosted Rosey's confidence when he told reporters, "They don't know how well Roseboro throws. They can go, but he'll cut them down."

Roseboro made Alston sound like a prophet. He threw out every Chicago runner that tried to steal in the first two games. With the

Series tied at one game apiece, Landis finally swiped a base in Game Three, but Johnny caught Aparicio, Fox, and Rivera to erase multiple threats. "Johnny's arm was a major factor in winning that pivotal third game which saw Chicago make 12 hits, have four walks and one hit batsman yet lost 3–1," Bob Laughlin wrote. The Dodgers won the Series in Los Angeles, a gift to the city the team's second year in its new home. Roseboro had only two hits but was considered one of the stars for his superb defensive play, a theme that would define his big league career.

Johnny spent his World Series money on a new Thunderbird for Jeri and an Austin-Healey for himself, an extravagance that he couldn't quite afford, but it would be years before he came to terms with his fiscal irresponsibility. Johnny and Jeri also had their first child, Shelley, in June. Johnny considered her a bigger thrill than winning the pennant and the World Series. He spent hours playing with her and talking to her. He loved to watch her fall asleep on his chest.

Having started a family, the couple moved out of Compton to south LA in 1960. Roseboro's batting fell off that summer, dropping to .213, the lowest of his career for a full season, and the Dodgers finished fourth, but Johnny's defensive play continued to improve. In 1961 he won his first Gold Glove. He also raised his average to .251 and made the All-Star team.* The Dodgers finished four games back in second place. Jeri and Johnny had another daughter, Staci, born in February 1961. Johnny thought Jeri was a good mother, but he felt a strain in their marriage. She loved being a baseball player's wife, going to the games and mixing with the other wives. A natural introvert, he did not talk about what bothered him, and the resentments smoldered.

---

* He played in the second game of the two-game edition, going 0–3 in a game ended by rain after nine innings even though the score remained tied 1–1.

Johnny was so quiet in the clubhouse that his teammates nicknamed him "Gabby."* "If he says 'Hello,' he sounds like he's chattering," legendary *Los Angeles Times* columnist Jim Murray observed. Gabby did socialize with his teammates, often playing cards, though he preferred the solitude of the cinema and sometimes watched four movies in a single day. When he decided to speak, he often displayed a sharp wit. For instance, he likened the spitball to "a drunk passing out suddenly and sprawling on the floor." He didn't have to say much to pitchers: a glare or a smile let them know his thoughts. He often used his humor to settle them. When Larry Miller made his major league debut in Cincinnati, he was understandably nervous. He got two quick outs on pop-ups then gave up a double and a home run. The Reds' next batter, Frank Robinson, smacked a vicious line drive back through the box that carried to the center field wall. Roseboro called time out, sauntered to the mound where the rattled Miller feared his major league career might end with his debut, and said, "I think you're playing Robinson a little too close."

Another time in Philadelphia, Roseboro and Dodgers pitcher Dick Egan, who had been struggling, watched Richie Allen take batting practice. The Phillies' star slugger, who had a fondness for booze, seemed so inebriated he bumped into both sides of the narrow door before making it into the batting cage. But then he awed Egan with the way he smashed balls into the bleachers. Later, with Los Angeles losing, Egan was called on in relief with Allen on deck. "I was freaking out and grabbed Roseboro," Egan said. "What about Richie?!"

"Don't worry," Gabby replied calmly. "He's probably sober by now."

---

* Pitcher Roger Craig, Roseboro's teammate from 1957 to 1961, claims he came up with the nickname, but Roseboro credits Dodgers pitcher Ed Roebuck with dubbing him "Gabby."

Sure enough, Allen grounded out to third.

By 1962 Roseboro had established himself as one of the best defensive catchers in the majors and a team leader. Not the rah-rah sort, but the type that motivated teammates to play their best with his own consistent and competitive play. "John did everything possible to win," Ken McMullen, his teammate for three years in Los Angeles, said. "He expected everyone to play the game with passion and dedication as he did." They respected Roseboro, never wanting to let him down. "I loved the guy—as a person, friend, and teammate," Stan Williams reflected after Roseboro's death, echoing the unanimous sentiment of his teammates. "John was hard not to like." He played to win, and so did they. "Winning is the aim," Roseboro wrote. "Winning games, not sportsmanship trophies for fair play."

The fastest catcher in the league and regularly the top base stealer among them, Roseboro was part of "the Swift Set," the Dodgers quintet rounded out by Maury Wills, Jim Gilliam, Tommy Davis, and Willie Davis, so named for their swiftness on the base paths (Wills swiped a record 104 bases in 1962 and Roseboro stole 12 in 15 tries, the most by a National League catcher since 1928). "Rivals in haberdashery, partners in shower stall three-part harmony, walkie-talkie radio hams and strummers of eclectic musical instruments, these five friends (and occasional enemies) kept the Dodgers clubhouse rollicking throughout the 1962 season," David Plaut writes in his book *Chasing October: The Dodgers-Giants Pennant Race of 1962*. *Sports Illustrated* noted, "There was fierce competition among them for the distinction of being the best-dressed Dodger." Vin Scully, the voice of the Dodgers, singled out Roseboro with his Brooks Brothers suits as "the Iviest guy in the league." Jim Murray chimed in: "He is as fastidious as Queen Elizabeth. When he comes on the field, even his baseball shoes have a high enough shine to shave by. He buffs them between innings."

The five black men on the Dodgers felt the solidarity of race, understanding the subtle prejudices among teammates. "We had ways of checking out white players," Wills said. "If a guy smoked, you could offer him a puff of your cigarette. Or you could offer somebody a bit of your sandwich or a swig of your drink. The guys who accepted were all right. The guys who were prejudiced would rather die than take a puff or a bite or a swallow." Though there were white guys who wouldn't share a cigarette with one of the Swift Set, the Dodgers didn't suffer the racial divide that other teams like the Giants did. Perhaps because they had had a head start on integration with Jackie Robinson's debut in 1947, the Dodgers felt more like a family with its occasional squabbles but overriding sense of unity.

Roseboro had emulated Campanella in his catching style, showing his target the same way and calling pitches in a like manner. He also mimicked Campy when it came to taking a stand—or not—on racial issues. Much as he chafed under the taunts and attitudes and segregation of baseball and the country as a whole, Johnny absorbed the prejudice rather than take pains to dismantle it. That was Campy. One time when the team stopped to eat on the road coming back from a game, the restaurant management insisted the black players sit behind a screen in the back of the room. Had Jackie Robinson been there, he would have led the march out. Campanella, though, accepted the terms and ate his meal. "He was sort of our leader, but he was not a man of action where race was concerned," Johnny wrote. He could say the same about himself.

There was plenty of overt and covert racism inside and outside of baseball at the time. Jeri often didn't go to spring training with her husband because there was nowhere for a black woman to stay in Vero Beach. When she did go she could not sit with the white players' wives in the segregated stadiums of the South. Baseball cards depicted black players like Roseboro as white in their back-side cartoons, the color of Crayola's peach-hued flesh tone, as though Topps and others had only one color in mind for ballplayers, which was typical of the insensitivity of the day. One time in Houston,

Roseboro crossed the street against a red light. A traffic cop said nothing to the white guys who crossed in front of him but yelled at Johnny, "Back on the curb, boy."

"What about them?' Johnny said, gesturing to the white guys.

"I'm not talking to them," the white cop replied. "I'm talking to you, boy."

Johnny sized up the old, doughy officer. He could drop him with one punch but considered the consequences of doing so. Johnny stepped back to the curb.

"That's where the hate comes from," he wrote later. "I don't hold on to hate, but I know where it's at."

He sympathized with those fighting for civil rights. He could understand their motivation. But he wasn't ready to join them. Shortly after the 1961 baseball season opened, the Freedom Riders had taken to the roads. Hundreds of black and white college students and supporters filled buses that traveled along interstates throughout the South to test new federal laws that banned segregation at rest areas and other public transportation facilities. The nightly news featured images of the resistance they encountered, showing young people with faces bloodied by angry mobs and one bus torched by attackers. Plenty of Americans pushed back on the drive for civil rights. One hundred years after the Civil War, the country remained divided on racial issues, though Roseboro was not one to take sides openly in the debate. He was more likely to take his seat quietly at the back of the city bus than seek confrontation alongside the likes of the Freedom Riders.

Johnny found a way to come out of himself in front of the camera. The Dodgers' move to Los Angeles had provided opportunities for several players to answer the call from nearby Hollywood. Over the years, Johnny had small parts in several films, including *Geisha Boy, Get Fisk,* and *Experiment in Terror.* He also made appearances on several television shows: *Mr. Ed, Dragnet, Burke's Law,* and *Marcus Welby, M.D.* He liked doing those appearances, but they did not translate into lucrative endorsements. Jeri enjoyed the chance to hobnob with Hollywood stars. She worked on John Kennedy's 1960 presidential campaign with the wives of Milton Berle, Nat King Cole, and Steve Allen. She also brought Johnny to parties at their houses. After being dragged onto the dance floor and embarrassed by another player's wife, Johnny told Jeri, "I'm not going to any more of these goddamn parties."

The Dodgers provided plenty of entertainment for Hollywood in 1962, winning 102 games their first season in their new stadium in Chavez Ravine. They held first place for 95 days, up until the final day, which saw the season end in a tie with the Giants. While federal troops occupied Ole Miss to squelch the uprising over James Meredith's matriculation, Los Angeles and San Francisco began a three-game playoff. They split the first two games, each team winning at home, but the Dodgers faltered in their 165th game of the year and lost 6–4. Though Juan Marichal declared that his team's comeback resulted from divine intervention, the Dodgers suffered more of a hellish dejection. They locked the press out of the clubhouse, and instead of celebrating with the champagne on ice, they used it to take the edge off the agony of defeat. Roseboro didn't imbibe. He simply dressed, walked past the reporters without a word, and drove home. He had played a fine season, which included a home run in the All-Star Game, but the team's collapse soured it all. "It was a very long winter, having to explain what happened to us," Roseboro wrote.

The Dodgers collectively may not have played as well the following season, but they fared better, thanks in large part to Sandy Koufax with his MVP, Cy Young Award–winning summer. He won 25 of 30 decisions, allowed fewer than two runs per game, and led the majors in strikeouts, shutouts, and victories. Roseboro caught his second no-hitter (he had caught Koufax's first no-hitter in 1962) against the Giants on May 11 when Koufax bested Marichal. Roseboro had become Koufax's catcher of choice. "With him out there, I felt like I was never alone," Koufax said. They worked so well together that they sometimes went four or five games without Sandy shaking off one of Rosey's signs. Johnny shared this telepathy with other Dodgers pitchers. He didn't even have to use signs with Roger Craig, whom he knew so well he just gave the target and Craig tried to hit it. The entire pitching staff had come to trust Johnny's sharpened awareness of their strengths and the liabilities of the batters they faced. "He knew every pitcher and what they were capable of doing," said Ron Perranoski, Roseboro's teammate with Los Angeles and later Minnesota. "He seldom came out to the mound. I had to call him out if I needed him. And then he'd crack a little joke to take some of the pressure off."

Despite Johnny's good relations with the Dodgers' white pitchers, racial tensions in the country continued to worsen. In May Koufax's no-no over Marichal was overshadowed by the images playing that week on television. Birmingham commissioner of public safety Bull Connor had ordered the use of fire hoses and police dogs to turn back people marching for desegregation in Alabama's largest and most segregated city. The scenes of water jets blasting the shirts off the backs of bystanders and German shepherds chomping on children caused international outrage. President John Kennedy called the action "shameful." The day of Koufax's no-hitter, someone bombed the hotel of Martin Luther King Jr., who had been held a month earlier in a Birmingham jail. By the time King delivered his famous "I Have a Dream" speech in Washington late that summer, it was clear that the racial conflict in America loomed much larger than the national pastime's annual fall classic, though that did not diminish interest in baseball.

When the Dodgers won the pennant to face the Yankees, Brooklyn fans delighted that dem bums would return to New York to play in the World Series. The Dodgers players, on the other hand, felt trepidation rather than nostalgia. The Yankees were two-time defending champions and had won six of their seven matchups against the Dodgers. Simply practicing in Yankee Stadium intimidated Roseboro. "I can't ever recall feeling as tense as I did during our off-day workout in that big ballpark," he wrote. "You don't want to fuck up, of course. There's always that. But there was more than that this time."

Maybe his nerves put some extra pop in his bat. His first time up, in the second inning, he faced Yankee ace Whitey Ford with two runners on. Ford hung a curve that Roseboro clobbered over the right field fence. With Koufax striking out a World Series record 15, Johnny's dinger was enough to beat the Yankees 5–2. "His three-run homer off Whitey Ford early in the first game of the World Series got the Dodgers off to a flying start, and they never looked back as they swept four straight from the Yankees," George T. Davis wrote in the *Los Angeles Herald-Examiner.* Roseboro had delivered several clutch hits over the season, including a grand slam in Pittsburgh in September that helped the team stay in first place. Dodgers general manager Buzzie Bavasi gave Roseboro the credit he often didn't receive: "I think John Roseboro was more valuable to us in 1963 than anytime, although he hit for a higher average the two previous seasons. He's an unsung hero of the club."

When a reporter asked him later if the World Series home run was the most memorable moment of his career, Roseboro said in typical fashion, "No. My biggest thrill was receiving that check after the World Series."

Bavasi gave Roseboro a $3,000 raise for the 1964 season, upping his salary to $30,000. His manager paid him with praise. "Nobody can block a plate any better than Roseboro or get away faster on an opponent's bunt," Walt Alston said. "Roseboro can run faster than Campy, throw as hard and hit with as much power—though not as often. He's coming into his own."

After five and a half seasons in the majors, Roseboro had not erased Campanella from the memory of Dodgers fans, but he had quieted his critics and contented them with his play. He appreciated Alston's affirmation and Bavasi's backing. That spring, though, he had developed calcium deposits in his knee, an occupational hazard, and the team physician made him sit out part of spring training. Nobody accused him of jaking, because nobody played through more pain than Rosey. He shrugged off busted fingers, broken toenails, bruises everywhere from foul tips, and constant knee pain with humor. He figured he took about three foul tips a game, on average "one bleeder and two stingers." He knew they were coming. "The only thing I don't know is which finger. It gets to be kind of a game, like guessing what the dealer has in blackjack." His job required so much soaking afterward in the clubhouse whirlpool that teammates called it "the USS Roseboro." "Seventeen years in this business, I've never seen anybody like Roseboro," Dodgers trainer Doc Anderson said. "And I've seen some tough catchers. I don't know how he takes the beating he does."

He won respect and a reputation for durability and toughness. "Roseboro plays when 90 percent of the ballplayers couldn't," Alston said. "He'll get hit on the shoulder point with a foul tip and won't even rub it. He's absolutely fearless." Pitcher Joe Moeller, whose ball moved so much it was hard for Roseboro to catch, commented, "He had probably the highest threshold for pain of any person I knew. He would take a foul tip off his finger, look down at it, swear at me, and walk off the field with his finger completely covered in blood then return the next inning."

Roseboro was behind the plate on Opening Day despite the pain in his knee, which would keep him from taking batting practice all season and had to be drained regularly. In July a foul tip caught him on the middle finger of his throwing hand and tore the flesh back to the knuckle. *Los Angeles Times* columnist Jim Murray said the finger looked like "a peeled banana." Roseboro took 15 stitches at the hospital but was the first one at the ballpark the next day. Alston sent him home. "He'll be back before almost anyone else would be," Dodgers trainer Bill Buhler said. "He can stand more pain than any man I know." Sportswriter Bob Hunter of the *Los Angeles Herald-Examiner* added, "While John sustains an inordinate number of injuries, he recovers so rapidly that his durability has become almost a legend."

Gabby's toughness was most evident in plays at the plate. "There was no question that John Roseboro was the boss," Bavasi said. "He had more courage than any catcher I ever saw. On a close play at home, nobody'd ever score because he'd block the plate with his entire body. He was the Rock of Gibraltar."

Unfazed by the contact, the former linebacker crouched low and hit runners so that they remembered it. One collision with Orlando Cepeda knocked the Giants' star out with a knee injury. "He was trying to hurt me, so I hurt him," Roseboro wrote. "I hit him with a cross-body block, caught his leg and almost broke it." When the Cardinals' Daryl Spencer tried to take him out, Roseboro sent Spencer somersaulting. "He lit on his butt and bounced a couple of times," Johnny wrote. When Cincinnati pitcher Jim Brosnan tried to run over Roseboro, he failed. "He hurled himself at me, and I hit him in the middle and raised him into a full flip and he landed flat on his back with a hell of a jolt," Roseboro recalled.

His ruggedness in blocking the plate became legendary. "He is so strong that a base runner would just as soon charge a moving streetcar as John Roseboro," Murray wrote. "Where most players block the plate, Roseboro gets the ball and charges up the line like [Los Angeles Rams All-Pro linebacker] Les Richter. It sometimes delays the game while they sweep up the kayoes. They had to unscrew Julian Javier's neck one night last year when he hit the Roseboro shins and his head suddenly hit his shoulders."

Roseboro was unapologetic for his rough play. "Between those white lines it was a war zone," he said. "You can say, 'Hi, how are the wife and kids?' before the game, but once it starts, I'm gonna try to beat your butt and you're gonna try to beat mine. I can't become intimidated or leery of being hurt. I got a reputation as a guy who would hurt other guys, and they'd come into me cautiously, which was the ideal situation for me."

Roseboro's reputation also provided security for his pitchers and gave them confidence to pitch effectively inside. "I never worried about knocking someone down because I knew they would never get to the mound with John behind the plate," Moeller said.

Johnny took boxing lessons and studied karate. He liked to think of himself as a tough guy. But off the field he wasn't. Those closest to him, his wife and children, saw the tender side. "He wanted to be a tough guy, but I don't think he could hurt anybody," Jeri said.

Despite his injuries, Roseboro had his best season in 1964. His decision at the beginning of the year to swing for contact rather than power paid off with a .287 batting average, the high-water mark of his career. He had only three home runs but 24 doubles, another personal best. He also threw out 60 percent of runners trying to steal, tops in the league. The Dodgers, however, did not fare as well as a team. They lost more games than they won and finished in sixth place, 13 games back.

On July 2, 1964, President Lyndon Johnson signed the Civil Rights Act. The new law, which made discrimination based on race, color, religion, or national origin illegal, had widespread implications for players like John Roseboro and Juan Marichal. But it did not eliminate bigotry, and in some ways it inflamed racial tensions. Two weeks later, when a white New York police officer shot and killed a 15-year-old African-American boy in front of his friends on Manhattan's Upper East Side, the incident sparked six nights of rioting in

Harlem and Bedford-Stuyvesant. Over the next six weeks, race riots followed in Philadelphia, Rochester, Chicago, and three New Jersey cities. One hundred years after the Civil War, the sequel seemed to be playing out in a wave of guerilla urban violence.

CHAPTER FIVE
Summer of Fury

THE SPECTER OF VIOLENCE OVERSHADOWED THE FIRST DODGERS-GIANTS matchup of 1965. Malcom X had been murdered in February. Two weeks later, police in Selma turned a march for voting rights into Bloody Sunday. Also in March, the United States had sent its first troops to fight in Vietnam after launching Operation Rolling Thunder, an aerial bombing campaign of North Vietnam. And civil war had broken out in the Dominican Republic.

Violence always lurked when the Giants and Dodgers played, dating back to the first encounter in 1889 between the New York Giants and the then Brooklyn Bridegrooms in a best-of-11 championship series that initiated the nation's oldest rivalry in professional sports, one soiled by beanballs, brawls, and bad blood. A winner-take-all intensity charged the ballpark every time the two teams squared off. Giants players felt the surge the moment they arrived in enemy territory two weeks into the 1965 season. "When you stepped off the plane in Los Angeles, you could *hear* the electricity," San Francisco's power-hitting first baseman Willie McCovey said. "Even the skycaps at the airports were all wrapped up in the rivalry. It carried over to the hotel and finally the ballpark. The tension was always there."

The atmosphere and tradition pushed the players to compete at a higher level. "Those of us who have been around a while always play this series just a little harder, and it's contagious among the young players who aren't as familiar with the background," explained the Dodgers' hard-throwing pitcher Don Drysdale, who would figure into both ends of the anger in that first series of 1965.

Specific personalities had stoked the rivalry over the previous seven decades. Brooklyn owner and president Charles Ebbets resented that his star pitcher, Joe "Iron Man" McGinnity, had defected to the Giants in 1902 and wanted in every way to beat them. John McGraw, who became the Giants manager that year, targeted Ebbets with frequent insults at the park and in the press. Ebbets lobbied the league (unsuccessfully) to punish the insolent manager. The stakes escalated in 1914 when McGraw's former teammate turned nemesis, Wilbert Robinson, became the Brooklyn skipper, a position he held for the next 17 years; the two rivals didn't so much play games as wage battles. After the Giants won the World Series in 1933 and the Dodgers finished 26½ games back, McGraw's successor, Bill Terry, responded to a reporter's question about the Dodgers prospects in 1934, "Brooklyn? Is Brooklyn still in the league?" The Dodgers retaliated by defeating the Giants in the final two games of the season to spoil New York's pennant chances while Brooklyn fans waved "We're still in the league" banners at the Polo Grounds. Seventeen years after that, Dodgers manager Charlie Dressen provoked the same revenge when he announced midseason 1951, "The Giants is dead." That resurrected New York with a winning spree (39 of 47 games) that eliminated the Dodgers' 13½-game lead, the coup de grâce coming off Bobby Thomson's bat in the last inning of the three-game playoff with the "shot heard 'round the world."

When the two teams played one out of every seven games against each other—22 times each summer—the spikes came up, the fastballs shrieked inside, and the benches often cleared. In 1951 Giants pitcher Sal Maglie, known as "the Barber" for the close shaves he regularly gave batters, knocked down the Dodgers' Jackie Robinson. Robinson bunted the Barber's next pitch down the first baseline, and when Maglie bent over to field it, Robinson smashed into him with a vengeance that emptied the benches. Four years later, Maglie again brushed back Robinson who again bunted. This time, the Barber avoided fielding the ball even though Robinson slowed to give him the chance to reach it. Instead, Robinson knocked over Giants second baseman Davey Williams, who was covering first. Alvin Dark, then the Giants shortstop, bowled over Robinson at third base later in the game, jarring the ball loose from Robinson's grip, and the two grappled. In 1953 Ruben Gomez, the Giants' notorious "beanball king," plunked the Dodgers' Carl Furillo, who was contending for the batting title, in the wrist. Figuring Leo Durocher had ordered the pitch, Furillo charged the Giants manager. In the brawl that followed, someone stepped on Furillo's hand, breaking a bone, and he had to sit out the next 10 days (though he did end up winning the batting title with his .344 average). Such was the intensity the rivalry inspired.

On April 29, 1965, a playoff atmosphere permeated the Los Angeles ballpark, with both teams poised to be top contenders for the National League pennant. The Dodgers had reinforced their already strong pitching corps—Johnny Roseboro said in spring training he thought this was the best Dodgers team he had ever played on—and the Giants relied on the strong bats of Willie McCovey, Willie Mays, and Jim Ray Hart. Drysdale took the mound at Chavez Ravine that Thursday night against Juan Marichal. Juan had won his last three starts after losing a 1–0 decision on Opening Day. He had already thrown two shutouts.

But that night required focus beyond the Dodger Blue. Five days earlier, the rumblings of revolution that Juan had heard two months previous in the Dominican Republic were realized. Rebels loyal to Juan Bosch—who had won the election in 1963 but been ousted shortly afterward in a coup—pushed aside the military-imposed junta and set up their own government. The next day, Marichal could barely breathe. As often happened with him, the stress manifested itself in a physical ailment. This time, it attacked him in the sinuses. But he started the game against the Mets. Dominican military forces loyal to the ousted junta staged a countercoup. The people of his country who tuned into the broadcast of the Giants-Mets game found solace in Marichal's success that night—until static bewitched their radios. The Western Union operator at Candlestick Park knew that something had gone wrong in Marichal's country when he lost contact with the two Santo Domingo radio stations seized by the rebels. Marichal continued to strike out Mets batters and blanked New York, but the news from his country shook him after the game.

He and Alma worried about their families. Juan could not call his mother and siblings to check on them. The farm had no telephone. Letters took a week each way. He went to the San Francisco consulate to read the Dominican papers, but they were three days behind. The best he could make out was that bands of soldiers and insurgents stalked the capital's streets, looting and executing hundreds—so many that the Dominican Red Cross workers buried them where they fell—but he could not be sure that his and Alma's families were safe. Even though his wife's family did have a telephone, the fighting interrupted phone service and it sometimes took days to make contact. On April 28, the day before Juan was scheduled to start against the Dodgers, President Lyndon Johnson dispatched several thousand US Marines to the Dominican in Operation Power Pack.

The President explained to congressional leaders and later to the American people on television that he wanted to protect the 2,000 American citizens in the Dominican Republic and prevent the spread of communism in the Caribbean. No one wanted another Cuba, did they? The specious Red threat provided a good cover for the protection of $150 million of American investments. The deployment of US troops made the nightly news, which Juan watched with alarm. By the 29th he had still not heard from his family. Not knowing unnerved him. As much as he tried to concentrate on the batter in front of him, he could not suppress his worries.

The Giants took a 1–0 lead in the second inning when Drysdale walked McCovey and then gave up two singles. Marichal grounded out to end the threat. The next inning, Drysdale faced Willie Mays. Roseboro knew the Giants' best hitter had an Achilles' heel. "He hated to be hit by pitches," Roseboro wrote. "He especially hated to bat against Drysdale because Don would drill him." Johnny liked Willie—the two were friends off the field—but the only loyalty any player had in those Dodgers-Giants duels was to his own team, and his only aim was to beat the other. Even when Mays came to the plate sweet-talking him, Roseboro didn't hesitate to call for an inside pitch.

With Drysdale he didn't have to. The Big D thrived on throwing hard inside. He had been tutored in intimidation tactics by one of the best—Sal Maglie had ended his career with the Dodgers and found an eager pupil in the young Drysdale. Over the course of his 14-year career, the 6-foot-5 Drysdale set a record for hitting batters (154) that still stands. He knocked down countless more. Fines and suspensions from the league president didn't deter him. "He liked to teach hitters respect by knocking them down," Roseboro wrote. "He was the meanest, most intense competitor I ever saw."

Sure enough, Drysdale delivered a fastball under Mays's chin. "What's wrong with that motherfucker?" Willie whined to Roseboro. "Why does he want to hurt me?"

Johnny laughed. "Willie, he don't want to hurt you. He just wants your respect."

Willie grounded out harmlessly to third base.

The majority of the 30,219 fans in Dodger Stadium loved seeing their pitcher smear the Giants' star in the dirt. The animosity agitated them as much as it did the players. In one game Dodgers shortstop Maury Wills tried to turn a double play but beaned Giants runner Jim Ray Hart when Hart didn't slide. Hart lay on the ground, the Giants stormed the field, and a Los Angeles woman in the left field seats clobbered a female Giants fan over the head with her shoe.

That dimension of the rivalry dated back to the beginning, too—to the late 19th century, when the fisticuffs between the two sides were as likely to involve fans as players. Ebbets Field, where Giants outfielders had to dodge rocks and other missiles thrown at them, became an equally dangerous place for Giants fans. In New York the Dodgers and Giants were the only two major league teams from the same town competing in the same league. One couldn't be neutral; the rivalry demanded you choose a side. If you loved the Bums, you hated the Jints—and vice versa. The circumstances tampered with the character of otherwise good people. Legend has it that Monsignor Woods, a Catholic priest from Brooklyn respected for his charitable works, declared in 1923, "I hate the Giants!" Whether or not he actually said that, the legend speaks to the grip the rivalry had on those it possessed.

In 1938 a postal worker named Bob Joyce sought comfort at a Brooklyn saloon after his beloved Dodgers had lost to the Giants. He didn't find it from the bartender, William Diamond, who needled

Joyce. Frank Krug, a patron and Giants fan, spiced up the taunting with his own comments.

"Shut up, you bastards," Joyce said. "Lay off the Dodgers."

Not surprisingly, that only incited more teasing. The laughter chased Joyce out of the saloon. He soon returned with a revolver and shot the bartender in the stomach. When Krug tried to intervene, Joyce plugged him in the head. After police arrested him, Joyce pleaded a temporary insanity brought on by rage from hearing the ridicule directed at his Dodgers.

The rivalry also took shape from the character of the two boroughs where it originated. Glitz against grit: Broadway, Park Avenue, and the Upper East Side versus Flatbush, Bed-Stuy, and Prospect Park. Dodgers fans resented the urbane elitism of the Giants' following; Giants fans disdained the blue-collar vulgarities of the Brooklyn faithful. The move to the West Coast changed the complexion but not the intensity of the rivalry, which accentuated the animosity intrinsic between the capitals of Northern and Southern California. "Los Angeles and San Francisco had long sustained a mutual disregard, hatred blended with a tinge of jealousy for what one town possessed that the other did not," David Plaut writes in *Chasing October.* Columnist Herb Caen of the *San Francisco Chronicle* characterized the reciprocal hatred as one of congenital convenience, "a reflex built in at birth. It is firmly a part of the mystique of each city, and why not? It's fun to have an object of automatic disdain so close at hand."

Plaut details how the pundits from the two places reflected their constituents' views with the mud they slung up and down the coast. The *Los Angeles Times'* Jim Murray criticized the loose morality and weather to the north: "San Francisco isn't a city—it's a no-host cocktail party. It has a nice, even climate: it's always winter." His compatriot Melvin Durslag at the *Los Angeles Herald-Examiner* poked fun at the town's new team in its early years: "San Franciscans [who expect a pennant] are advised to stay away from coarse foods

. . . avoid stimulants that irritate the stomach walls . . . if seized by a choking feeling, lay quietly and well-covered until the physician arrives." The *San Francisco Chronicle*'s Art Rosenbaum sniped back with "Smodgers," referring to the LA smog, and the "city whose women would attend the opera in leopard shirts and toreador pants if indeed they attended the opera at all." Caen threw in the remark, "Isn't it nice that people who prefer Los Angeles to San Francisco live there?"

There were those who thought the move across the country or expansion in 1962, which reduced the times the teams faced each other every summer to 18, might dull the intensity of the rivalry, but it remained robust in California. Alvin Dark, who had played for the Giants in New York and managed them in San Francisco, said, "I don't care where you play these games, the Dodger-Giant rivalry is always intense." The move simply built upon what was already there. "You can talk all you want about Brooklyn and New York, Minneapolis and St. Paul, Dallas and Fort Worth," said Joe Cronin, who was born in the City by the Bay. "But there are no two cities in America where the people want to beat each other's brains out more than in San Francisco and Los Angeles."

A scorer's decision exposed the mutual enmity in 1959. Giants pitcher Sam Jones, perhaps better known for chewing a toothpick on the mound than he was for his sweeping curveball, worked a no-hitter into the eighth inning at the Los Angeles Coliseum (where the Dodgers played their first two seasons in California) when his shortstop bobbled a ground ball and didn't attempt a throw to first. *Error,* Jones thought. Obvious error, many witnesses concluded. But the official scorer, Charlie Park of the *Los Angeles Mirror-News,* ruled base hit. The San Francisco newsmen in the press box lambasted him, but Park resisted their appeals. The *San Francisco Chronicle* observed that there are "dark and secret things unrelated to reality and governed by no law of man or nature that happen all the time in the Los Angeles Coliseum . . . Whatever the explanation, the facts are intolerable to San Franciscans who regard baseball as a sane pastime, bound by logical rules, fairly imposed. They don't like to have indignities inflicted on Sam Jones' no-hitter."*

Even the groundskeepers became complicit in the indignities. Dark employed them to thwart Maury Wills's speed in 1962, the year Wills set the Major League Baseball mark for most stolen bases in a season (104). The Giants manager instructed Candlestick Park groundskeeper Matty Schwab to douse the base paths, ostensibly to keep the loose dirt from swirling, but obviously to slow down Wills and the rest of the speedy "Swift Set." Murray complained that if Schwab had sprayed any more water "the Red Cross would have declared second base a disaster area." Of note, the Giants players voted Schwab a full $7,290 World Series share that season for his contribution to their success.

In the fourth inning of the game on April 29, 1965, the Dodgers' Tommy Davis pleased the locals with a triple that drove in a run to tie the score. Two innings later, Wills singled, moved to second on a bunt, stole third, and scored on another Tommy Davis hit (this a single to center field), and the Dodgers led 2–1. Perhaps Marichal's concentration had slipped. Herman Franks lifted his pitcher for a pinch hitter in the seventh (ending Juan's streak of nine complete games going back to 1964) and replaced him with Bobby Bolin. Juan remained on the bench, intent upon the outcome of the game he had started against the hated Dodgers. When Drysdale knocked down

* Jones did notch a no-hitter in his career: Four years earlier, pitching for the Chicago Cubs, he no-hit the Pittsburgh Pirates on May 12, 1955. But he had another no-hitter in 1959 taken away. He had no-hit the Cardinals on September 26 through seven innings when rain stopped the game. His effort was initially recorded as a no-hitter only to be rescinded by Major League Baseball in 1991 when it decided games had to go nine innings for pitchers to be credited with a no-hitter. Perhaps not coincidentally, Toothpick Sam's second nickname was "Sad Sam."

Mays with another inside pitch in the top of the eighth, Marichal seethed.

Juan had been around long enough to have internalized the enmity. Each player felt a personal stake in what *Time* characterized as "baseball's bitterest rivalry." They didn't forget the hard slides, the inside pitches, the angry words of those games. "The grudges got carried not only from game to game but from year to year," Wills wrote in his autobiography, *On the Run*. "It was like a war all the time."

In the days before free agency mobilized players and fertilized fraternization between opponents who had formerly been teammates, the rivalry stuck because teams remained almost the same from year to year, which thickened the players' loyalties. As with any long-standing conflict where the next generation inherits the elders' feud, the veterans inculcated the younger players with their hatred—to the point where they saw red in orange-and-black or Dodger Blue. "We hated the Giants," Carl Furillo said. "We just hated the uniform."

So when Don Drysdale led off the eighth and Bobby Bonin retaliated with a slow curve that thumped him on the posterior, everyone expected it. But the pitch was not enough to assuage Marichal's sense of injustice. "For the five years I've been in the league, I've seen too much of this sort of thing," Juan said afterward in the clubhouse. "He [Drysdale] has hit Mays and Cepeda and has knocked just about all of us back from the plate. I do not say he tries deliberately to hit us, but he has good control and shouldn't be that wild. This stuff has got to stop. I'll do something about it if he continues. Somebody's going to find out we can protect our hitters. Next time he comes close and I'm pitching, he'll get hit. And real good, too."

Sportswriter Arnold Hano interpreted Marichal's statement as more than an idle threat: "The young Dominican declared war [on Drysdale]." National League president Warren Giles also took Juan seriously. Giles warned that any pitcher deliberately "protecting" his hitters would be assessed a $1,000 fine.*

Drysdale, meanwhile, did nothing to mollify Marichal or the other Giants. Rather, the Big D incited his antagonists with the retort, "I'm only about sixty feet away from them in any direction. They know where I am. If they get me, they better get me good or I'll take four guys with me, and I don't mean those .220 hitters, either."

Marichal lost the first matchup 2–1. The Dodgers came away from the series with three wins in four games. The two teams met again in San Francisco four days later on May 7. Johnny Roseboro had a big game, going 3-for-3, with his biggest hit coming in the eighth, a leadoff single that eventually became the winning run in the Dodgers' 4–3 victory. That same day, the Dominican Republic's civil war became *Time* magazine's cover story. The American press widely supported the president sending troops to intervene in the region for the first time in 40 years. "If ever a firm hand was needed to keep order, last week was the time and the Dominican Republic was the place," *Time* stated, referring to Santo Domingo as "a city gone berserk in the bloodiest civil war in recent Latin American history."

The marines did not readily succeed in restoring order. The rebels included a loose collaboration of Bosch loyalists, aspiring communists, opportunistic insurgents, and defiant army soldiers battling the military junta's air force and US Marines in a chaotic urban guerrilla war that ranged from one neighborhood to another. Ad hoc execution squads lined up victims against walls, snipers fired at US helicopters, and a mob paraded the head of a police officer on

---

* Marichal made $60,000 in 1965. The modern equivalent of Giles's threatened penalty would be a $304,167 fine to Giants pitcher Tim Lincecum, who made $18,250,000 in 2012.

a pole like a trophy. Bodies littered the streets. The smell of rotting flesh hung pungent in the air. In the hospitals doctors operated on the wounded by flashlight and without anesthesia. "Santo Domingo was a city without power, without water, without food, without any semblance of sanity," *Time* reported.

Juan couldn't read these reports—many of them sullied by misinformation—without worrying about his family. Nor could his wife, Alma. They had allegiances on both sides. Alma's brother was a lieutenant in the military, and her sister had married an officer. Juan had friends among those revolting and those resisting. They craved a stable government for their country and wanted their loved ones to be safe. "With troops in the streets and people being hurt and killed, it gives you a strange feeling to talk political abstractions when you are thousands of miles away, playing baseball for a living," Juan wrote. He felt powerless being so far from his loved ones during the war. The anxiety overwhelmed him. His sinus troubles persisted. He was scheduled to start the third game of the second series with the Dodgers on Sunday afternoon, going up against Sandy Koufax, but while throwing his warm-ups before the game, he fought for breath. Franks substituted Gaylord Perry for Marichal.

Jesus Alou popped a two-run homer off Koufax in the bottom of the fourth to give the Giants a 2–0 lead that delighted the 40,596 fans at Candlestick. Los Angeles countered with a two-run homer of their own by Willie Davis in the sixth. The Dodgers took special satisfaction in the home run off Perry, who had hit two of their batters. Franks pulled Perry in the seventh after he gave up two singles. Giants reliever Masanori Murakami hit Roseboro with the first pitch he threw all season. That loaded the bases. Murakami struck out the next batter for the second out, but then Franks brought in the right-handed Marichal to face the left-handed-hitting Wally Moon. Juan hadn't felt fit to pitch but, as he often did, pushed himself to play through his malady. Not so well at first. He gave up a single that scored one runner and almost another who was thrown out at home. Though the run counted against Perry, Marichal had given up the hit that put the Dodgers ahead 3–2.

In the Giants' half of the eighth, Koufax walked Mays, gave up two singles that tied the score 3–3, and left the game. Two sacrifices and a single by Marichal put the Giants up 6–3. Juan walked the first batter in the top of the ninth but then struck out the next two and got the final out on a fly ball to right field for the win. Koufax, despite striking out 11 batters in seven innings, gave up five runs in his worst outing of the season to date and took the loss. Still, the Dodgers remained in first place, five and a half games ahead of the Giants, who were mired in eighth place with an 11–13 record.

The teams did not play each other again until June 15, when Marichal faced Drysdale in their first meeting since they had traded taunts in the papers. The Giants had found their winning stride, going 20–13 since Marichal beat the Dodgers on May 9, and climbed up to third place, though they remained five and a half games behind their first-place rivals. Marichal had won nine games, led the league with four shutouts, and allowed only 1.85 earned runs per nine innings. Drysdale had won 11 games, the most of any NL pitcher.

The civil war continued in the Dominican Republic, and President Johnson kept funneling marines to the cause. By the end of May, 20,500 US troops occupied the island, about half the number of those in Vietnam. But the factions on both sides complicated negotiations and rendered a ceasefire impossible. Riflemen sniped at suspected enemies in Santo Domingo, rebels launched mortars at marine positions, and government tanks rolled through narrow capital streets blasting houses suspected of harboring rebels. From his perch in Puerto Rico, deposed Dominican president Juan Bosch blamed the United States for the messiness of the situation.

Americans began to question and criticize Johnson for aligning himself with "a military junta that is widely hated," and it became clear that "the Dominican people—not just a handful of communists—were fighting and dying for social justice and constitutionalism," as the *New York Times* pointed out. Marichal's sinuses raged unabated. *Time* referred to his condition somewhat dismissively with the comment that he had been bothered by "an allergy his doctor blamed on the revolution in his native Dominican Republic."

But the strain on Marichal was serious. On television he saw the scenes of his countrymen rioting, stealing from stores, killing one another. The images disturbed him. "There's no way you can concentrate while that is happening in your country," he said. The Braves rocked him for nine runs in less than four innings, one of the worst outings of his career, in late May. He and the Alou brothers received word at the end of the month that their families were safe—for the moment. Juan's sinuses continued to trouble him. Sneezing fits shook him so violently that when he was driving he had to pull over his car until they passed.

More than 50,000 fans filled Dodger Stadium on Tuesday, June 15, for the Marichal-Drysdale rematch. Neither pitcher hit any batters. Both delivered top performances. Drysdale pitched a complete game, gave up only two runs, and cracked two hits of his own. But Marichal outdid him, scattering five hits over nine innings, allowing only one run, and getting a hit himself. San Francisco won 2–1. But the Dodgers took the next two, and the Giants left Los Angeles six and a half games back.

Two weeks later, they met again in San Francisco, once again Drysdale against Marichal. The 35,000-plus San Francisco fans booed Drysdale and cheered merrily when the Giants scored a quick run in the first inning. But then the two pitchers took turns retiring batters quickly with strikeouts and ground ball outs. When Marichal gave up a single in the third, he induced the next batter to ground into a double play. When Willie McCovey singled in the fourth, Roseboro threw him out trying to steal.

But the Dodgers battery came undone in the fifth. Drysdale committed two errors on the first two batters. Roseboro made another to let a run score. Then Johnny let a ball get by him, and the runner advanced. A walk and two singles later, the Giants led 5–0. Drysdale buckled down for the final four innings, retiring 12 batters in succession, striking out 4 of them. Roseboro atoned by singling during a Dodgers rally in the seventh and making it to third but did not manage to score. Marichal got Drysdale to ground out weakly with the bases loaded to end the threat. Juan was simply too good for the Dodgers that day, shutting them out on six hits. The victory marked Marichal's 10th consecutive win over the Dodgers at Candlestick. Los Angeles remained in first place, but the Giants had whittled the gap to two and a half games.

Juan was selected as the National League's starter for the All-Star Game in Minnesota on July 13. In his last start before the game, he blanked the Phillies 4–0, his seventh shutout and 14th victory of the season. He lowered his ERA to 1.55 even with a nine-run barrage over three and two-thirds innings in Milwaukee. Despite the distraction of the civil war back home and his sinus trouble, he was pitching one of the finest seasons of his career.

His teammates on the NL All-Star squad included Drysdale and Koufax. For all the attention given to his matchups against Drysdale that season, Koufax remained Marichal's true counterpart for the distinction of being the major league's best pitcher. That season the *Sporting News* referred to "the great Marichal" as "the best right-hander in the league" with his "magnificent mastery." Koufax was, simply, "the Left Arm of God." While Koufax blew batters away with his supernal fastball and curveball, Marichal baffled them with his patented mix of pitches and impeccable control. Sandy racked up strikeouts; Juan preferred the efficiency of ground ball outs. "It takes at least three pitches to strike a man out," he said. "It only takes one for a ground ball." However they achieved it, Marichal and Koufax were equals in success: From Opening Day 1961 to the Midsummer Classic of 1965, both had won 91 games.*

Equals in success, they were a study in contrasts: Marichal was married with children, a dark-skinned Catholic Latino and sometime practical joker who set off stink bombs on airplanes. Koufax was a highly desired bachelor, a light-skinned Jew from Brooklyn and a man of incalculable reserve. Marichal employed a variety of windups, most notably his signature high leg kick, to sling his arsenal of 13 pitches—including a fast slider, a jumping fastball, a sinking overhand curve, a breaking sidearm curve, and a nasty screwball—all with precise control. He had another weapon: his willingness to tickle batters inside. Koufax, on the other hand, used an amazingly efficient windup to throw his curve and fastball, the only pitches he needed to dominate the opposition. Koufax modeled understated emotion; Marichal displayed a flash temper.

They had started against one another only twice, both times in 1964, splitting decisions, though Koufax could claim the edge with his no-hitter. "No other head-to-head mound rivalry ever seemed more destined to fire the fan's imagination," Peter C. Bjarkman writes in *Elysian Fields Quarterly*. The two would square off for the rubber match in August—with everlasting consequences.

---

* Over 16 seasons Marichal would win 243 games and lose 142 for a .631 career winning percentage (51st on the all-time list). Koufax went 165–87 through 12 seasons, a .655 winning percentage (22nd all-time).

After curfew that night on a darkened street in Santo Domingo, a short line of cars carrying representatives of the Organization of American States' negotiating team drove out of the rebel zones. The talks had stalled, stymied by the "bitter hatred" that divided the two sides. An American reporter observing the cars' retreat was suddenly startled by a civilian rebel with a rifle. The reporter took a nervous step backward. "Tell me," the rebel accosted him. "How did Marichal do today in the All-Star Game?"

The reporter was relieved to be able to tell the man with the rifle that even though Sandy Koufax picked up the win with an inning of scoreless work, Marichal took home the game's MVP Award for his three innings (the maximum the rules allowed a pitcher to throw in the game) of one-hit, shutout pitching. Marichal also singled and scored in the National League's 6–5 triumph. The rebel walked away satisfied, and the reporter's heart rate eventually stabilized.

The violence remained centralized in Santo Domingo, but the effects spread nationwide. Bank closings hampered the country's already weak economy. Resolution seemed remote, the conflict's escalation more a certainty. "After thirty-one years of savage Trujillo dictatorship and subsequent vacuums, the hatred of the Dominican Republic runs deep, and there are thousands of people on both sides who are just aching to have at each other," *Time* reported in August.

Juan continued to fret and to win. In his first outing after the All-Star Game, he shut down the Astros 7–0 for his 15th win and 8th shutout. Joe Morgan, Houston's future Hall of Fame second baseman, said of Marichal afterward, "There's only one more in his class, and I'm not so sure about him [Koufax]." On August 4 Juan beat the Cincinnati Reds 4–3 in 10 innings. In his 17th win of the season and 100th of his career, he struck out 14, his high mark for the summer. He had pitched 18 complete games and allowed only 1.65 earned runs per nine innings. His performance had been remarkable; given the circumstances, it was absolutely amazing.

Meanwhile, in Los Angeles, Roseboro wasn't repeating his success of the previous year. He had put together an eight-game hitting streak in April, but his aching back took him out of the daily lineup. He had some timely hits, like his eighth-inning single that produced the winning run against the Giants in May, but he was putting up a lot of oh-fers in the box scores, the worst being an 0-for-7 night in Houston in mid-May. By July 5 his 33 RBI were second-best on the team, but he was hitting only .239. The frustration that ensued may have prompted a falling out with one of his best friends on the team.

Maury Wills and Johnny had been roommates on the road and good friends for six years. They both enjoyed playing various musical instruments, from the ukulele to the banjo, though Wills showed more talent and didn't hesitate to tease Roseboro about his musical shortcomings. They also enjoyed dressing up for a meal on the road and generally got along well. "He was a charming guy with a gift of gab, a very appealing person and roomie," Johnny wrote. But Wills had a weakness for women, and the more success he had on the field the more he enjoyed in the bedroom. Finally, one night during the first week of July in Cincinnati, after Rosey had waited two hours to call his wife while Maury wooed a woman on the phone from midnight to 2 a.m., Rosey asked Alston to switch him to a room with Willie Davis. "He [Wills] gets into so much business I can't get my rest," Johnny explained. "I love him like a brother, but I got to get away from him."

"It's like a divorce," Wills told a reporter. "Roseboro packed up and went home to mother."

Johnny wasn't a playboy in the fashion of his ex-roomie, but he was no monk, either. He and his wife endured frigid spells that he warmed with other women, occasionally accepting the overtures of groupies who wanted to make it with a ballplayer. Jeri knew ballplayers cheated on their wives. She once showed up unexpectedly in Johnny's hotel room saying she simply wanted to surprise him, though he suspected she wanted to catch him being unfaithful. She didn't, though her radar was astute even if her timing was off. Johnny had an affair with a graduate student in Chicago that lasted several years and ended after Jeri found one of the woman's love letters. Jeri lit into Johnny, but he did not admit any more than she read. He would later meet a woman that would end their marriage.

Two weeks after his breakup with Wills, Roseboro fell into a slump. His parents came out to visit during a home stand, but all they saw was their son's futility during an 0-for-19 spell that lasted five games. His average fell to a disappointing .211. He managed a hit on July 27, but Walt Alston dropped Roseboro to eighth (from fifth) in the batting order and even sat him a couple of games the final week of July.

Roseboro's hitting picked up some during August. During nearly the first three weeks of the month, going into a critical series with the Giants, he went 9-for-34, a .265 clip. Not great, but an improvement on his July. His biggest contribution remained his defensive play. That season he posted a stellar .994 fielding percentage, allowed only eight passed balls—his best mark since 1958—and threw out nearly half of the runners who tried to steal on him.

On August 6 the Dodgers played the Reds in Cincinnati, Roseboro went 1-for-3 with two walks, and President Johnson signed the Voting Rights Act in a ceremony that heralded the new law as the completion of the Emancipation Proclamation, eliminating voter qualification tests and adding more than one million African Americans to the voting rolls. Referring to slavery's legacy in America, Johnson said, "Today we strike away the last major shackle of those fierce and ancient bonds." But the stroke of the president's pen did not erase the prejudice. That week, white thugs beat five civil rights workers in Americus, Georgia; night riders burned two black churches in Slidell, Louisiana; and white neighbors of Chicago mayor Richard Daley pelted demonstrators outside his house with eggs and tomatoes. Despite the landmark legislation, racial tension remained taut throughout the nation.

The Dodgers returned to Los Angeles for an eight-game home stand beginning Tuesday, August 10. Koufax won his 20th game of the season, which spurred talk about the possibility of 30 wins. No one had reached that mark since the Cardinals' Dizzy Dean in 1934, three decades prior. But Koufax had 12 remaining starts, and it seemed possible the way he was pitching. Roseboro thought he might make it; he expected Sandy to win every start. "He was the best I ever saw," Johnny wrote simply. "I think what set Sandy apart from all the other pitchers was his ability in his prime to throw his stuff so hard and with such accuracy." The upbeat mood of Angelenos, whose team had been in first place for 99 days, took an abrupt turn the following night.

Around 7 p.m. on Wednesday, Lee Minikus, a white California highway patrolman, clocked a gray Buick doing 55 in a 35-miles-per-hour zone on Avalon Boulevard. Minikus gave chase on his motorcycle and pulled over the Buick near 116th Street in the midst of the Watts neighborhood. The driver, Marquette Frye, a 21-year-old black man, and his stepbrother, Ronald Frye, 22, had been drinking screwdrivers that afternoon. Officer Minikus smelled alcohol on their breath. He asked Marquette to perform a field sobriety test. Marquette complied but was unable to walk a straight line. The patrolman informed the driver that he was under arrest for operating a motor vehicle under the influence.

The traffic stop had attracted a small crowd of 25–30 people, drawn to the flashing lights on a hot, lazy evening. Marquette had entertained them by joking with Minikus, who had bantered back.

Their repartee had been polite, jovial. The crowd had laughed. Marquette's mother, Rena Frye, changed that.

Barely 5 feet tall, she pushed through the crowd, which was growing steadily. She had been cooking rabbit in her apartment a block away when someone told her that the police had arrested her son. Rena lit into Marquette about his drinking. Her anger ignited his and recast the situation. The white Officer Minikus and his two white colleagues who had answered his routine call for backup suddenly became symbols of a century of oppression, and the moment reminded Marquette and the other African Americans in the Watts neighborhood of past incidents when white cops confronted black citizens. "Those motherfucking cops ain't going to take me to jail," Marquette screamed, and he flattened himself against a building along the sidewalk. When Minikus stepped toward him, Marquette shouted, "Don't touch me, you white motherfucker," and swung at him.

It got ugly. Officer Minikus and one of his colleagues reached for Marquette to handcuff him. He ducked away. The crowd snarled. The third officer called for reinforcements. The struggle to subdue Marquette on the sidewalk persisted. The skirmish attracted more onlookers. The call for backup summoned more than two dozen squad cars. One of the white highway patrolmen struck Marquette with his baton and split the skin above his eye. Blood spilled onto the young black man's face That riled the crowd. The law had wounded one of their own, and those who witnessed it abandoned respect for the law.

A 20-year-old woman spat on a highway patrolman. Another officer grabbed her, his arm around her neck. The crowd moved in, ready to lynch the white men. The cops raised their batons. The crowd threw rocks. They smashed windows of passing cars. They grabbed white passengers from cars caught in the snarl and beat them. They chanted to the law, "Get out, Whitey!" One cop cussed, "Nigger." They beat him. The Watts riot had begun.

It raged for six days. Looters emptied stores. Mobs burned buildings. Hospital workers scurried to treat the wounded. The city morgue tallied the dead. The governor called in the National Guard. That week, Watts resembled the streets of Santo Domingo.

The LAPD arrested Dodgers outfielder Willie Crawford, who lived near Watts, on suspicion that he was involved in the riots. Because he was black. Police Chief William Parker, who valued morality and respect for the law and whom *Time* declared "the most respected law enforcement officer in the United States after J. Edgar Hoover," explained with a poor choice of words that the riots started when "one person threw a rock and then, like monkeys in a zoo, others started throwing rocks." Others were more sympathetic to "the Negro's unbridled rage" that sparked "fires of hatred and frustration." Some even took pride in the "bloody outburst." President Johnson denounced the violence as a setback for civil rights. "A rioter with a Molotov cocktail in his hands is not fighting for civil rights any more than a Klansman with a sheet on his back and a mask on his face," Johnson said. "They are both lawbreakers, destroyers of constitutional rights and liberties, and ultimately destroyers of a free America." Yet for those who felt impotent under decades of oppression, violence seemed the only recourse. "The only way we can get anybody to listen to us is to start a riot," one black man in Los Angeles said. "As long as we lie down we are going to get kicked."

The players at Dodger Stadium could see the smoke 10 miles away where angry African Americans chanted, "Burn, baby, burn." Team management announced that fans who feared coming to the ballpark could exchange tickets for a September game. The stadium scoreboard listed highway exits closed by the rioting. The day the city imposed martial law, August 14, Koufax won his 21st game, but the violence had almost rendered baseball irrelevant to Roseboro, a black man living in south-central Los Angeles. When he picked up the newspaper, he skipped the sports section for the first time in his life and read the latest reports of the violence, which pained him.

"It's bad for my race," he said. On the field he had to remind himself that his job mattered. "I'd wake up in the morning and say to myself, 'Why are they playing games?'"

His drive home from the ballpark took him past the fires and fighting and shook him. The rage and violence that had collected and exploded here was unlike anything he could have imagined in Ashland 30 years earlier. The riots laid bare to him the bitter truths of racism that he had missed in his youth. He was dismayed that the anger and frustration had erupted into such destruction to property and life.

One night that week, word spread of a protest march that would pass in front of the Roseboro house on its way to a nearby park. Worried what might happen along the way, Johnny gathered the guns he had collected over the years and sat guard by his front door, prepared to protect his family and his property. It turned out that he didn't have to fire a shot—the march never happened—but the conflict tormented him. Wasn't there something he could do to help the people of Watts? They had shot the comedian Dick Gregory when he tried to intervene. They had scorned Martin Luther King Jr.'s attempt to pacify rioters. But Roseboro was a Dodger, a professional ballplayer. Maybe he could reach folks on a different level.

When one of Jeri's cousins, who worked with youth in a local community center, called to ask Johnny if there might be a way to get kids away from the violence, he responded immediately. While helicopters zipped over Watts and television stations showed scenes of the fires, Johnny coordinated buses to take boys and girls out of the danger zone and bring them to Dodger Stadium, where he bought their tickets. It was the little he could do to provide the children some temporary relief.

But Rosey knew he couldn't squelch the hatred and the violence. By the time the Dodgers headed north to San Francisco for a four-game series with the Giants, the riots had caused $40 million in property damage, claimed 34 lives, and left another 1,032 people injured. The wounds cut even deeper.

Despite Johnny's misgivings, the game went on. But the players, like America itself, had shed some of their innocence. Try as they might to stay focused on baseball, they could not ignore their humanity. "I suggest that the temper of the country has risen in the last few years because of broken dreams and broken promises, because of frustration," *New York Times* sportswriter George Vecsey observed in *Sport* magazine. "I also suggest that ballplayers—no matter how sheltered—are affected by the temper of our times, whether they know it or not." He concluded that the national pastime reflected the violence in society.

Indeed, beyond the brushbacks and taunts traded by Marichal and Drysdale, several other violent incidents had already marked that season. A month earlier, Philadelphia teammates Frank Thomas and Richie Allen had argued so vigorously that Thomas smacked Allen on the shoulder with his bat. In May Roberto Peña of the Cubs had gone after Dodgers pitcher Bob Miller after being hit by a pitch, and Roseboro had forcefully come between them. That same month, even the gentleman Sandy Koufax had struck Lou Brock in the ribs with a fastball. No one seemed safe in the summer of fury.

Juan continued to worry about his family in the Dominican. He wrote to them, but two weeks passed between his posting a letter and receiving a response. "It was a long wait," he said. His teammates, the Alou brothers, suffered the same worry. "We just wanted the season to be over so we could go home and see our loved ones," Juan said.

Amazingly, despite his fragile emotional state, Juan continued to dominate on the mound. On the eve of the Giants' four-game series with the first-place Dodgers, he blanked the Mets 5–0 on three singles, marking his ninth shutout of the season. He improved to 19–9 with a league-leading 1.73 ERA. Koufax had won two more games than Marichal, but Juan had five more games left to play, which meant at least one more start than his rival, and his significantly stingier ERA and nine shutouts seemed to give Juan an edge in the Cy Young competition. If Marichal could keep up this pace and his

Giants could edge the Dodgers, he stood an excellent chance to win his first Cy Young Award.

But the situation at home had skinned his nerves raw. In August he barked at the official scorer at Candlestick over a decision that didn't go his way. The Saturday before his ninth shutout, he had lost his ninth game to the Phillies by giving up three runs in the eighth inning. He turned his temper against home plate umpire Lee Weyer in an argument over the strike zone. Weyer did not eject Marichal but did write him up. Juan's teammates obviously noted his condition. "I really don't think Juan should have been playing at all," Willie Mays later told the *New York Times*. "He was pretty strung out, full of fear and anger, and holding it inside."

So when the Dodgers traveled to San Francisco for another series between the bitter rivals, it wasn't simply two teams contending for the pennant.

CHAPTER SIX
Bloody Sunday

THURSDAY AFTERNOON, AUGUST 19, 1965, JUAN MARICHAL WALKED across the outfield grass toward the entrance of the Giants clubhouse at Candlestick Park after his team had finished taking batting practice. The Dodgers players had started coming out for their turn. Juan spotted John Roseboro near the right field bullpen. "Hi, Johnny," he said.

"Hi, Juan."

The two men knew each other from five years on opposite sides of the Dodgers-Giants rivalry. They had also been teammates for two games as National League All-Stars in 1962. Johnny had caught Juan for two innings in the second game, when Juan had thrown two wild pitches. They did not share the connection that Juan did with fellow Latin players or Johnny did with fellow African-American opponents like Willie Mays. They paused for a moment to exchange pleasantries more perfunctory than personal. That day's competition would supersede any sympathy from their connection.

The Dodgers had arrived in San Francisco with the slimmest of leads over the Giants, their 70–51 record a .579 winning percentage, placing them slightly ahead of the Giants' .578. With only six weeks remaining in the season, the two teams were engaged in the National League's tightest pennant race to date, with the Milwaukee Braves and Cincinnati Reds also in contention. The team occupying first place had changed four times in the previous week. Pittsburgh and Philadelphia also figured into the race. The four-game series at Candlestick gave both the Dodgers and the Giants the chance to secure their position and push the other out of contention. *Time* reported on the pennant struggle that week: "The tension was terrific—especially in San Francisco."

Nearly 36,000 fans, some of them Dodgers faithful who had driven up the coast for the confrontation, came out to the ballpark by the bay for Thursday's game. Roseboro doubled in the seventh to drive in a run and tie the game 3–3. The Dodgers added two more runs in the next inning, but Giants catcher Tom Haller smashed a two-out, two-run homer off Don Drysdale (making an unusual relief appearance) in the bottom of the ninth to send the game into extra innings. Dodgers leftfielder Lou Johnson homered in the top of the 15th, and Roseboro singled to drive in an insurance run. After Ron Perranoski shut down the Giants in the bottom half, the Dodgers had increased their lead over the Giants in the standings to a game and a half.

Before the first pitch Friday night, Maury Wills spied that the San Francisco groundskeepers had spread dirt mixed with peat moss near home plate to soften the surface—and slow him down. He grabbed a board and scraped away as much of it as he could. He pointed out the spot to the umpires. "I don't believe this should be allowed," he said.

He worked his revenge on the Giants when he led off the fifth inning. He showed bunt. Haller, behind the plate for the Giants, leaned forward, ready to pounce on the ball. Wills yanked back his bat and nipped Haller's mitt. Interference, the home plate ump ruled and sent Wills to first. The Giants protested: "How can that be interference? Wills tried to do that. It wasn't Haller's fault." But the call stood.

The Giants didn't like it. They led 4–1, thanks in part to Mays's two-run homer in the third, but wanted to even the score in subterfuge. Matty Alou led off their half of the fifth. He squared to bunt, then pulled back like Wills had, trying to flick Roseboro's mitt. His teammates thought he succeeded and so did some reporters, though home plate ump Al Forman let it go. The distraction caused Johnny to miss the catch. The ball struck him in the chest like a punch. "Weasel bastard," he growled. "If somebody hurts me, I'm going to get one of you guys."

The Giants in the dugout jumped on Roseboro. Marichal, Matty's best friend, yelled from the steps, "Why do you get mad? Haller doesn't get mad."

Johnny glared at Juan. "You sonofabitch, if you have something to say, come out here and say it to my face!"

Juan stayed where he was next to manager Herman Franks and glared back.

"If he doesn't shut his big mouth, he'll get a ball right behind his ear," Johnny told Alou, who relayed the message to his friend.

Jim Ray Hart added a solo homer that put the final score at 5–1 and brought the Giants back to within a half game of their rivals. Roseboro, 0-for-4 on the night, remained sore afterward. On his way to the team bus, he came upon the Giants' Orlando Cepeda in the parking lot. "Tell Marichal that if he has the guts to tangle with me, fine," Johnny said. "But if not, he should quit wolfin' at me from behind the manager's back."

In Saturday's matchup, with more than 42,000 on hand, Roseboro got some satisfaction in the top of the seventh. With one out, one on, and his team trailing 2–3, Johnny homered to put the Dodgers up 4–3. Mays tied the game with a solo homer in the eighth. The game continued with playoff intensity into the 11th when Wes Parker hit a two-out, two-run shot over the right field fence that put the Dodgers up for good 6–4 and again increased their lead to one and a half games.

The series climaxed on Sunday with the rare marquee matchup: Juan Marichal versus Sandy Koufax. Fans slept outside the stadium in a line for tickets. When Candlestick opened its gates, 42,807 poured through the turnstiles, the largest crowd of the season. More than a million more tuned in to the Channel 11 television broadcast back in Los Angeles. The game promised something to remember.

Danger portended. On the Dodgers' bus ride back to the hotel Saturday night, Johnny had remained on edge. The stress of the series, following the previous week's riots in Watts, had spiked his natural competitive spirit. Talking with Lou Johnson and Jim Gilliam about facing the Giants' ace the next day, Johnny said Marichal better watch himself "because I won't take any guff from him."

Sunday afternoon, Juan ran to the mound, the way he always did. He dusted his hand with the rosin bag once, flopped it behind the rubber, tossed his warm-up pitches, and was ready. His arm felt good, even in the relatively cool bay air, near 70 degrees under a high sky. The wind swirled a paper wrapper behind home plate. The stadium throbbed with anticipation. The Dodgers had never beaten Marichal at his home park; he had defeated them 10 straight times at Candlestick. Two years earlier, in their only previous showdown in San Francisco, Marichal had defeated Koufax.

The drama began with Juan's first pitch. Maury Wills beat out a bunt down the third baseline. Like most pitchers, Marichal hated the base-hit bunt more than a home run. The long ball was simply a power swing the batter gambled on correctly; the bunt taunted the pitcher, like spitting on his shoes. Juan did not tolerate anyone showing him up, especially on his first pitch. Wills had laid down the gauntlet for the day.

Juan retired the next two Dodgers, but cleanup hitter Ron Fairly stroked a double to score Wills. That steamed Juan. He got the next batter but returned to the dugout already down 1–0.

Koufax struck out the Giants' side.

Juan ran back to the mound to start the second inning. After recording the first out, he gave up a double to first baseman Wes Parker. That brought up Johnny Roseboro. He had already contributed to the series with a double, a homer, and four RBI. He was pleased to be showing more confidence at the plate in light of his recent slump. The catcher promptly singled to drive in Parker and increase the Dodgers' lead to 2–0. Marichal chafed. Eight batters, and he had already allowed more runs than he had averaged giving up over nine innings the entire season. He fanned Koufax to face the top of the order again, Wills.

Juan had an insult to even. He fired a fastball high and tight. Shoulder high.

From first base Roseboro watched the ball hone in on Wills. That wasn't right. Relieved to see Maury flop before the ball could hit him, Johnny was peeved that Marichal had thrown at his friend. Even though the two roommates had split up, Johnny did not want to see Maury hurt. Wills, the Dodgers' team captain and emotional leader, didn't like it either. He rose slowly and dressed down Marichal with a long look.

Wills lined out to end the Dodgers at-bat. When Los Angeles took the field, Roseboro wanted to set things straight with the Giants' first batter, Willie Mays, San Francisco's equivalent of Wills as team captain and emotional leader. Johnny didn't want Koufax to hurt him; he just thought the situation called for Sandy to send a message that they wouldn't tolerate Marichal throwing at the Dodgers' batters.

Crouching behind home plate, Roseboro flicked his index finger, a sign for Koufax to put the batter in the dirt. Despite popular legend, Koufax believed in the practice of intimidating opposing hitters and protecting his teammates. He didn't throw at their heads because he feared hurting them, but he was willing to deliver his own messages. Three months earlier, in a game against the Cardinals, after Lou Brock had bunted his way on, stole second and third, then scored on a sacrifice fly, an angry Koufax pointedly plunked Brock in the ribs with fastball.

Koufax wound up and sailed a fastball well over Mays's head to the backstop. He later told reporters, "It was a lousy pitch. I meant it to come a lot closer." But he had fulfilled his duty, even if it was merely a token gesture.

The Giants managed a run to make it 2–1.

Marichal took note of Koufax's missive over Mays's head. He resented the way Dodgers pitchers—mostly Drysdale but now Koufax—threw at his teammates. When Dodgers right fielder Fairly returned to the plate in the top of third with two out, Marichal was also thinking of Fairly's first-inning double that had scored Wills. He delivered an inside fastball that sent Fairly diving to the ground. The Dodgers fans in the overflow crowd—and there were plenty of them that afternoon—hollered in protest. Giants fans cheered. Juan thought Fairly had overreacted—the pitch hadn't been that close.

But Matty Alou later observed about his friend, "Juan wanted to fight all day. He had the devil inside him that day."

Marichal's pitch roiled the Dodgers bench, where manager Walt Alston and the players were convinced Marichal had thrown at Fairly. He had put two of their teammates in the dirt. They jumped on him with shouts and taunts.

Home plate umpire Shag Crawford warned both teams. No more. "Another one like that, and the pitcher's out of here."

That didn't stop Koufax from approaching Roseboro. "Who do you want me to get?"

Johnny didn't want Sandy ejected. "I'll take care of it," he said.

Marichal led off the Giants' half. He knew baseball's code called for Koufax to put him down, but he wasn't sure Sandy would do it, especially after Crawford's warning. Still, he was uneasy stepping into the box 60 feet from baseball's hardest thrower. If ever there was a time for a pitcher to deliver an inside fastball that screamed "You can't throw at our guys," this was it.

The fans anticipated the showdown. The tension on the field crackled through the stands.

Crawford felt it, too. He crouched behind Roseboro, his hand on the catcher's back, poised to eject Koufax if his pitch came too close.

Twenty-one-year-old Tito Fuentes, who had played his first major league game only four days earlier, watched from the on-deck circle, clutching his bat. The rest of the Giants peered intently from the bench and the outfield bullpen.

Koufax curved a pitch across the plate. Crawford called it a strike. Juan exhaled. He prepared to swing at the next pitch. Roseboro called for a fastball. Low and inside. Sandy delivered. Juan held off.

Johnny intentionally dropped the ball, moved behind Marichal to pick it up, and whizzed his throw past Juan's face. Marichal later said the ball clipped his ear. He turned to face Roseboro. "Why you do that, *coño?!*" he demanded.

Roseboro, one of the strongest men in baseball, had decided that if Marichal challenged him, he was going to "annihilate" him. The 5-foot-11, 195-pound Roseboro dropped his mitt and stepped toward Marichal. "Fuck you and your mother!"

Juan saw the catcher in his mask and chest protector advancing on him. He recalled Roseboro's threats, repeated by Alou and Cepeda. Fear took over.

Marichal raised his bat over his helmet and brought it down toward Roseboro's head like he was splitting firewood. The blow did not strike squarely but did open a two-inch gash above Johnny's left eye.

Johnny's rage erased his formal training in karate and boxing. He lunged at Marichal like an alley fighter.

Juan retreated and stiff-armed Johnny with his left hand. The two ended up between home plate and the mound. Roseboro flailed at Marichal with punches. Juan chopped at him with his bat. He pried Roseboro's mask loose. Johnny knocked off Juan's helmet, which flew toward first base and bounced on the grass. Juan nicked him again with the bat, and Johnny landed a single right to Juan's face.

Koufax rushed from the mound and raised his hands behind Roseboro, the ball tucked in his glove, trying to calm Marichal's bat, which Juan twirled with his right hand.

Charlie Fox, the Giants third base coach, ran in to separate the pair but then leaned back to get clear of Marichal's bat. Fuentes raced from the on-deck circle, forgetting to leave his bat behind. Fox, Fuentes, and Koufax seemed intent upon separating the pair but hesitated to come between the two and be struck themselves. For one sickening instant Fuentes gripped his bat with both hands, looking like he was going to use it as a weapon, just as Juan had.

The benches and bullpens emptied. The players surged toward the sparring pair on the grass in front of the mound. The 42,807 fans, initially stunned by the sight of Marichal clubbing the catcher, leaped to their feet and shouted.

Plate umpire Crawford attempted to subdue the two. He placed a hand on both of them, his mask still on. Initially, he'd been astonished—*did he just do that?!*—but then he moved in, worried Juan was going to swing his bat at the players and coaches closing in on him. Crawford, a combat vet from World War II, noted that no one else dared step between the two men.

When Juan swung his bat and Johnny stumbled to his left, Crawford saw his opening. He wrapped his arms around Marichal from behind and the two tumbled to the ground, Marichal on top of Crawford, still clutching his bat. "I didn't want them to take the bat away from me," he later said. "I know if they take the bat away then everybody will hit me."

Johnny regained his footing. Big Willie McCovey held out his forearm but Roseboro slipped past. Koufax had yielded to Crawford and tipped toward Fuentes, who let go of his bat and did not attack him. Both focused on Marichal. A gaggle of players and coaches surrounded him. The majority seemed more interested in breaking things up than in taking sides and joining the fracas. They were horrified by what they had just witnessed—a player had never clubbed another on the field with a bat—and by the sight of the blood streaming from the gash on Roseboro's head. The blood covered the left side of his face. Many on the field thought Juan had crushed Johnny's eye. "There was nothing but blood where his left eye should have been," Alston said.

In the squirming melee, players grabbed at Marichal on the ground, trying to wrest away his bat or strike him. Dodgers rookie pitcher Mike Kekich reached one arm around Marichal's neck but did not deliver a punch. Kekich had been getting a drink of water and had not seen the altercation begin. Afterward, when he heard how Marichal had struck his teammate, he said ruefully, "I could have punched Marichal silly. I blew it."

Dodger Lou Johnson, a black man and Roseboro's friend, sprinted in from left field and threw punches at anyone in a Giants uniform. McCovey smothered him in a bear hug from behind but was not able to contain him indefinitely. Relief pitcher Howie Reed, a white player, went "berserk" trying to get at Marichal. He yanked at those on top of Juan so he could get a piece of him. Still on his back, Juan fended off Reed with kicks, spiking him on the left thigh. Juan also caught Johnson in the ankle with his spikes, opening a cut that would leave a scar. It took several men to constrain Reed.

Roseboro tried to push his way through to Marichal, still on his back, though he had rolled away from Crawford. Someone stepped on Crawford's hand and cut it.

The crowd packed into the stands watched the mayhem unfold on the field. The fans were set in their loyalties, and the violence only stirred the fury of the bitter rivalry. Mays worried that if Roseboro in all his rage reached Marichal, the fans would leap the low railing and set off a full-blown riot on the field. He scrambled toward Johnny, losing his cap and getting kicked in the head on the way.

Mays wrapped his arms around his friend from behind and tugged. "Johnny, stop it," Willie pleaded. "Stop fighting. Your eye is out."

Mays pulled Roseboro away, and the wounded man stopped struggling. Willie grabbed a fistful of jersey under the bloodied chest protector and led him away from the swarm around Marichal. The blood streaked Johnny's face. It flecked Mays's jersey. Johnny gingerly touched his hand to his head and looked at the blood on his fingers. They met Dodgers trainer Doc Buhler behind home plate. Willie tenderly pressed a towel to his friend's forehead. "This never should have happened," he said. "Nobody should hit anybody with a bat."

Tears slid down Willie's cheeks.

Doc Buhler examined Roseboro's wound. Johnny did not feel the pain yet. He just felt angry that he had landed only one punch.

His teammates and coaches gathered around while Mays wiped the blood from his hands with the white towel. Koufax faced him with his hands on his hips and a look of bewildered concern.

Meanwhile, back on their feet, Crawford lectured Marichal, who gestured in his defense. His Giants teammates and coaches looked on.

Roseboro suddenly burst from the trainer, tore past Mays, and rushed back for another shot at Marichal. This time, Preston Gomez, the Dodgers' third base coach from Cuba, grabbed him and pulled him away, with Roseboro jawing at Marichal.

Juan yelled back, "You want some more?"

That incited Dodgers coach Danny Ozark. In the initial scuffle he had tried to separate opponents, but when he heard Marichal mocking Roseboro, he wanted to tear him apart. "He's a goddamn nut," Ozark later said. "A guy like that would hit a woman." Several Giants had to block Ozark from their pitcher. Somebody decked him with a punch.

San Francisco pitching coach Larry Jansen, one of the few men Juan could trust at the moment, put his arm around Marichal's shoulder and led him off the field.

The Candlestick fans booed Roseboro on his way to the dugout. He flashed them the finger.

Johnny wanted to stay in the game, but Alston insisted he have his head tended to. "You get that fixed up," the manager said.

"Shit," Roseboro said and removed his gear.

To get from the visitors' dugout on the third base side to the clubhouse entrance in right field, he had to walk across the outfield. The fans taunted him ferociously. He bent over and patted his rear—*Kiss my ass.*

Once inside the clubhouse, he started to feel the pain. His head "throbbed like a toothache." Doc Buhler wanted to stitch the wound, but Roseboro didn't want him sticking a needle in his scalp, so the trainer closed the cut as best he could with butterfly bandages. The gash would later require 14 stitches at the hospital.

Johnny heard that Russ Hodges, one of the Giants' broadcasters, had said Roseboro swung his mask at Marichal. Not so. The accusation infuriated Roseboro. "It made me mad on top of mad," he said.

He was ready to go after Marichal again in the clubhouse across the hall, but did not make a move to plow through the dozen policemen guarding each entrance.

Crawford ejected Marichal. A policeman escorted him to the clubhouse. A couple of teammates checked on him. His jersey was torn open and he had a few scratches on his chest but was not hurt. He settled at the desk in the clubhouse office and listened to the game on the radio.

Play resumed with Jeff Torborg behind the plate for the Dodgers and San Francisco police officers patrolling the dugouts and field. They would remain stationed there until the final out. No one wanted the riled fans leaping the railing. Crawford told Koufax, "Whatever you do, don't throw at anyone. We don't want a riot here."

With police officers also guarding the two clubhouses, Juan heard Giants broadcaster Lon Simmons's description on KSFO that Bob Schroder finished Marichal's at-bat and struck out. Fuentes then flied out deep to left. But the incident had rattled Koufax. He walked Jim Davenport and McCovey in succession. That brought up Mays.

The crowd booed. They did not approve of his role in the brawl, crossing enemy lines to tend to Roseboro instead of fighting for his side. That prompted *Los Angeles Herald-Examiner* sportswriter Bud Furillo to comment, "San Francisco always has been a 'Kill the Umpire' town, but what kind of cannibals roam in Candlestick these days?"

Mays appeased the fans somewhat when Koufax threw his fastball over the middle of the plate, waist high—exactly where he didn't want to put it. Willie stroked the ball 450 feet into the left field bleachers. His 4th homer of the series, 38th of the season, and 491st of his career put the Giants up 4–2.

Ron Herbel took Marichal's place on the mound. He shut out the Dodgers on three singles for the next five frames.

Out the doorway and into the corridor that connected the two clubhouses, Juan could see Mays going into the Dodgers clubhouse between innings to check on Johnny. Once the adrenaline subsided, regret crept in. Juan was sorry he was out of the game. Sorry for what he had done. At the same time, he thought, Roseboro had been wrong to throw the ball so close to him. That could have killed him. He had lost his head wanting to defend himself. Still, he was sorry it had all happened.

Franks came in and told Marichal he should leave for the airport and that some policemen should accompany him. Just to be safe. Juan agreed and joined the team that night for its flight to Pittsburgh.

Roseboro also left early, escorted by police. Two of San Francisco's finest disguised the Dodgers catcher in a Giants cap and led him out of the stadium to a taxi stand, where Johnny and the team's traveling secretary, Lee Scott, caught a cab to the airport.

The Dodgers managed a run in the ninth, but the Giants hung on to win 4–3, finishing the series where they had started it, a half game behind their rivals. By the time the game ended and police allowed reporters into the clubhouse, both Marichal and Roseboro had left the ballpark. But they would never escape that afternoon.

CHAPTER SEVEN

This Ain't Over

NO ONE COULD REMEMBER A PLAYER STRIKING ANOTHER IN THE HEAD with a bat. Word spread widely and rapidly. The bulletin scorched the wires from Candlestick to the other parks in the league. Mets announcer Bob Murphy read it during the live WOR-TV broadcast of New York's game: "Juan Marichal hit John Roseboro on the head with a bat following knockdown pitches to Wills and Fairly. Roseboro left the field bleeding over the left eye." First came shock, then indignation.

Back in Los Angeles, 10-year-old Roger Guenveur Smith was one of the million or more fans watching the televised broadcast of the game.* He had spread his baseball cards of the starting players on the

* In accordance with the practice of the time, the home game was not broadcast in the San Francisco area.

living room floor the way he always did. The lineup included one of his heroes, John Roseboro. Roger had met Roseboro at a community event and Johnny had signed an 8-by-10 glossy photograph of himself in his catcher's gear. Roger treasured that autographed photo.

Suddenly his mother screamed. Then the mayhem and Roseboro's head, the blood dark on the black and white screen. "I took it personally," Roger said. Nine days earlier, he had stood in front of his father's motel, the Palm Vue on Western Avenue and 39th, and watched the liquor store and pawn shop across the street burn. Now he plucked Marichal's card from the carpet, a head shot of the pitcher in his SF cap grinning and looking to the side. With absolute rage Roger set the cardboard effigy aflame. "Burn, baby, burn," he chanted.

KTTV, Channel 11 in Los Angeles, which had broadcast the game, replayed the incident on the evening news that Sunday, but then the station destroyed the videotape, per the Dodgers orders. "They said it was for the good of the game," KTTV sport director Bill Welsh said. "That re-showing the tape wouldn't be good for baseball."

Jeri Roseboro had the game on but had stepped outside to be with her daughters. They were splashing in the pool with a babysitter. When she heard the commotion from the television, Jeri retreated inside. She saw the fighting on the screen, the trainer tending to Johnny, her husband bleeding. The images horrified her. Jeri locked the door. She didn't want the girls to come inside and see what was happening. She hadn't liked Marichal before, thought he was arrogant beyond what was acceptable in a pitcher, and now she trained her fear and anger on the man.

Once Johnny had left the game, she called the Dodgers clubhouse but could not reach him. It calmed her some to hear Vin

Scully, the voice of the Dodgers, address her directly during the broadcast, "Jeri, John's okay."

She finally did reach Johnny in the clubhouse. He assured his wife that Scully was right. He had not lost his eye. It was only a flesh wound on his scalp. He told her he was going to leave the park early with Lee Scott to go to the airport and grab a bite to eat. That's when she knew her husband was all right, when she heard he still had his famous appetite.

After the Dodgers' flight took off for New York and a four-game series with the Mets, Johnny played in the regular poker game with his teammates. The cut on his head continued to seep blood. When talk turned to the fight, he said, "I don't believe in turning the other cheek."

The media wanted more when the plane landed at LaGuardia at 4:30 a.m. A reporter asked Roseboro if he planned to finish the fight with Marichal when the Giants and Dodgers played for the last time that season on September 6 and 7. "No," Johnny said softly. "But it's not easy to forget when somebody splits your head open."

He finally got to bed at the hotel around 7 a.m. but woke with a monster headache. The reporters crowded into his room on the 15th floor of the Roosevelt Hotel. He talked to them seated on the edge of his bed still in his blue pajamas. He occasionally pressed his hand to the bandaged patch on his head. He told them his version of events, said that his throw had not touched Marichal, that Marichal had clubbed him when he took a step toward him. "As far as I'm concerned the incident is forgotten," he said. "I'm not thinking about getting him or looking for him or anything like that."

Everyone wanted to talk about it, and suddenly Gabby had a lot to say. Later that day Roseboro appeared on Les Crane's television show, the square white bandage on his scalp in stark contrast to his black hair, and repeated his diplomatic message with a caveat: "In my opinion it's all over. If anything has to come of it from me, then they can forget it because there will never be another incident between Marichal and I *unless*"—here he tilted his head to look at the host—"he makes a mistake and starts something and of course I'll be there when it happens. But as far as being vindictive or anything like that, it's just almost forgotten."

Almost? "My wife didn't like my head being bashed open too well." He smiled. "But she'll get over it."

Meanwhile, National League president Warren Giles was also at the Roosevelt Hotel conducting his investigation into the incident, talking to the managers of each team and the umpires by telephone. When a Los Angeles reporter asked Roseboro what he thought Marichal's punishment should be, Johnny confided in him, "He and I in a room together for about ten minutes."

Roseboro wanted to play in that night's game but didn't. His headache drove him to the hospital for X-rays, which revealed no fractures. "Nothing was there," he joked.

While Roseboro talked, Marichal stayed quiet. He had kept to himself on the Giants' flight to Pittsburgh and napped fitfully.

Roseboro's telling his side of the story and displaying his bandaged wound to the New York media cast him as the victim and Marichal as the villain, roles that the majority of the public outside of the Bay Area accepted. "If Marichal is permitted to continue in Major League Baseball, the game will never be the same to me," Harry Evans of Los Angeles wrote to the *Los Angeles Times*. Joseph Danvers of Monterey Park, California, called the paper to insist that Marichal be "disqualified from baseball or placed in an asylum." They represented the hundreds who voiced their opinion to the ball club, the newspaper, and the National League president's office with advice for how Giles should deal with Marichal.

The San Francisco press deferred judgment. "What he did was a terrible thing, yet I don't think anyone in San Francisco really criticized him," said Nick Peters, a beat reporter covering the Giants at the time. "I think he had the benefit of the doubt because we all knew what a good guy he was, and we gave him that."

Elsewhere, the press hammered Marichal. They condemned his "brutal attack" as "atrocious," "reprehensible," "outrageous," "disgraceful," and "cowardly." Howard Cosell called it "dastardly." A *Los Angeles Herald-Examiner* headline declared, Juan Disgraces Baseball. Even if Marichal had been afraid that Roseboro was going to attack him, Arthur Daley wrote in the *New York Times*, "It has to be a pretty warped instinct, though, for one ballplayer to flail another on the skull with a bat."

The day after the incident, Giles, having concluded his inquiry, sent Marichal a telegram: "I am sure you recognize how repugnant your actions were in the game. Such actions are harmful to the game, have no place in sports and must be dealt with drastically. . . . My investigation indicated there were underlying currents by others throughout the series, but your sudden and violent action Sunday was unprovoked and obnoxious and must be penalized." His penalty: a $1,750 fine and eight playing dates. Giles stipulated that the team could not pay the fine, that the money must come from Marichal himself and be paid prior to his reinstatement.

Giles's interpretation that Marichal's action was "unprovoked" seemed to exonerate Roseboro, laying the blame squarely on Marichal. The fine, a record amount at the time,* underscored the drastic measures the league president felt he must take. Giles said he calculated the amount based on what he thought Marichal would earn during the term of his suspension.†

When Juan arrived at Forbes Field on August 23 for that evening's game with the Pirates, reporters wanted his reaction. He tried to avoid them and kept mumbling, "No comment." After an hour

* Ted Williams had been fined $5,000 for spitting at fans in Fenway Park in 1956, and Babe Ruth had been fined $5,000 for reporting out of shape in 1925, but both of those fines had been imposed by the players' clubs. The $1,750 levied by Giles against Marichal was the largest amount either league had fined a player.

† To put it in contemporary terms, the same percent applied to Tim Lincecum's $18,250,000 salary in 2012 would be $532,292.

and a half of that, Giants manager Herman Franks finally convinced Marichal to tell his side of the story. The club released a statement in Juan's name that read: "First of all, I want to apologize for hitting Roseboro with my bat. I am sorry I did that. But he was coming toward me, with his mask in his hand, and I was afraid he was going to hit me with his mask, so I swung my bat." The statement went on to explain how the anger between the two teams had mounted with Maury Wills and then Matty Alou taking swipes at the catchers' mitts and Roseboro delivering threats via Alou and Orlando Cepeda. It recounted how Roseboro had deliberately dropped the ball and then thrown it back close by Marichal's head, and asserted that the ball "ticked" Marichal's ear. The statement repeated that Roseboro had taken off his mask and Marichal was afraid he was going to hit him with it.

The statement ended, "I am sorry but many times our players on the Giants are hit by pitches and sometimes hurt, and nobody says anything then." The final line echoed Marichal's comments after Drysdale had thrown at Willie Mays earlier in the season. It hinted that the Marichal-Roseboro conflict was not an isolated incident but one layered in the history of the long-running feud between the two teams. Juan sat at a table in the clubhouse with Franks at his side. He fiddled with a deck of playing cards while the manager clarified events for the reporters and complained that his star pitcher's suspension would hurt his team.

When the press asked Roseboro for his reaction, he said he had not taken off his mask. Video footage and photographs show that Roseboro did indeed have his mask on until the scuffle reached the grass in front of the mound and Marichal pulled it off. Roseboro admitted that he had challenged Marichal and Franks in the shouting between the catcher and the Giants bench on Friday night but denied that he had ever threatened Marichal. He also asserted that the ball he threw had not ticked Marichal's ear. "How does he know I dropped the ball on purpose?" he demanded angrily and added, "If

Marichal doesn't want to get in a fight on the field, he should keep his mouth shut."

While no one approved of Marichal hitting Roseboro with his bat, there were those, primarily in the Bay Area, willing to forgive him and support him. The Archdiocese of San Francisco wrote an open letter to Marichal in its newspaper expressing support for the weekly communicant: "We see young boys in school yards and all over the Bay Area imitating your high leg-kick delivery. Whether they know it or not, they also imitate your behavior. One thing they learned this week is the manliness of your public apology. It suggests that your basic character is as big as your baseball talent."

California Secretary of State Frank Jordan thought the $1,750 fine was too large for the crime and offered to start a campaign to raise the funds to cover it. One San Francisco woman actually did begin collecting money to pay Marichal's fine.

Some supporters remained blindly partisan. Giants fan R. A. Kelly wrote to the *Los Angeles Times,* "Every time the Dodgers play in San Francisco and lose a game, they start to whine. I'm getting so I hate the Dodgers. Hitting with a bat is inexcusable, I know, but some of those whiners really deserve it."

There were also those who saw the incident as more nuanced, not so clearly black and white, despite their obvious allegiances. Giants radio broadcaster Lon Simmons, who had been calling the game on KSFO radio, thought the two players should share the blame. "It was wrong for Marichal to hit him with the bat, but that was a lethal weapon Roseboro used, throwing the ball from that distance," Simmons said. He considered Juan's use of the bat an impulsive act of self-defense. He also insisted that Roseboro started the incident—provoking Marichal by throwing the ball so close to his face—while his counterpart in Los Angeles, Vin Scully, persisted in the belief that Marichal had been the instigator. "I thought the punishment was really unjust with Roseboro not getting anything," Simmons said. "They were both involved, both liable."

The Dodgers protested what they considered Giles's leniency. "He should get kicked out of baseball," said Ron Fairly, one of the Dodgers whom Marichal had put in the dirt during Sunday's game. "He should have been suspended 1,750 days and fined eight dollars. Using a bat is the same as going out with intent to kill. If I'd done something like that on the street, I'd have been arrested. He should be arrested, too."

"I thought it was a real gutless decision," said Maury Wills, the other player Marichal knocked down. "I think the punishment should have been much more severe."

"This ain't over," said Dodgers outfielder Lou Johnson, who had jumped into the fray and been spiked by Marichal. "I'm going to get me one of them." Indeed, in the inning after Marichal and Roseboro had fought, Johnson had slid hard into Tito Fuentes at second base, but San Francisco's shortstop had sidestepped the challenge.

Giles tried to justify his decision—which he called the toughest he had ever made—by explaining that he wanted to take into account how Marichal's suspension would affect his team's pennant chances. He factored in the World Series money at stake and the fact that Roseboro had not been seriously injured. "If I'd have been influenced by the calls and wires I received, I'd have had him shot or put him out [of baseball] for life," Giles said. "But you can't penalize the other twenty-four guys or the club itself. You want to penalize a guy for a terrible thing like this, but you also want to be fair."

Reaction to the National League president's justification was as widespread and mixed as it was to the punishment he levied. Most seemed to think Marichal deserved a longer suspension, but they believed Giles had been wise to take the long view. "Pitching an entire club out of the race—which the permanent loss of Marichal would have done—is a little too stiff a deal to hand out for the misdemeanor of a single player," Chester L. Smith wrote in the *Pittsburgh Press*. Others found fault with Giles's reasoning. "It would appear that the penalty is determined by the position of the player's team in the pennant race, rather than by the severity of his crime," Dr. Karen Koziara of San Jose, California, wrote in a letter to the editor of the *Sporting News*. "Pretty sad justice." Sandy Koufax also observed, "If it had happened in April, he probably would have been suspended for thirty days."

The incident and its aftermath dominated national news in late August, overshadowing other events, such as President Johnson signing a law that imposed penalties for burning draft cards, Gemini 5 returning to earth after a record 120 laps around the earth, and Casey Stengel announcing his retirement. *Sports Illustrated* ran an oversize photo—a page and a half wide—in its August 30 edition that showed Marichal with his bat raised over his head, Roseboro tumbling to his knees in front of him, and umpire Shag Crawford reaching to subdue Juan with a very concerned Koufax and others looking on. The image depicted Marichal as the criminal and Roseboro as the casualty. So did the text: "Giants' pitcher Juan Marichal, swinging his bat like a headsman's ax, had opened a two-inch gash and raised a swelling the size of a cantaloupe on the left side of Roseboro's head." *Life,* the nation's most popular magazine, ran a two-page spread in its September 3 edition under the headline A Pitcher Goes to Bat Against the Catcher with a sequence of four photos showing Marichal swiping Roseboro and Roseboro punching Marichal along with a larger shot of Juan on his back with his spikes up after being tackled by Crawford. The most arresting image, though, was the one blown up to cover almost two pages that showed Mays holding a fistful of Roseboro's jersey and leading him away while Johnny, blood drizzled down the side of his face and his chest protector, studies the blood on his hand after touching it to his wound. The small section of accompanying text read in part:

"Pitcher Juan Marichal of the Giants suddenly lashed out with his bat (*top pictures*) at catcher John Roseboro of the rival Los Angeles Dodgers, who fought back bare-handed."

In the days before the 24-hour news frenzy fed by Twitter, countless websites, and CNN, Fox, MSNBC, et al., these photos prominently displayed in widely distributed magazines placed the story in the forefront of the nation's consciousness. For most Americans these were the only images they saw of the incident. The visual and textual depictions further influenced public opinion that Marichal was the villain and Roseboro the victim. The *Sporting News*, known as "Baseball's Bible" because it was considered the primary authority on the national pastime (and perhaps because of the moral tone it frequently adopted), excoriated Marichal in an editorial dated September 4, 1965. Declaring that Giles's punishment was too lenient and that a 30-day suspension would have been more effective, the weekly granted that Marichal's teammates and Giants fans deserved consideration in determining the sentence "but their importance pales when one ponders the possible consequences of an act as vicious as Marichal's. To us it appears an open invitation to a Marichal type for a repeat performance."

A "Marichal type" suggested a similarly impetuous Latino. The reference was widely understood in a culture rife with stereotypes. Earlier in August, *Sports Illustrated* had published an article about the infusion of Latin players in the big leagues that reflected the nation's attitude, suggesting that "they"—as though all Latinos were alike—displayed reckless individuality, must be managed carefully because of their pride, and could be easily manipulated. "Caribbeans in general have the reputation for being temperamental, and the ballplayers are no exception," the article asserted. Marichal's actions were filtered through the lens of this widespread attitude.

The *Sporting News* editorial condemned Marichal from a position of cultural arrogance: "Baseball in America would enjoy the status of cockfighting if its players descended to Marichal's fighting style." The statement jabbed at a pastime that enjoyed widespread popularity and acceptance in Juan's homeland. The editorial also chastised him with a condescending tone: "A baseball bat is a deadly weapon; even a child knows that." And it showed no compassion for Juan's emotional state: "In Marichal's defense, some have mentioned worry over the turmoil in his native Dominican Republic and the super-charged atmosphere surrounding a collision of pennant contenders. These alibis might carry weight if Marichal had used his fists. They are a mockery when viewed alongside his actual defense. There is no excuse for Marichal's actions."

The *Sporting News* editors weren't the only ones who deferred to stereotypes in berating Marichal. "These young Caribbean hot bloods absolutely must be taught restraint," Bob Broeg pontificated in the *St. Louis Post-Dispatch.* "In a situation like that, you act first and think later," William Chapin wrote in the *San Francisco Chronicle.* "Especially if you're a fiery Dominican."

Dick Young, the often contrarian columnist for the *New York Daily News,* objected to what he perceived as prejudice biasing his colleagues' opinions: "I am frightened . . . by what my hysterical fellow journalists want to do to Marichal. They want to lynch him. . . . These fine noble members of a fine, noble profession, these men who decry emotional violence of any kind and plead constantly for level-headed calm—these men have formed a mob. They want to drag Marichal into the street and hang him from a telegraph pole.

"I wonder if the mob would be shouting so if his name weren't Juan Marichal. What would the mob shout, I wonder, if his name were a nice Nordic name like Frank Thomas, which it just happened to be a couple of months ago. I seem to recall that Thomas hit Richie Allen on the side of the head with a bat and the only penalty he got was being sent to Houston, which is pretty drastic, I'll grant you . . . but I didn't hear the mob screaming for Frank Thomas's head or calling him a savage."

Young was referring to the incident earlier that season, in July, when the Philadelphia Phillies' Frank Thomas had an altercation with his teammate Richie Allen and swung his bat at him, striking Allen in the shoulder, not the head. Giles did not take any disciplinary action, though the Phillies sold Thomas to Houston only days later. That incident did not receive national press coverage or universal condemnation for many reasons—one of them may very well have been that Thomas was a white man born in Pennsylvania.

In truth, Juan wasn't a "young Caribbean hot blood" or a "fiery Dominican." He was competitive, yes, but also a man of deep faith, sweet natured and fun loving. The afternoon of August 22, he got caught up in a moment of passion at a time when he was emotionally fragile. That does not excuse his behavior—he would be the first to say that—but it does help one understand that his action was uncharacteristic, not a natural reflection of his personality but an aberration. Perhaps that is why it would haunt him so.

Despite the portrayals of him as the victim and the outpouring of public sympathy in his favor, Roseboro knew he wasn't blameless. "Of course I provoked the incident," he later wrote in his autobiography. He missed two games but was back behind the plate on August 25 with 14 stitches across his scalp. And, despite his qualified conciliatory tone in interviews and joking remarks, he remained righteous and unwilling to admit his part. A week later, he filed a suit in Los Angeles Superior Court against Marichal and the Giants seeking $10,000 in general damages and $100,000 in exemplary and punitive damages. The suit charged that Marichal "did without provocation commit assault and battery against the plaintiff with a deadly weapon, that Roseboro was severely injured and was caused pain and suffering." Roseboro defended the disingenuous suit by telling the press, "My decision to take this action is due not only to the brutal attack upon my person [which he repeated was unprovoked] but, just as important, is due to the fact that some severe actions should be taken against a man who not only set a bad example for millions of baseball fans throughout the world but apparently from recent statements has attempted to defend and justify his outrageous conduct."

When his anger softened his conscience would work on him.

The day after the incident, when Juan received Giles's telegram rebuking him, he also started receiving "threatening, obscene and vulgar" telegrams and letters that persisted past the end of the season. The following day, the company that made Saxon Apple Juice replaced Marichal with Willie Mays promoting the drink on billboards throughout Los Angeles. And everywhere, it seemed, Juan heard the journalistic chorus condemning him.

He had wanted the chance to explain himself to Giles but cancelled their meeting after the league president told the press that he had not talked to Roseboro or Marichal or any of their teammates because "you don't accomplish anything by talking to the players." Marichal probably figured Giles already had his mind set and would not give any weight to what he had to say. Perhaps more significantly, he remembered what had happened when Ford Frick had fined him and other Latin players for playing in the Caribbean exhibition two years earlier. Marichal did not expect any understanding from the organization that had threatened to suspend him for playing in his own country.

The public condemnation stung. Even worse was the personal torment. He replayed the moment over and over in his mind. He couldn't help but wonder what would have happened if he had dropped his bat, swung instead with his fists or pushed Roseboro away or even poked the bat into Roseboro's gut—anything but swung the bat the way he had. Try as he did to shove these thoughts away, Juan couldn't escape the guilt and shame and remorse that swamped him. Not even prayer could wash away those feelings.

Phil Pepe of the *New York World-Telegram and Sun* speculated how deeply the public reaction would affect Marichal, knowing that the punishment would not be measured in games or dollars but in much more personal terms. "There is the humiliation," Pepe wrote. "Juan is a decent and sensitive man, who must know by now that he performed a dastardly act. And if he does not know it, he will hear about it, you can be sure. He will face public scorn and in the jungle that is baseball, opportunists will not let him forget what he did. The damage it will do to Marichal, psychologically if not physically and financially, is immeasurable. Life could be miserable for him from now on, and that is the real punishment."

Arthur Daley of the *New York Times* raised the same question, wondering if Marichal would be able to survive not the suspension but the scorn. "Can his temperament withstand the derisive reminders he is bound to get in the days and years to come?" Daley asked.

Marichal continued to dress for the Giants' five games in Pittsburgh, three in New York, and on to Philadelphia. He brooded for three days but then resumed his pregame running regimen in the outfield, and he pitched batting practice for six days. He even smiled gamely for photographers. But he sat impotently in the dugout while his team played. He could do nothing to help the Giants. They had left San Francisco half a game behind the Dodgers, but with Juan on the bench, they didn't win a game until Friday, August 27, and won only three of ten during the length of Juan's suspension. The eight "playing dates" ended up including two doubleheaders, makeups for rainouts that extended Juan's suspension until September 2 and covered ten games.

Franks had said that the loss of his ace for any period "would murder the club." The Giants pitching was already thin. The team carried two "bonus baby" rookies who took up valuable roster space but whom Franks couldn't trust in critical situations. Gaylord Perry hadn't reached his potential yet. The team picked up the 44-year-old Warren Spahn, but he lost more games than he won. Trailing the Pirates 8–0 in the first game of a doubleheader, Franks was so desperate that he called upon outfielder Matty Alou to pitch two innings.*

During the time of Marichal's suspension, the Dodgers also faltered, but despite the Giants' chance to pull ahead, they didn't—or couldn't—without their Cy Young candidate. When Marichal returned on September 2, the same half game separated the two rivals in the standings. Juan felt responsible for how poorly his team had played during his suspension. "He had fretted over how he might make up for his loss to the team," sportswriter Arnold Hano wrote. "During his inactivity, the Giants had played horrible ball. In a strong sense, it was Marichal's fault. He had to make amends. Not just pitch well. Pitch doubly well." So before Juan started the first game of a doubleheader that Thursday afternoon, he told Franks, "If I win my game, I will pitch the second game, too."

On the eve of his return, he had learned about Roseboro's lawsuit. It bothered him that Roseboro painted Marichal's action as unprovoked, but Juan would not talk to the press about it, except to say about the monetary demands, "I wish I had that much, half that much, a quarter that much, but I don't."

Juan knew this start was not just another game. The 30,410 fans at Connie Mack Stadium wouldn't let him forget it. Those who thought his action had been atrocious, outrageous, cowardly, and criminal, who thought he should not be back pitching so soon or should have been banned for life or even thrown in jail—those people

* Surprisingly, Alou gave up three singles but no runs and notched three strikeouts, twice fanning Willie Stargell.

booed Marichal when he was announced as the starting pitcher, when he took his warm-up pitches, when he ran to the mound to start the game, and every time he came to bat. He tried to shrug off the contempt but could not ignore it. He had not been booed like that before. He felt sorry all over again. But they hadn't seen what happened, they hadn't been there for the series, hadn't witnessed the buildup to that moment on Sunday. They didn't have family in the Dominican Republic during a civil war that worried them sick. No, they had just seen the photographs, the ones that made Juan look like a hatchet man, just read the convicting opinions in the paper, and so they booed. And booed. And Juan wept inside.

He pitched well but not well enough to win his 20th game. He lasted seven innings, struck out eight, gave up four runs on seven hits, and took the loss. "I was not sharp," he told reporters after the game. Accustomed to a large workload—he had already logged 237 innings through the first four and a half months of the season—the layoff had hurt him. He did not have to make good on his promise to pitch the second game, which the Giants won to remain one game behind the Dodgers.

The following day, the Giants headed to Chicago. In the Dominican Republic, after 3,000 Dominicans and 31 US servicemen had died in a little more than four months, the warring sides accepted a provisional government until elections could be held in the spring. Nine thousand US troops remained in the Dominican Republic to make sure the truce held. Juan was pleased but would feel complete relief only when he could be with his family again.

Marichal usually pitched every fifth day, so ordinarily his next start would be on September 7. But the Giants were scheduled to play two games in Los Angeles on the 6th and 7th and Giles feared that if Marichal pitched in Dodger Stadium, that could set off a riot the magnitude of those in Watts. So he prohibited Marichal from even traveling with his team to Los Angeles. Not wanting to wait another six days to pitch after his 10-game suspension, Marichal coaxed Franks into letting him start in Chicago September 5 after only two days of rest. Before the Giants left Philadelphia, Juan received a letter that threatened him if he pitched at Wrigley Field. Chicago FBI agents circulated through the stands during the first game of the series but did not apprehend any would-be assassins. Marichal pitched a complete game that Sunday to defeat the Cubs 4–2.

Juan was disappointed that he couldn't pitch in Los Angeles. He didn't want his absence to hurt the team further. And he didn't think it was fair that Giles had banned him the additional games. "I don't think it's right," he said. "We're trying to win the pennant." The Dodgers, on the other hand, would not have minded the chance to get their revenge against Marichal on the mound. "It doesn't make any difference to us where he is," manager Walt Alston said. "Truthfully, we would have felt better playing against him and beating his brains out." The Los Angeles skipper was speaking metaphorically one presumes, though one couldn't be sure, which probably made Giles seem prudent.

The Giants won both games in Los Angeles without Juan and pulled even with the Dodgers in first place. Back in San Francisco, the fans embraced Marichal on September 9 in his homecoming against the Astros. They cheered him warmly when he ran to the mound. Their affection buoyed him. His teammates also had his back. With two outs in the fourth inning, Marichal had not allowed a hit. Houston's Walt Bond drove a ground ball up the middle. Giants shortstop Dick Schofield snagged the ball behind the base but, off-balance, had no play. Wanting to keep Marichal's no-hitter going, he shoveled the ball to second baseman Maxie Lanier, who turned and threw blindly to first. They didn't get the runner, who reached with the Astros' first hit of the game, but they did show Juan how much he meant to them. "That crazy play those guys made behind me—an utterly foolhardy and impossible try to get the ball to first—gave me one of the warmest feelings I have ever had in my pitching career,"

Marichal wrote in his first book. "And you should have heard the applause from the crowd!"

Juan won the game, his 21st, and recorded his 10th shutout, best in the majors, but Koufax obscured his heroics by pitching a perfect game the same day. The Giants had a slim half-game lead over the Dodgers, but Koufax moved to the forefront as the prime candidate for that year's Cy Young Award.*

Roseboro hadn't caught Sandy's perfect game. Alston had given him the day off. But a strange thing had happened to Roseboro after his fight with Marichal: He had started to hit. The baseball. In the 10 games between his return and Koufax's perfecto, Johnny had gone 14-for-36, a blistering .389 average. But Johnny's hitting surge and Sandy's perfect game notwithstanding, the Dodgers had not played like a pennant winner. In the three weeks since August 22, the Dodgers had won 10 games and lost 12.

Marichal won his 22nd game on September 13 against Houston, but he wouldn't win again that season. The Giants' 14-game winning streak, which had stretched their lead over the Dodgers to four and a half games, began to crumble with Marichal's next start. He could not find his rhythm against the Braves in Milwaukee, giving up two early home runs to Hank Aaron. Franks pulled Marichal with one out in the fourth and the Giants trailing 5–1. Juan came undone in those final four starts, losing three of them and giving up an inordinate number of home runs (eight). Since coming back from his suspension, he had been reluctant to pitch inside, and power hitters took advantage of him. Post-suspension, he gave up a home run every five innings as opposed to averaging only one every 16 innings prior to his fight with Roseboro. His ERA those final four games was 6.45, almost quadruple his league-best 1.78 through August 22. In Juan's final start of the season, on September 30, the game was tied 2–2 (Marichal had given up two solo home runs) when he smacked a

* Koufax finished the season 26–8 with a 2.04 ERA, 27 complete games, and the Cy Young Award.

double in the top of the eighth. He swung too wide around the bag. When he dove back, he jammed his left thumb and broke it. He had to come out of the game. He didn't pitch again in 1965.

The Giants faltered along with Marichal, going 8–8 the final two weeks and two days of the season. Their lead dwindled steadily with each of Marichal's starts. They were up by four games as late as September 20, but the Dodgers went on a tear, winning 15 of their last 16 games, and claimed the pennant, two games ahead of the Giants. Roseboro credited Koufax, who set a major league record that season with 382 strikeouts. When they needed to win, they did. "We had confidence," Roseboro wrote. "He gave us confidence."

San Francisco's general manager Chub Feeney, on the other hand, blamed Giles for the Giants losing the pennant. He didn't think his team had been able to recover from the loss of its ace for 12 games and that Juan had not pitched with the same effectiveness when he returned, especially his final four starts. Feeney was not alone in that opinion. "The ten-day layoff cost Marichal his great year," sportswriter Jim Ellison observes in his essay "Juan Marichal: After the Incident." "He was an indifferent pitcher the rest of the way, winning three games and losing four; he was hit freely. His usually impeccable control was off. The man who came back, against the wishes of at least half the country, was not the man who swung his bat in anger on Sunday, August 22, in Candlestick Park. He was a sad and confused young man, saddled with a $110,000 lawsuit and a haunting memory to contemplate through the long nights."

Almost a month to the day since Marichal struck Roseboro, another Dominican lost his head with bat in hand. Pedro Gonzalez, the second baseman that Ramfis Trujillo had let the Yankees assign to Licey when he denied their request for Marichal, had been traded to the Indians earlier in the season. On Monday, September 20, in Cleveland, bottom of the fifth inning, Gonzalez faced the Tigers' Larry Sherry. Sherry threw an inside pitch that caught Gonzalez's bat when he ducked out of the way. Gonzalez believed that the Detroit manager, Charlie Dressen, often had his pitchers throw at black hitters. When Sherry's next pitch came inside again at his head, Gonzalez's rage spurred him to the mound. He swung his bat at Sherry. Some say the lumber caught the pitcher on the leg; others say the swing missed. Players rushed in quickly to subdue Gonzalez before he could seriously harm Sherry.

Once again, the summer of fury had erupted in a moment of violence on the diamond. It did not receive the national attention that the Marichal-Roseboro moment had, probably because neither player involved was as big of a star and the Indians-Tigers rivalry was nothing compared to the Giants-Dodgers. Also, with both teams more than a dozen games out of first place, the confrontation lacked the context of a pennant battle. And, of course, Gonzalez hadn't spilled blood the way Marichal had.

But the authority's response was still swift and severe. American League president Joe Cronin suspended Gonzalez for the rest of the season, 13 games, and fined him $500, substantially more as a percentage of his salary than the amount levied against Marichal.* The fact that it had occurred in the wake of Marichal's action no doubt compounded the punishment for Gonzalez's crime. "I'll do anything to stop the use of bats in baseball controversies," Cronin said. "We just can't have any more of this. It is our job to stop physical violence, and we will punish fighting of any kind."

Not only had a player taken a bat to another—again—it was a Dominican player, which only seemed to confirm the earlier indictments of Marichal as being part of a rogue class of "Caribbean hot-bloods" and "fiery Dominicans." These incidents could be the

* Gonzalez earned $10,500 in 1965, compared to Marichal's $60,000.

kernel that formed the basis of the stereotype. Or the classification of Dominicans as hot-bloods could be an exaggeration extrapolated from several incidents. To get at the truth would require a significant study and sensitive cultural analysis, as Jim Kaplan suggests in *The Greatest Game:* "We would have to . . . determine if the number of Latinos involved [in violent incidents] was greater than their percentage of the baseball population. Further, we'd have to explore the effect of poverty and prejudice on Latino players and wonder how Anglos would behave if they were from the same background." Regardless, Gonzalez had delivered Marichal another derisive reminder of his own guilt.

Meanwhile, Johnny and the Dodgers were delighted to be back in the World Series. After the Twins won the first two games, Roseboro contributed to his team's critical Game Three victory with a stolen base and two RBI on a pair of singles. Johnny had another hit in the deciding Game Seven, pitched and won by Koufax. With six hits Roseboro batted .286 in the Series, by far his best performance in any of the four Fall Classics he played. "Because of our comeback, it was an especially satisfying series," he wrote.

The 1965 season had ended—in success for Roseboro, disappointment for Marichal—but the implications of their altercation had not ended. For the two of them, the sun would never set on August 22, 1965.

CHAPTER EIGHT

That's Not How the Story Goes

UNDER THE HOT PHOENIX SUN, UNCERTAIN WHAT TO EXPECT, JOHNNY Roseboro gripped his bat more tightly than usual. Juan Marichal glared at the hitter 20 paces away and fingered the ball in his hand. Somebody had wanted them to shake hands at the plate beforehand, but neither one volunteered to initiate a staged truce. This duel, their first meeting since last August 22, had drawn a crowd of curious onlookers that jammed the nearly 8,000 seats, stood beyond the right field screen, swarmed the slope past the left field fence, and perched on the hill across the street. Runners poised on first and second with one out in the top of the second of a scoreless spring training game, but there was far more than an RBI or two at stake that Sunday afternoon of April 3, 1966. San Francisco sportswriter Harry Jupiter captured the mood: "It was like the crowd that packs the Indianapolis Speedway every Memorial Day. Nobody wants to see anybody get hurt or killed, but if it's going to happen . . ."

Everywhere Juan went that winter in San Francisco and back in the Dominican Republic, all anyone wanted to talk about was the fight. The letters kept coming. The taunts were incessant. No one would let him forget.

Meanwhile, Johnny, still troubled by what had gone down in Watts, had offered his services to the LAPD "in any capacity." The police department hired him as a community relations officer to soothe relations between the police and the people that the riots had scorched. He spoke to students at schools, kids in juvenile detention, seniors at community centers, and congregations at churches. They listened to his message of viewing the police as fellow human beings and engendering mutual respect. "He's winning friends in the field for the LAPD," Bud Furillo noted in the *Sporting News*. But his audience's first question invariably seemed to be about the fight with Marichal.

The questions continued into spring training at Vero Beach. Juan's apology had not appeased Johnny. It had come through the press, not in person. "But even if he had come to me face to face, I wouldn't have been impressed because apologies in my book don't make up for the original deed," Johnny told *Los Angeles Herald-Examiner* columnist Melvin Durslag. "There are too many people in this world who do terrible things intentionally and feel they can ease out of trouble with an apology."

He still thought about retaliating. It frustrated him that Juan had scored the decisive blow. Johnny said if he had landed several convincing punches himself, he probably would have considered them even and not filed the lawsuit. But, having come out on the losing end, he wanted some sort of vengeance. He, too, had replayed the fight in his mind many times, wishing he could have altered the outcome, thinking how he should have applied his training in the sweet science, that he should have parried and grabbed. "Instead I started flailing away with crazy punches, throwing a lot of street rights," he told Durslag in spring training. "This isn't the way to neutralize a man with a weapon. But I lost my head."

And now here they stood, face-to-face again, having swapped weapons, Johnny with the bat, Juan with the ball. The naked sun blazed upon them.

Juan's first pitch missed outside. The second high. Cautious.

Johnny took the next for a called strike, then fouled one off. Patient.

Juan delivered a 2–2 slider belt high. Johnny stroked it cleanly to right.

Jesus Alou, the Giants right fielder and Marichal's roommate, charged in to play the line drive on its first hop, but the ball leaped over his head and continued back to the fence where hundreds stood. Johnny sped around the bases and beat the throw to the plate. He had legged out an inside-the-park home run, good for three runs in the Dodgers' eventual 8–4 victory—a small drink of revenge but not enough to quench his thirst.

During the off-season, when the Dodgers' Sandy Koufax and Don Drysdale had famously teamed up to demand more money, $235,000 between them, Marichal believed his 22 wins, 10 shutouts, 2.13 ERA, and All-Star Game MVP performance deserved a significant raise. He asked for $80,000 in 1966, increasing his '65 salary by a third. Giants general manager Chub Feeney, who blamed the team's late collapse the previous summer on Marichal's suspension, did not think Marichal deserved a raise at all. He pointed out that Juan had lost his last three games and the Giants had finished two games back. The team offered Marichal the same $60,000 it had paid him in 1965.

That offended Juan. "Juan seldom gets angry," his wife, Alma, said. "It takes a lot for him to get angry about something, but when he does get angry, he will stay angry for a long time."

Marichal came down to $75,000 but insisted it was that or nothing. He would quit baseball before accepting the Giants' insult of an offer. Spring training started without him.

One Giants official thought Marichal should wise up and accept the club's offer. "What's he going to do?" the official scoffed to a reporter. "He isn't going to make $60,000 in the Dominican Republic cutting sugarcane."

When Juan read the comment in the newspaper, it further infuriated him. "Lots of people earn good livings in the Dominican Republic," said Marichal, who had been buying up the land around his family farm outside Laguna Verde. "I can earn a lot of money growing crops on my farm. In the United States there are those who think all Latin Americans are peasants. Well, we are not. I will do very well here without playing baseball for the Giants."

Feeney finally realized Marichal did not intend to budge and signed him for $75,000. Marichal pitched only 13 innings in Arizona, but he was ready for Opening Day. Physically, if not emotionally. More than the insults from the Giants during his salary negotiations, the condemnation, the suspension, the derogatory comments, his own remorse had all hardened something inside. The smile that puffed his cheeks shone less frequently. He withdrew, became sullen.

Once he finally had arrived in spring training, Juan opened up to a writer he trusted, Harry Jupiter of the *San Francisco Examiner*, in an article that would be published in the June issue of *Sport* under the headline Juan Marichal's Hard Fight to Redeem Himself. Juan said he decided to talk because, "When it happened, only Roseboro's side of the story was emphasized. I don't think my side was ever really considered by Mr. Giles or anybody else." In the article he repeated his version of events. "Look, I never in my life ever thought of hitting anybody with a bat," he said. "But in that second, when the ball brushed against my ear, the thought I had was that it could have killed me. Unless you experience something like this, you can't understand the feeling I had at the moment."

Even after talking about it, he still felt isolated with that feeling—and those he'd had afterward. People wondering how the incident with Roseboro would affect Marichal noticed the different demeanor and perhaps a subtle change in his pitching. He was afraid to throw inside. He didn't want to hit a batter. Which set Willie Mays against him on Opening Day.

After Mays had homered, Cubs pitcher Bill Hands aimed a fastball at Mays's head in his next at-bat that Willie barely escaped. He got up and took several steps toward the mound before he could be restrained. Marichal had never seen his teammate so mad. But when a payback pitch came due against the Cubs' leading hitter, the best Juan could manage was a weak toss over Ernie Banks's head. "It was just nothing," Juan admitted. "And everybody knew it."

After the game Mays confronted Marichal. "I'm trying to win for you. How am I going to do it if you won't protect me?"

"He's a nice guy," Juan said lamely.

"So am I," Willie fumed.

But, more than his teammate's anger, Marichal feared the wrath of National League president Warren Giles if he struck a batter with a pitch.

The Giants and Dodgers played their first regular season matchup in Candlestick exactly a month after their Phoenix exhibition. Roseboro had started haltingly at the plate, 9-for-43 in the young season. He faced Marichal in the second inning with one on and one out. The threat of danger did not permeate the atmosphere that Tuesday evening the way it had in Phoenix, but the animosity was present. Prior to their fight, Roseboro had done well against Marichal, better than against most pitchers, going 21-for-71, a .296 average. This time Roseboro did not hit the ball. Marichal struck him out.

His next at-bat, Roseboro reached on Marichal's error, when Juan dropped the ball. His next time up, he singled. But with an 8–1 lead and two outs in the top of the ninth, Marichal induced Roseboro to fly out to the shortstop to end the game.

Two weeks later, they squared off again at Chavez Ravine. It was Juan's first time in Los Angeles since August 22. The Angelenos booed Marichal vehemently when his name was announced, a thunderous roar from 53,561 zealous fans. Marichal did his part to quiet them by slapping two hits and pitching 10 innings of one-run ball until he was replaced by a pinch hitter in the 11th. Roseboro went 0-for-5 against Marichal, but the Dodgers won in the 13th, bringing them within four games of the league-leading Giants after five weeks of play.

The cut on Johnny's head had closed, the small scar obscured by his curly black hair, but Juan's wound could not be stitched shut. "You see a lot of scars in baseball," Philadelphia manager Gene Mauch said one day when talking about the Giants pitcher. "On the face, on the chin, on the cheeks. On the legs and arms sometimes. We don't know about this scar. This one might be someplace in Juan Marichal where you can't see it." Mauch drew an *X* across his heart.

Fans continued to taunt him, "Hit anybody with a bat lately?" Letters stained with racial ugliness continued to arrive. On the mound he heard the boos. The antipathy was anathema for a man who desired others' affection. "Juan needs love," Jesus Alou said. "You see, we Dominicans do not play just for money but for appreciation."

Marichal seemed determined to show them that he could overcome the derisive reminders and the internal wound with his performance. Through the end of May he was 10–0, having won every start except for the game against the Dodgers when he came out after 10 innings and one earned run. He had pitched nine complete games and four shutouts. His ERA stood at 0.80. *Time* magazine placed him on the cover of its June 10, 1966, issue and tagged him "the Best Right Arm in Baseball."

The qualified praise came in deference to the Left Arm of God, though the article did declare that "Better than Koufax or not, Juan Marichal without question . . . is the most complete pitcher in the game today, or any day." The magazine based that assessment on his assortment of pitches and how he used them. Two weeks earlier, the Mets' Chuck Hiller, who, as Marichal's teammate in 1962 had become the first National Leaguer to hit a grand slam in the World Series, told the *San Francisco Examiner,* "As far as I'm concerned, he's better than Koufax. Sandy may be quicker, but he doesn't have the pitches Marichal does."

Tom Sheehan, a pitcher-turned-scout for the Giants, had pointed out to Marichal his recent tendency to pitch away from the batter rather than inside. "I am glad he said this, because a lot of it was subconscious—I did not want to make a mistake and hit a batter, with the Roseboro thing so recent in people's minds—so I was not going for the inside," Marichal wrote. "It is bad for a pitcher not to use the inside part of the hitter's area, but double bad for a *control* pitcher not to do it." Once Sheehan alerted Marichal and he made the necessary correction, he became, once again, a complete pitcher.

The civil war ceasefire had promised elections now about to take place in the Dominican, which renewed Juan's anxieties in June. Marichal had become one of the biggest landowners in the Dominican Republic, having acquired 1,065 acres where he grew hay, beans, plantain, rice, and corn in addition to raising 300 dairy and beef cattle. Given his position as a landowner and connections to Trujillo through his in-laws, he supported the conservative cause headed by Joaquín Balaguer, whose political posters touted the presidential candidate as "the Marichal of the Palace."* Balaguer's backers solicited Juan to sign his name to an advertisement in the Dominican papers that urged his fellow countrymen to vote to "bring peace to all so that we can have revolution without blood." Referencing the ad, *Sports Illustrated* snarked that Marichal "perhaps mindful of the good example he ought to be setting, has not bloodied an opponent with a baseball bat all season long." In the days leading up to the election, the sinus troubles that had bothered Juan in 1965 returned. Balaguer's victory in the elections, which were free of disturbance, provided some measure of relief.

Fluke injuries dogged Marichal the next two months—his pitching hand caught accidentally in a car door, a turned ankle, and a line drive off his foot—but he continued pitching complete games and winning. By the time the Giants played the Dodgers again, on August 27 at Candlestick, Juan was 18–5 with a 2.18 ERA. Only one game separated the two teams in the standings with the Giants ahead in the pennant race, though they still trailed Pittsburgh by half a game. Roseboro had picked up his average by cutting out batting practice, which he said threw off his timing, and was batting .298, better than he had ever hit over an entire season. He worked a full count off Marichal in the second with one on and no outs, then lined a single to center. Another single and sacrifice scored a run and moved Roseboro to third. Maury Wills laid down a surprise bunt, but Giants third baseman Jim Hart threw out Johnny at home to get Marichal out of the inning.

After Hart homered, Don Drysdale, whom Dodgers manager Walt Alston had again started regularly against Marichal all season, knocked down Willie Mays. It was Drysdale's turn to go down when he led off the fifth. "He may be wondering . . . whether I will retaliate by putting him down the way he put Mays down," Marichal wrote in his first book. "The setting here in Candlestick is the same, almost to

* Juan's cousin, also named Juan Marichal, was Balaguer's running mate.

Juan Marichal, heralded as "the Best Right Arm in Baseball," won 191 games in the 1960s, 27 more than Bob Gibson, 33 more than Don Drysdale, and 54 more than Sandy Koufax. NATIONAL BASEBALL HALL OF FAME LIBRARY, COOPERSTOWN, NY

In September 1965 *Los Angeles Times* columnist Jim Murray wrote, "John Roseboro is at the moment the Most Valuable Player in the National League, if not baseball." NATIONAL BASEBALL HALL OF FAME LIBRARY, COOPERSTOWN, NY

In 1952 Johnny posed with his parents at their Ashland home at 407 West 10th Street for a story in the *Ashland Times-Gazette* about Roseboro signing with the Dodgers. PHOTO COURTESY OF SHELLEY ROSEBORO

In the uncertain times that followed the assassination of the dictator Rafael Trujillo, Juan left spring training in 1962 to marry his sweetheart, Alma Rosa Carvajal, in the Dominican Republic. PHOTO COURTESY OF MARICHAL FAMILY COLLECTION

The Marichal family in 1970: Alma, Elsie, Juan, and Yvette. PHOTO COURTESY OF MARICHAL FAMILY COLLECTION

Roseboro with Roy Campanella, whom Johnny loved like a second father. One of the hardest things Roseboro had to do was take over his mentor's position after Campy's career-ending car accident, which left him paralyzed. NATIONAL BASEBALL HALL OF FAME LIBRARY, COOPERSTOWN, NY

Roseboro tags out Gino Cimoli of the St. Louis Cardinals. Buzzie Bavasi, the Dodgers' general manager, called the catcher—whose toughness behind the plate was legendary—"the Rock of Gibraltar." UPI

Roseboro fiddling with a guitar at a party hosted by actor Robert Cummings. Johnny liked to play and sing, but his roommate Maury Wills teased him about his limited musical talent. PHOTO COURTESY OF SHELLEY ROSEBORO

The Roseboros at home in 1968: Jaime, Johnny, Staci, Shelley, and Jeri. PHOTO COURTESY OF SHELLEY ROSEBORO

Los Angeles pitcher Sandy Koufax and catcher John Roseboro celebrate the Dodgers' improbable sweep of the New York Yankees in the 1963 World Series.
© AP/AP/CORBIS

Giants vs. Dodgers, the bitterest rivalry in sports, grew more bitter on August 22, 1965, after Roseboro buzzed Marichal and Marichal clubbed Roseboro.
© BETTMANN/CORBIS

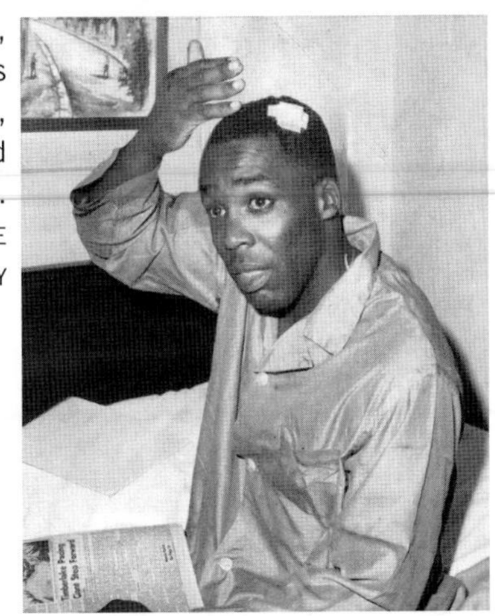

The morning after the fight, Roseboro gave an impromptu press conference at the Roosevelt Hotel, still in his pajamas, and showed reporters his bandaged wound.
NATIONAL BASEBALL HALL OF FAME LIBRARY, COOPERSTOWN, NY

Ten-year-old Dodger fan Roger Guenveur Smith was so upset by what he witnessed that he burned this 1965 Topps card of Marichal.
COURTESY OF THE TOPPS COMPANY, INC.

Dodgers manager Walt Alston with Marichal at Dodgertown in Vero Beach, Florida, after Juan signed with the Dodgers in March 1975. Alston once told his team to leave Marichal—the Dodgers' archenemy—to him if a fight broke out.
© BETTMANN/CORBIS

John Roseboro and Juan Marichal became unlikely teammates in the Dodgers' old-timers' game in August 1975.
DIAMOND IMAGES/GETTY IMAGES

With a flourish of their Sharpies, the two men transformed photos of their fight into a testament of reconciliation. © BETTMANN/CORBIS

On July 31, 1983, the day he was inducted into the National Baseball Hall of Fame, Juan said in Spanish, "I accept the honor conferred on me today in the name of my family and my country, the Dominican Republic." NATIONAL BASEBALL HALL OF FAME LIBRARY, COOPERSTOWN, NY

Johnny and Barbara in Los Angeles circa 1999. She helped him find his way out of his darkest time. PHOTO COURTESY OF MORGAN FOUCH-ROSEBORO

Johnny horsing around with his grandnephew Alex and daughters Shelle and Nikki. Nikki said, "I could not have asked for a better father." PHOTO COURTES OF MORGAN FOUCH-ROSEBORO

In 2005 the San Francisco Giants unveiled a statue of Juan Marichal th immortalizes his signature high leg kick. It joined statues of Willie Mays and Willie McCovey outside the San Francisco stadium. © 2013 S. F. GIANTS

After reconciling, Marichal and Roseboro occasionally appeared together at card shows. PHOTO COURTESY OF MORGAN FOUCH-ROSEBORO

the day, as a year ago when the Roseboro episode occurred. I get him to a count of one ball and two strikes—now he must *really* be wondering—for you could waste a close pitch if you were of a mind to." But Juan decided not to risk another altercation, another suspension, another regret, and grooved a fastball that Drysdale watched for strike three.

Roseboro didn't manage another hit—Juan struck him out in the sixth—and Marichal picked up his 19th win. He threw only 106 pitches (74 percent for strikes) in what he considered one of his best and most important games of the season. "After all the doubts, after all the worries about Marichal in the big ones, I can still pitch," he wrote.

For Roseboro, his single was the second of only two hits he managed off Marichal after August 22, 1965, but he remained strong at bat and behind the plate. He finished the season with a .276 average, second highest in his career, 23 doubles, also second best in his career, and won his second Gold Glove. By September *Los Angeles Times* columnist Jim Murray had fingered Roseboro as the reason for the Dodgers success. "John Roseboro is at the moment the Most Valuable Player in the National League, if not baseball. He is the Dodgers' glue and has been for nearly ten years. If the fans don't know it, the league does. From dugout to dugout, the advice goes, 'Don't mess with John Roseboro.'"

Murray praised Roseboro for being a "no-nonsense, show-up-for-work guy" who was "conscientious—and ballplayers who are, are in shorter supply than .400 hitters." He claimed Roseboro was even more valuable than Mays because, as a catcher, Roseboro was more involved in the defense. "You have to win the pennant to win the MVP," Murray wrote. "But, if they have an award for Most Valuable Human Being, I know where my vote would go."

Not many dwelt on the anomaly of a black man directing the defense, but Roseboro's leadership was unusual at a time when, in some states, African Americans could not marry Caucasians, were denied housing, and were routinely passed over for employment. A time when there had not been a black US Supreme Court justice, CEO of a Fortune 500 company, or US president. A time when there had not been a starting African-American quarterback in the modern NFL and fewer than a handful of regular African-American catchers in Major League Baseball (Elston Howard, Earl Battey, and Roseboro's predecessor Roy Campanella). At a time when many white Americans believed that blacks lacked the intelligence and leadership skills the position required, Roseboro proved them wrong.

The Dodgers did end up winning the pennant, overtaking the rival Giants for the last three weeks of the season. Roseboro did not win the MVP Award; he finished 13th in the voting. Koufax carried the team through the final weeks, including a victory on the final day of the season with only three days' rest in a must-win situation. He ended his last season by leading the majors in wins (27), complete games (27), innings pitched (323), ERA (1.73), and strikeouts (317). Marichal had a terrific season, going 25–6, giving him the best winning percentage in the majors, pitching 25 complete games with four shutouts and posting a 2.23 ERA, but, once again, "the Best Right Arm in Baseball" had fallen short of Koufax. Marichal had beaten the Dodgers three times in 1966 but never had the chance for a head-to-head rematch with Koufax.

Juan went home while Johnny and the Dodgers went to the World Series. Koufax had nothing left, however, and the Baltimore Orioles sent Los Angeles packing in four straight. The team headed to Japan to play a series of exhibition games, but what they had thought would be a victory tour "turned into a wake," Roseboro wrote.

The funeral occurred the following summer. With Koufax retired and Wills exiled to Pittsburgh (traded after he abandoned the Japan tour), the team sank to the depths of the National League, finishing 73–89, 28½ games back in eighth place, better only than the bottom-feeding Astros and Mets. Johnny had a decent year, batting

.272 in 116 games, but he was 34 years old, packing a few extra pounds and feeling the years spent catching in his knee and shoulder. It dawned on him that he was expendable, especially from a woebegone team. Sure enough, in late November 1967 the Dodgers dealt him to the Minnesota Twins along with pitchers Ron Perranoski and Bob Miller for shortstop Zoilo Versalles and pitcher Mudcat Grant. Johnny understood that the trade made sense—the Dodgers needed a shortstop to replace Wills—but emotionally he felt rejected. He cried at the news.

He would be 35 in May. Could he still play? The doubt shadowed him to spring training with his new team.

On a winter evening following the 1966 season, the president of the Dominican Republic invited Señor Juan Marichal to his residence. Joaquin Balaguer pinned the nation's "citizen supreme" medal on Juan's chest. The political payback for Marichal's support did not diminish the sincerity of his countryman's esteem. The moment symbolically restored Juan's hero status in his native country.

But his reputation remained tainted in the United States. With Koufax retired, Marichal reigned as Major League Baseball's best pitcher in 1967. Chub Feeney could not blame the Giants' previous late-season stumble on his ace, and Juan was not feeling as angry and stubborn, so they agreed on a $100,000 salary for 1967—a level finally commensurate with his talents, though still behind Drysdale, who had won only 13 games in 1966 (and lost 16) while collecting $110,000. But the Dominican pitcher's legacy had begun to calcify. "An Angeleno remembers only the sight of Marichal's bat against the side of John Roseboro's skull," Furman Bisher observed in the *Atlanta Journal.* "How's that for injustice, for the greatest pitcher in baseball to be remembered for a hit that didn't even make the Baseball Guide?"

Marichal published his first book, *A Pitcher's Story: The Greatest Pitcher in the Major Leagues Tells the Inside Story of His Rise to the Top,* authored with San Francisco sportswriter Charles Einstein, which recounted parts of the 1966 season and explained his part in *l'affaire* Roseboro by excerpting Harry Jupiter's article from *Sport.* With Koufax retired it was not only the opinion of Marichal, Einstein, and Bisher but widely accepted that Juan currently held the title of "greatest pitcher in the game." The book seemed to be the pitcher's reply to the questions about whether his temperament could withstand the aftermath of that event.

Another publication distracted Juan that summer. In late July the *Saturday Evening Post* published an article by Al Stump that cast Marichal as discontented, victimized by the system and game. It detailed his troubles, from the city of San Francisco making him tear down a greenhouse in his backyard to spectators booing him. "They [the boos] hurt," Stump quoted Marichal. "Trouble with baseball is that always they want more, more, more . . . without thinking of what suffering they bring a player who happens to be down." Stump identified prejudice as the underlying cause of the Latino's problems. "Inequality seems to be an obsession with Marichal," Stump wrote. "He believes that he and the rest of the major-league Latins are victims of a subtly functioning prejudice."

Marichal claimed Stump had misquoted and unfairly characterized him, dismissing the article as "*muy, muy, muy malo.*" The writer had indeed made factual errors and embellished facts. Marichal's attorney claimed his client had been libeled but did not file a suit. The profile may have been more caricature than a realistic portrait but at its core probably contained the truth that Juan had felt the sting of prejudice and resented it.

His trouble played out on the mound. He lost his first three games of the '67 season, getting hammered for 13 earned runs in 18⅓ innings. He won his next eight starts but after that lost more games than he won. Another fluke injury—liquid sprayed into his eye when he cut open a golf ball—and a pulled hamstring hampered him. What hurt worse, though, was the sense Juan had that the front office did not take his injuries seriously, perhaps dismissing them with the stereotype of Latin players as malingerers. "They thought I was jaking," Marichal said. "This simply is not true." Rumors bubbled up that the Giants might trade him after the season.

Before Johnny and Jeri left Los Angeles, they added a son to their family. Though he loved his daughters deeply, Johnny had always wanted a son. He and Jeri decided to adopt. They visited an adoption agency near their home. Johnny spotted a small boy sitting on the floor surrounded by toys. From among all of the toys, the boy selected a Nerf football and held it in his little hands, as if to show Johnny. "That's my boy," Johnny said.

Jaime, five years younger than Shelley and seven younger than Staci, completed the family. Johnny's instincts for Jaime's athletic ability proved accurate. He would go on to star in high school and play seven seasons of professional baseball.

But the move to Minnesota also meant Johnny had to say goodbye to his parents. John Sr. and Geraldine had moved out to the Los Angeles area after the 1965 World Series, and Johnny had bought them a house in Pomona. The elder Roseboros had enjoyed the chance to be closer to their grandchildren and vice versa. Johnny, still very close to his parents, also loved having them around. The trade spoiled all that.

Minnesota made Roseboro appreciate Los Angeles. The Twins had a talented roster—witness Harmon Killebrew, Tony Oliva, Rod Carew, Dean Chance, Dave Boswell, Jim Perry, et al.—"but they were a troubled team, full of bickering and bitterness," Roseboro wrote. Whereas the Dodgers had blended well, the Twins divided into racial and ethnic cliques. Roseboro observed that the Latinos, like the Venezuelan Cesar Tovar, who was making only $17,000 in 1968 despite finishing seventh in the MVP voting the previous season, were "badly underpaid and understandably bitter." The blacks were treated worse. The American League in general did not seem as welcoming to African-American players as the National League, which had hired more Negro League players than the American League after Jackie Robinson's debut with the Dodgers. The Twins in particular made things tough on black players because of their owner, Calvin Griffith, whom Roseboro called "the least likable person I met in baseball." In 1978 Griffith would say under the influence that he had moved the Washington Senators to the Twin Cities because Minnesota had only 15,000 black residents. "Black people don't go to ballgames," Griffith said. "But they'll fill up a rassling ring and put up such a chant it'll scare you to death."

Roseboro found that Griffith "acted as though he was a plantation owner and the rest of us were slaves." Johnny's bat weakened against unfamiliar pitchers in a new league, but he played strong behind the plate, winning the respect of his team's pitchers. "I shook him off only once during the opening game in 1968 against Washington and that guy got a base hit off that pitch," said Twins ace Dean Chance, who had won 20 games the previous season. "That man [Roseboro] is all right." But Griffith, who had acquired Roseboro's contract along with the catcher, thought the Dodgers had overpaid him. Los Angeles general manager Buzzie Bavasi had, in fact, raised Johnny's salary to $60,000 before trading him to the Twins to soften the blow. The following spring, when Roseboro did not sign Griffith's contract, which would have slashed his pay by 33 percent, Griffith sent him a letter that said, in effect, "Boy, where else can you work and make $40,000 a year? Take this, or you'll never work again."

Roseboro pointed out that the maximum cut allowed by the collective bargaining agreement was 20 percent, or $12,000 in his case, so that's what Griffith offered next. Johnny tried holding out, but Griffith didn't budge. Johnny finally accepted the cut but didn't forgive the cutter. That summer, 1969, Billy Martin took over as the Twins manager. Roseboro liked Martin's gambling style and winning spirit. He didn't like Martin's aggressiveness in ordering pitchers to throw at batters or the way he criticized them, and Johnny told him so. But playing under Martin, his hitting picked up. Roseboro's average fluctuated between .285 and .320 much of the season, finally dipping to .263 at the end due to fatigue. Roseboro also improved the pitching staff, which he had discovered when he arrived in Minnesota "didn't know how to set up batters, knock people on their butts, and stuff like that. It took me a year to where we were cooking," Johnny said. "Dave Boswell and Jim Perry won 20 games that year because they learned how to follow my direction. That's not being egotistical. That's because I knew what I was doing." To back that up, he could point to the spot on the American League All-Star team he earned that season.*

The Twins won the American League West division† but lost the league championship series to the Orioles. Griffith fired Martin, who had bloodied Boswell's face in a bar fight in August, and released Roseboro, whom he thought he was still paying too much damn money. Roseboro initially challenged his release, calling up American League president Joe Cronin to ask, "How in the hell can he release me when I made the All-Star team?" But he found out no rules prevented Griffith from making roster decisions guided by stinginess or stupidity. In the end, Johnny realized, "It was the best thing that ever happened to me."

---

* Roseboro replaced starting catcher Bill Freehan of the Detroit Tigers in the seventh inning and flew out to center field in his only at-bat of the AL's 9–3 loss in Washington.

† 1969 was the year the American League and National League expanded to 12 teams each and both leagues split into two divisions.

Marichal came back strong in 1968. On July 28 he drove in the winning run with a Baltimore chop over the third baseman's head in the 11th inning to win his 19th game of the season. More significantly, it marked the 95th time in his last 96 wins that he had gone the distance, a feat the *Houston Chronicle* called, even in those days when starters routinely pitched complete games, "one of the most amazing statistics in baseball." Marichal did it by taking special care of his arm. He squeezed a rubber ball to strengthen his hand and arm but didn't lift weights because he wanted to maintain his flexibility. After games he soaked in a hot shower for 15 minutes with a towel wrapped around his arm. He ran to keep his legs strong and his conditioning up. He won 26 games that season, losing only nine, but he felt like he could have won 30 with more run support from his teammates.* He had notched five shutouts and allowed only 2.43 earned runs per nine innings. He had made a convincing comeback from his subpar '67 season.

Good as Marichal was in 1968, yet again another pitcher eclipsed his performance. The St. Louis Cardinals' Bob Gibson didn't win as many games, going 22–9, but he recorded 13 shutouts and posted a dazzling 1.12 ERA, which won him the National League's Cy Young Award and Most Valuable Player honors. Marichal and Gibson's dominance along with Denny McLain's 31 wins (making him the AL's Cy Young and MVP winner) in 1968 motivated Major League Baseball to lower the pitching mound by five inches—or 33 percent—the next season. Juan complained that the change disrupted his precision, and he struggled to keep his pitches down.

In May 1969 he pulled a muscle in his rib cage throwing a fastball in Houston. He finished the game but lost. He missed his next start and won the start after that by throwing sidearm because the

* Indeed, in six of the games Marichal lost, his teammates produced an average of only 1.17 runs.

pain wouldn't allow him to pitch overhand. He couldn't get past the sixth inning in his next two outings. Marichal recovered and pitched solidly, burnishing his record to 13–4, until he skidded in late July, losing four games in a row for the first time in his career. Pitching coach Larry Jansen sat him down to study some film and compare his motion from the previous year to his recent performances. They discovered he was not kicking his leg high enough and not following through as completely. After adjusting his delivery he finished the final five weeks 7–2 and pitched a game on September 12 against the Reds that he considered finer than his no-hitter in 1963 or even his 16-inning marathon against Spahn later that '63 season. He faced only 28 batters in a one-hit shutout against a team that included three future Hall of Famers: Pete Rose, Tony Perez, and Johnny Bench. "He was a master, a Rembrandt," Giants manager Clyde King said. Despite his four-game slump, Juan put up good numbers in 1969: a 21–11 win-loss record, eight shutouts, and 2.10 ERA, lowest in the majors. He was frustrated that his team finished second in the National League West but still had to endure perceptions that he was not a team player, perhaps lingering from Alvin Dark's earlier criticism. One scout noted, "Don't really think he cares if the Giants win the pennant. All he wants is about 25 games each year."

In February 1970, Roseboro and Marichal settled the lawsuit that Roseboro had brought against Marichal. Though the catcher had originally sued for $110,000, he agreed to accept $7,500 paid by the National Exhibition Company, which owned the Giants. Johnny's anger had dissipated, but the settlement did not appease either man's feelings. Remorse still troubled Juan. No matter how much he prayed for absolution, absent Johnny's forgiveness he still shouldered the guilt for his action. Roseboro, on the other hand, knew he had let Marichal absorb all of the blame for their fight, and that had started to gnaw at him. But he was not ready to ask forgiveness himself.

When Johnny's parents had moved out to California, his mother Geraldine had been able to transfer her employment to the J. C. Penney store in Pomona and keep working. Her heart troubled her at times, though she did not like to complain about her ailments, much like her son. She saw a doctor who prescribed her medication, but she stopped taking the pills when the prescription ran out—and landed in the hospital with fluid in her lungs in late January 1970. Jeri flew from Minneapolis to California to visit her at the Pomona Valley Community Hospital. After three days Geraldine was doing better, and Jeri flew home. But then a blood clot lodged in Geraldine's brain and killed her. She was 52 years old.

The death of his mother hit Johnny hard. It had come so unexpectedly. And early.

They flew back for the funeral at South Hills Presbyterian Church in Pomona. Johnny helped his father make the arrangements "and it was just terrible," he wrote. "It's a real ripoff, and they take advantage of poor people when they're pushed off balance." At the viewing, he stared at his mother, once a beautiful lady, reduced to "this waxy-looking woman with all the expression gone from her face." He could not push that image out of his mind.

He hated funerals and tried to get out of going to his mother's. He thought she would understand because they had joked with each other about not wanting anyone to go to their funerals. But the rest of his family insisted that he attend. So he did and wished his mother had more to her life and regretted that he had not shown her more of his love. "It became the ordeal I dreaded," he wrote.

The good news for Johnny that winter was that after Calvin Griffith set him free, he found a home with the Washington Senators. The owner, Bob Short, hired him to catch but also told him he was

Short's insurance policy in case his manager, Ted Williams, blew a fuse and quit suddenly. The situation appealed to Johnny, who thought he could still play and wanted to manage one day. Roseboro liked Williams. He enjoyed hearing his stories and picked up a lot from the master about the science of hitting. "He taught me more about hitting in a few months than I had learned in a lifetime," Roseboro wrote.

But it was too late. Johnny turned 37 in May. He was fighting his weight, nagged by shoulder and knee ailments, and not making contact. By late June he had managed only 11 hits. Williams called on him to pinch-hit occasionally but employed him behind the plate only a handful of times after that. They clashed when Roseboro argued with Teddy Ballgame about how to handle a young pitcher. Williams insisted the kid throw only curves.

"You can't ask that poor kid to learn in front of all those people in the stands," Roseboro said.

"Fuck the people," Williams said. "It's time the goddamn fastball pitcher learned to throw a curve."

"I can't catch that way," Roseboro said.

"Then you can't catch," Williams said.

By mid-August Roseboro wasn't catching anymore. Short told him he could try to find another team or stay on as a token coach for the rest of the season. The summer had been hard enough. His grief over his mother's death remained raw. Johnny had withdrawn from teammates, embarrassed by his failings, sensing that the other players thought he wasn't worth his inflated salary and feeling unhappy with the racial tensions among the Senators. Suddenly it had gotten worse.

This game he'd played since Bud Plank schooled him in the fundamentals back in Ashland, this game that had seen him into manhood, that had provided the platform for his skills to be watched and applauded and appreciated; this game that had given him two World Series and four All-Star Games, countless other memories, and that had been his means of earning a living—it was no longer his.

What then? He stayed—what other team would take in a washed-out, middle-age catcher?—because he needed the money. That proved worse than walking away clean because every time he pulled on the uniform knowing he wouldn't play and every pitcher he warmed up in the bullpen reminded him of how far removed he was from the glory days. Admitting that he could no longer play the game was the hardest thing he had done. "I spent many melancholy moments, lonely, feeling lost, wondering what I could do with myself, wishing I could go back twenty years to start all over again," he wrote. Of course, no one gets that chance.

That year, 1970, marked the end of Juan Marichal's dominance. The best pitcher of the 1960s would not be able to carry over his success into the new decade. From 1970 to 1976, when author Tom Wolfe dubbed the '70s the "Me Decade," would be pocked for Marichal by mediocre spurts, injuries, and comebacks—some successful but ultimately doomed.

An adverse reaction to penicillin given him to treat an ear infection kept him out of the 1970 season until May. He started slow, winning only three games while losing nine, and was left off the All-Star team for the first time in the past nine years. The sportswriters speculated that he was done, and Juan secretly worried they might be right. Then he found his fastball and control, staging a comeback that saw him win 9 of his last 10 decisions, including his 200th career win on August 28. He became the eighth pitcher to reach that plateau within only 11 seasons and the first Latin to win 200 games in the majors. But his ERA for the season had soared to a shocking 4.12, the first time in eight seasons it had been over three runs per game and the first time ever over four. The critics considered it a telltale mark.

Juan made a brief trip back to the Dominican Republic in the off-season to see his family but spent most of the winter in San Francisco working out with a personal trainer in the hope that superior conditioning would safeguard him at age 33 against injuries. He started the season 10–4 then stalled. For seven weeks he didn't win a game. He blamed bad luck but puzzled over what had really gone wrong. Finally, on August 10, he blanked Montreal, his 50th career shutout. He finished the season 18–11 with a respectable 2.94 ERA and again made the All-Star team. Perhaps most significantly, he pitched a complete game without giving up a run on the final day of the season when the Giants needed a win to edge the Dodgers. They lost in the league championship playoffs to the Pirates, but Juan showed he could still win in the clutch. At the end of the season, his .673 career winning percentage, based on his 221–109 record, stood as the best among all active pitchers. But like his 50th shutout, the .673 figure measured his success over time; those stats weren't indicative of his immediate effectiveness.

That season, even though Roseboro had left Los Angeles, Marichal further alienated himself from Dodgers fans. On September 13 at Candlestick with the Giants and Dodgers again in a race for first place and after Dodgers pitcher Bill Singer had hit two Giants batters, Marichal threw two purposeful pitches under Singer's chin. Umpire Shag Crawford, who six years earlier had tackled Juan after he clubbed Roseboro, warned Marichal, an automatic $50 fine. Two batters later, Juan hit Dodgers rookie Bill Buckner on the elbow with his first pitch. Buckner started toward the mound with his bat in hand. Crawford and catcher Russ Nixon quickly intervened. Crawford promptly ejected the pitcher and the batter. The Los Angeles press excoriated Marichal. *Los Angeles Herald-Examiner* columnist Melvin Durslag, who tagged Marichal as a player "known to reciprocate before there is provocation"—an unmistakable allusion to his altercation with Roseboro—wrote, "He never has learned to control his emotions as he does his breaking stuff" and that "despite their sentiments socially about Marichal, the Dodgers despise him in a game."

Just how much did they despise him? Before one heated series in San Francisco, Walt Alston had told his team, "If there's a fight tonight, I don't want one of you guys to dare touch that [expletive meaning Marichal deleted]. I'll be the guy, the only guy who takes care of him. Remember that. I want him." Alston did not get the chance, but he had made his feelings clear.

Marichal bickered with Giants owner Horace Stoneham about money before the 1972 season and held out once again. They finally agreed on a two-year deal worth $140,000 annually. But Marichal did not look like himself on the mound. He lowered his leg kick in his windup to ease the pain flaming in his back and the strain on his groin. After shutting out the Astros on Opening Day, he lost eight games in a row. He won with a complete game on June 2 but failed to go the distance again until August 22, when he pitched well but lost 0–1. His back hurt so badly at times that he said, "I just wanted to go to my room and cry." He missed a week while lying in traction in the hospital. He had a dismal season, 6–16 with a 3.71 ERA. The man who routinely hovered among the league leaders in complete games and innings pitched completed only six games and threw 165 innings, the fewest since his rookie year in 1960 when he was called up in July. Frankly, he looked like a has-been.

Late in the season, the Giants placed Juan on waivers to see who might be interested in the 34-year-old pitcher. No one bit, so Juan returned to the Giants in 1973. He had back surgery in October and spent the next four months wondering if he would be able to throw like he had before the pain. He worked hard to rehabilitate himself and report in top shape. He won on Opening Day with a complete game and thought he had another comeback in him. He felt he had regained his fastball and the ability to throw his sidearm curve. "I thought I was healthy enough to pitch like the old me, but I was never back to my old self," he wrote. He had another disappointing season, once again losing more games than he won (11–15) and giving up almost four runs per nine innings (3.82 ERA). This was not the Juan Marichal who had rivaled Sandy Koufax as the best pitcher in the game.

That December, Marichal received a phone call from Horace Stoneham. The Giants owner told Juan that he had sold him to the Boston Red Sox. What a blow. Like Roseboro before the Dodgers traded him, Marichal had known only one organization. He had been with the Giants for 16 seasons, the last 13½ in San Francisco. Now he had to move across the country to a different league.

He reported to spring training with the Red Sox in Winter Haven, Florida, but felt out of place in the strange uniform. He won a couple of games but was giving up a lot of runs when the thumb and two fingers of his pitching hand went numb in mid-May. He left the team to consult a San Francisco orthopedist. The problem was a disc in his back, but another surgery could end his career. Juan decided to rest. He rejoined the team in August and won three games before he was sidelined again, managing only two appearances for fewer than three total innings in September. He finished 5–1 but with a 4.87 ERA and the nagging certainty that he was done in the major leagues. The Red Sox confirmed his suspicions, releasing him in October 1974.

Juan went home to the Dominican Republic resigned that the end had come. He had his farm, four children, and a wife ready for a life together without baseball. But then his old friend Rafael Avila, the Dodgers' Latin American scout, visited him. Juan was a free agent, able to sign with whomever he pleased. Why not sign with Los Angeles? With Tommy John recovering from arm surgery, the Dodgers needed another starter.

The Dodgers? No, Juan said.

Don't you want to pitch again?

No, no, Juan said. I'm 36 years old. I'm retired.

But they have a good team, Avila insisted. They could go all the way.

Another World Series. That was tempting. And maybe he did have another season left in his arm. But the Dodgers? No.

Come on, Avila insisted. Come to spring training.

Juan weakened. A team wanted him. Never mind if it was his archrival, he was a ballplayer. That's all he had ever wanted to be since he started playing in Laguna Verde. Ballplayers played ball. The Dodgers offered him that chance.

In March 1975 he was posing for photographs in Vero Beach with Alston. Marichal wore a Dodgers cap and a home jersey with No. 57. Alston, the man who had once claimed dibs on beating up the Dominican, held up an away jersey with Marichal's name on the back. Both men smiled broadly.*

Whaaat?!

The news stunned the Los Angeles press and Dodgers fans. The papers reminded Angelenos of the fastball that had provoked Buckner in 1971, another aimed at Willie Davis's head in 1969 that had landed the centerfielder in the hospital, and, of course, the bat that had bludgeoned Roseboro. Always the incident with Roseboro. "How could they sign a guy who has done all that to us?" one Dodgers veteran player asked.

They needed another starting pitcher, that's how. "No one hated him more than I did," said Al Campanis, the Los Angeles general manager who had proposed the team sign Marichal, in trying to justify the deal to the doubting public.

"The inmates at Dachau would have named Hitler Man of the Year before Los Angeles would hire Juan," Melvin Durslag wrote. But when you are short of pitching and have a chance to win a pennant "you forget old wars," Durslag rationalized.

---

* Marichal actually wore No. 46 for the Dodgers when the season began.

In response to the obvious question, *What about Roseboro?* Juan was diplomatic. "I do not have anything against him," he said. "We can be friends right now."

Marichal knew what he was getting into, but he harbored another motive for signing with Los Angeles. Maybe, just maybe, if he pitched well enough for the team to succeed, he could win over his enemies. "I want to see if I can make the Dodger fans as well as the press forget about what happened," he said. Years later he added, "The only reason I signed with the Dodgers was because I wanted people to know I wasn't the type of person that wanted to hurt somebody over the head with a bat." Just maybe he could redeem himself.

Didn't happen. In his first start, against Houston on April 12, Marichal pitched three strong innings, but in the fourth he walked two; balked; gave up four hits, including a two-run homer; and trailing 5–2 with two outs uncharacteristically told Alston to take him out. Four days later against Cincinnati, he imploded in the third inning, allowing five hits, including another two-run dinger, and managed only one out. When Alston came to the mound with the Dodgers behind 3–0, Marichal told him he was done. "Go home and have a good night's sleep," the manager said. "I'll see you tomorrow."

"No, Mr. Alston," Juan said. "I just retired."

The next day, Marichal met with Campanis and told him if he couldn't pitch the way he used to, he didn't want to pitch and that pitching the way he had, he didn't think he could help the Dodgers. Campanis tried to talk him into staying, but this time Juan was certain that retirement was the best idea. He told the Dodgers to keep their money; he hadn't pitched well enough to earn what they had agreed to pay him. Juan said good-bye to the players and Alston in the clubhouse, publicly thanked the O'Malleys and Campanis and the fans for giving him a chance, and returned to his family.

Johnny Roseboro exhibited no schadenfreude at his one-time nemesis's flameout with his old team. Speaking to a reporter from his office where he worked for an insurance company, Roseboro said he bore "no resentment whatever" and had been rooting for Marichal to succeed. He had wanted others to give him the chance, hinting maybe it was even time to pardon Marichal. "I think people won't forgive that he beat us regularly, but the fight thing, that's something that happens every day in baseball," Roseboro said. "They can't get down on him because he threw close to hitters. He wouldn't be a great pitcher if he didn't. That's part of the game." Johnny said he had hoped Juan would win 15 games. "That would have solved a lot of problems."

Indeed, it would have soothed the anger of many Dodgers fans. But it wasn't how the story played out.

CHAPTER NINE

Johnny, I Need Your Help

JUAN MARICHAL BELONGED IN THE HALL OF FAME. HIS CAREER NUMBERS: 3,507 innings pitched over 16 seasons, 243 career victories, .631 winning percentage, 244 complete games, 2,303 strikeouts, 2.89 ERA. He won 20 games in a season six times and made nine All-Star teams. Placed in perspective, those numbers looked even more extraordinary. The consummate control pitcher, Marichal's strikeouts-to-walks ratio of 3.25 at the time was the best of any pitcher in the 20th century.* His 243 wins may have seemed modest compared to Cy Young's 511, but Marichal had won more games over his career than three quarters of the Hall of Fame pitchers, including Herb Pennock, Mordecai Brown, and Waite Hoyt. His

---

* This held true through 1980, the last season before he became eligible for the Hall of Fame. Through 2013 Marichal was 33rd all-time.

.631 winning percentage was higher than the majority of pitchers already enshrined, including Bob Feller, Carl Hubbell, Walter Johnson, Warren Spahn, and Cy Young. His 2.89 ERA was lower than that of more than a dozen Hall of Famers, including Dizzy Dean, Lefty Gomez, and Early Wynn. His 52 shutouts were then the ninth most all-time.* Against the best of the best—in the eight All-Star Games he pitched, when the players considered the outcome a matter of pride—he allowed the American League only one earned run. He also established himself as the dominant pitcher of the decade: His 191 wins during the 1960s were 27 more than Bob Gibson won, 33 more than Don Drysdale, and 54 more than Sandy Koufax. In short, Juan Marichal should have been a Hall of Famer on the first ballot.

But not everyone saw it that way.

When John Roseboro left baseball, it had not been on his terms. Disillusioned by how his career had ended with the Senators, he landed a job through a connection at the Security Pacific Bank back in Los Angeles. His role had him circulating through the black community schmoozing with business operators for $18,000 a year, a steep drop from his last salary in baseball. He had his own office, a secretary, and an expense account, but he hated it. He wanted to be back in the game. "Baseball gets in your blood," he said.

Roseboro let baseball people know his desire to coach, and the California Angels called. He wanted to be hired for his baseball acumen and leadership skills. The management wanted a black coach who could ease racial tensions on the team. It wasn't the ideal job, posting him in the bullpen and forcing him to take another pay cut

* In 2013 he was 18th on the list.

(a $17,000 salary), but if those were the terms he had to accept to get back into baseball, he was willing to do so.

Johnny figured it might be a step toward fulfilling his ultimate goal to manage. Naive hope hadn't blinded him—he knew organized baseball's tradition and modus operandi conspired against him as a black man. He knew how Major League Baseball recycled managers from a small pool of candidates. "There's always another job for these guys," he wrote. "They belong to a private, restricted club. They get hired, they get fired, they get hired again. It doesn't matter how mediocre you are. If you're a white Christian, welcome to the club. The good guys get the good jobs up front while blacks like Larry Doby, Willie Mays, Monte Irvin, Jim Gilliam, Jackie Robinson, Henry Aaron, Ernie Banks, and many more get paid off to stay on the sidelines in the shadows and do as they're told. If you're white, you can be in baseball all your life, but if you're black the time comes when you're just an ex-ballplayer."

Still, Johnny had reason to believe that he might one day be given the chance to run a ball club. Back in 1970 when Bob Short had hired him as Ted Williams's backup with the Senators, *New York Daily News* columnist Dick Young had written that Roseboro, "a highly intelligent and perceptive man," had what it took to manage in the big leagues and that Short was the man to hire him because he also had the guts to fire him, which certainly presented a barrier in many a general manager's mind, the anticipated public outcry over firing a black manager. Young reasoned that because Short had fired the Latino Hector Lopez from his position managing the Senators' Triple-A club, he would be able to fire Roseboro if needed. That scenario never played out, but at least Young's column validated Roseboro's aspirations.

Harry Dalton, the Angels general manager, reportedly considered Roseboro as a replacement when he fired his manager at the end of the season, but Dalton instead hired Bobby Winkles, a white man who had won three national titles coaching at Arizona State

University. The move prompted sportswriter Dick Miller to speculate, "Despite his lack of managerial experience, Roseboro might have had the job that went to Bobby Winkles if the franchise hadn't been located in the staunchly conservative Orange County."

Winkles did promote Johnny out of the bullpen to coach first base, though the ball field coaching boxes remained segregated: Dark-skinned ex-players could occupy the first base side, but the third base side, which required more thinking, was still seemingly reserved for whites. At the time, only one African American coached third on a regular basis in the majors: Gene Baker in Pittsburgh. By the following summer Baker was gone, and there were only six American-born black coaches in the majors, none of them on the third base side.

The racism in organized baseball that kept Roseboro on his side of the field rippled through the Angels club. One pitcher from the South frequently complained about the "goddamn niggers" on the team. He even beat up a white girl for dating one of his black teammates. The racial divide on the team ran too deep for Roseboro to mend. Despite Nolan Ryan throwing two no-hitters and breaking Koufax's single season strikeout record by fanning 383, the Angels had another lousy season, winning only 79 games and finishing 15 games back in the American League West.

In January 1974 the bottom fell out of the Roseboros' marriage. The bond had long been tenuous, but money stretched its limits. The drop in Johnny's income severely crimped their lifestyle. He had made some bad business deals along the way that complicated their mutual financial stress. Jeri wanted to go back to school to finish her bachelor's degree and even enrolled at Cal Poly San Luis Obispo to take courses, but she said Johnny discouraged it. Johnny complained that she spent her time volunteering for her daughters' Girl Scout troops and running the Angels' wives charity without bringing in any money herself. "She never worked a minute," he wrote. "She was too busy socializing." One morning in January

1974, Johnny snapped. He packed some clothes into his Camaro and left.

His departure hit the kids hard. Shelley was 14 years old; Staci, 12; Jaime, 7. Johnny tried to explain why he had to leave, but the children started crying and he could only hug them, unable to speak himself. Johnny visited when he could, but once spring training started, he was unable to see them often. Jeri accused him of abandoning his children. He accused her of turning them against him. She was bitter, having to sell the house and go on food stamps because Johnny couldn't afford enough child support. It was not an amicable divorce.

The Angels put Roseboro back in the bullpen for the 1974 season. He figured that was payback for the time the previous season when Winkles had told him to reprimand some drunken players harassing the stewardesses on a team flight. Roseboro thought that was the manager's responsibility, so he told Winkles to reprimand the players. And found himself back in the bullpen. Dalton gave Roseboro a $1,000 raise (to the measly annual amount of $18,000), but Johnny was not happy. With his primary responsibility answering the phone next to the relievers, he thought it was a bullshit job. But he realized his position. "As a coach, you have no bargaining power," he wrote. "You take what they want to give you or you go." He took it so he could stay in baseball and because there remained the faint chance "there might still be a future for me with the ball club." But when Winkles got fired midseason, the job did not go to Roseboro or Frank Robinson, another qualified candidate with the club finishing out his playing days; it went to Whitey Herzog—whose nickname seemed more apt to Roseboro than just coincidental—until Dalton could work out an arrangement with former Oakland manager Dick Williams. The new skipper brought in his own coaches for the next season, which meant Johnny was out of baseball, again.

Roseboro had been one of the best defensive catchers in the game and a competent coach, but he had not shown an aptitude for business. He had worked every off-season at various jobs, yet a string of bad investments over the years had drained his savings and left him in debt. He had invested in apartment buildings whose value depreciated in decaying neighborhoods. He tried flipping houses—sometimes by relocating them—but couldn't come out ahead. He started a travel agency that flopped. He opened a television retail store, but his partner cleaned him out, and he could not collect on a lawsuit judgment against the partner. He bought into a Union 76 station, even pumped gas and cleaned windshields himself, but was not able to stay ahead of the fuel bill. He started a record company but wasn't able to make any money on an album cut by Ike and Tina Turner. Another venture, a nightclub in Pomona, cost more to set up than it ever generated in revenue. The common theme throughout was bum partners blowing Roseboro's money.

After the Angels let him go, Roseboro auditioned for the sports commentator's spot on the *Today Show* but lost out to Bryant Gumbel. He tried to land a broadcasting job with a Philadelphia station but did not have the experience. He interviewed with Princeton to coach the baseball team but didn't get the job. He put out feelers in professional baseball but didn't catch any leads. He tried to get a job at United Airlines but it didn't pan out. He couldn't even find work as a security guard at minimum wage. He eventually had to file for unemployment. He couldn't afford his monthly $195 rent and had to move in with a friend. He ate cookies and drank soda for meals.

All the while, collection agencies pursued Johnny. He cleared only $2,500 in 1975, but his debts had multiplied to nearly $150,000. "The worst thing about being out of work is being in debt," he wrote. "You can't even starve in peace. They made my life hell, coming around and calling and threatening me with all sorts of things." Johnny was so desperate, he thought about holding up a store or mugging someone just to stave off the creditors. The days got so dark—hopelessly in debt, unable to make a buck, and estranged from his children—that in the summer of 1975 he fondled a .357 Magnum and contemplated plugging a bullet though his brain.

He might have pulled the trigger if it hadn't been for Barbara Fouch. They had met in Atlanta when he was still playing for the Dodgers. She worked as the publicist for the Office of Economic Opportunity with the task of promoting a tape Roseboro made urging kids to stay in school. Barbara was tall, thin, and beautiful. A college graduate and former model. But married, like Johnny.

Barbara split with her husband about a year before Johnny left Jeri. They talked frequently on the phone, commiserating about their troubles. When Johnny felt his lowest, Barbara seemed to be able to bring him up. They eventually decided what they had must be love. Barbara left Atlanta with her small daughter, Morgan, whom she called "Nikki," to be with Johnny in Los Angeles. Johnny suddenly had a family again. Which proved to be the tonic he needed.

Marichal and Roseboro met again in August 1975 at the Dodgers' fifth annual old-timers' game. Marichal had been a Dodger only briefly earlier that season, but he had agreed to return for the event, perhaps figuring he owed it to the team because he hadn't been able to help out in the starting rotation. Roseboro, amid the mess of his personal finances, welcomed the chance to be back in a Dodgers uniform and to see old friends. Almost 10 years to the date of their famous brawl, the two former combatants shook hands, though Johnny joked that maybe they shouldn't because then the sportswriters wouldn't have anything to write about. The two men even agreed to a joint television interview. "I'm not the type to do what I did that day," Juan said. "It is a game of passion. I've been sorry all these years that it happened."

No one knew, of course, just how sorry he was, how his guilt had invaded him, how he had prayed for forgiveness.

"Years go by," Johnny said. "You can't keep a grudge."

And he didn't, really. He wasn't the type. He did not resent anyone. Other than Calvin Griffith. He didn't resent the business partners who had betrayed him. He didn't resent his ex-wife. He didn't resent Marichal.

The two had not come completely clean. They had downplayed their feelings for the cameras. But it was the beginning.

When Johnny had scraped bottom, some former teammates had reached out to him, offering loans and support, but his pride had blocked him from accepting their help. One person he had let in was Don Newcombe, the former Dodgers pitcher who had known his own dark nights and encouraged Johnny to let go of his bitterness toward baseball and make his own way. No one had been able to help him like Barbara, though. When he was drowning in his depression, she threw him a life ring.

Johnny, Barbara, and Nikki, still a preschooler, settled into a house in the Crenshaw area, one of Los Angeles' respectable African-American neighborhoods. Johnny and Barbara married, and Nikki called Johnny "Daddy." The new couple set up a public relations firm, blending the popularity of Johnny's name and the experience Barbara had acquired. They opened Fouch Roseboro & Associates on Sunset Boulevard. Their client list steadily grew to include the Miss Black America contest, the author Alex Haley, and Andrew Young, then with the United Nations. Soon they were able to move into a larger office down Sunset Boulevard.

Johnny's relationship with Barbara, which Jeri knew predated their breakup, drove a bitter wedge between him and his soon-to-be ex and their children. After Jeri was forced out of their house, she did not tell Johnny where they had moved. In divorce court she returned the Christmas present he had given her. Barbara would remain the other woman, a troubling presence between them.

Los Angeles Times sportswriter Frank Finch suggested Johnny write a memoir. Jim Bouton's *Ball Four,* published in 1970, had inspired a genre of baseball tell-alls. Johnny added his, *Glory Days with the Dodgers and Other Days with Others,* to the collection in 1978. In addition to detailing his career, Roseboro confessed to occasional extramarital philandering, related arguments with Billy Martin and Ted Williams, and exposed some of organized baseball's racial troubles. But most significantly, he tried to set the record straight on his altercation with Juan Marichal. That's how he opened the book: "The thing I'm remembered best for is the Juan Marichal incident."

He knew he would not be remembered for his .249 career average. That his four All-Star Games, two Gold Gloves, four World Series performances, and the pair of Koufax no-hitters he caught had not seared themselves into people's memories the way that moment with Marichal had. So he addressed the incident up front rather than hide from it.

He reported the events in the four-game series that led up to Sunday's game, then admitted telling Koufax he would throw at Marichal himself and how he purposely threw the ball back close to Marichal's face, right in front of his nose. "It was intentional all right," Roseboro wrote. "I meant for him to feel it." He also admitted that he was ready to fight. "I was so mad I'd made up my mind that if he protested, I was going after him. He protested, so I started out of my crouch. . . . I went to hit him with a punch, and he hit me with his bat."

There it was. His admission of guilt. While Marichal had gone to the plate that day wondering if the pitcher might throw at him, he had no idea the catcher had plotted to intimidate him with a point-blank throw and intended to attack him. Johnny's version finally gave credence to Juan's explanation that he had been frightened and acted in self-defense. That provided Juan with a glimmer of validation. *See, it's like what I told you all along.* And it relieved Roseboro's guilt for having let Marichal absorb all of the blame for the past 13 years. "John felt that because Juan suffered, he suffered, too," Barbara said.

Other than the odd appearance at events like the August 1975 Dodgers old-timers' game, Marichal did not have much to do with baseball after retiring. For the first two years, he stayed in San Francisco and played a lot of golf with his friends Matty and Felipe Alou. He also enjoyed being with his wife and four daughters, to whom he had said good-bye so many times during his playing days. And he spent a lot of time watching baseball games on television, feeling estranged from the game and a bit lost. He tried moving his family back to the Dominican Republic, but the girls, ranging in age from 7 to 15, had been raised mostly in the United States and had difficulty adjusting to the Caribbean culture. The Marichal family came back to San Francisco with plans to buy a house outside of the city, but when a deal on a property they liked fell through, they returned once again to the Dominican Republic. He sold insurance for a while. He and Alma had two more children, another girl in 1980 and a son in 1981. They built a house in the Dominican Republic, and that became their family's home.

Juan still attended church on Sundays, said his prayers in the morning and evening, recited the Psalms—"My help comes from Yahweh, who made heaven and earth"—and tried to live by the principles set out in the Bible. His mother had taught him right from wrong and that when he did something wrong, he should pray for forgiveness. He was so proud of the many things he had accomplished in his baseball career—the 243 career victories, .631 winning percentage, 244 complete games, 2,303 strikeouts, 2.89 ERA—but one regret persisted. He had become friendly with Roseboro but still carried the guilt. So he often prayed for God's forgiveness. He also prayed that God would help Johnny forgive him. "It was hard for me to live with that on my conscience," he said.

More than 20 years earlier, during his second summer playing professional baseball in the United States, Juan had visited the Hall of Fame with some Springfield teammates. He had been awed then by the giants revered there. And he couldn't help but notice the absence of Latin players among them. Now, on the other side of his playing days, he wanted his career to culminate in the Hall of Fame. To be enshrined among the game's immortals, to be anointed one of the legends, to be granted his plaque in the pantheon. The dream of that young island boy who had wanted his mother to hear his name on the radio had matured to this, his desire to be honored as one of the greatest of all time, a distinction he believed he had demonstrated during his 16 seasons in the big leagues.

Marichal certainly had had a career worthy of the Hall of Fame, but in 1981, his first year of eligibility, he received only 233 votes or 58.1 percent. Seventy-five percent was required for induction. He finished behind Bob Gibson, Don Drysdale, Gil Hodges, Harmon Killebrew, and Hoyt Wilhelm. Gibson was the only one who received enough votes (84 percent) to make it in.* But even Gibson could not believe Marichal had not made it. No way did Gibson think he was 104 votes better than his former rival. "He was the greatest pitcher I ever saw," Gibson said.

---

* Each voting cycle, qualified members of the Baseball Writers' Association of America name no more than 10 eligible players whom they consider worthy of Hall of Fame honors. To be enshrined a player must be named on at least 75 percent of the voters' ballots.

The most obvious knock against Marichal was that he had never won a Cy Young Award. Despite the fact he had been the most dominant pitcher throughout the 1960s, someone had always outshone him in his best individual seasons.* It also hurt that in his best seasons his team never won the pennant. There were plenty of pitchers in the Hall of Fame who had never won a Cy Young Award and plenty who had won the award but not been inducted, yet it did seem a costly omission on Marichal's curriculum vitae.

Marichal's style also came up short when contrasted against his contemporaries. As a control pitcher with an abundant variety of pitches who preferred the efficiency of a groundout to the flamboyancy of a strikeout, he lacked the overpowering fastball of Koufax, the intimidating approach of Drysdale, and the rapid working pace of Gibson. Frank Robinson, the power hitter who became the first player to win MVP awards in both leagues, "once complained that you couldn't appreciate Marichal like you could Koufax," writer Peter C. Bjarkman observes. "And it was a complaint shared by Sixties' fans as well, who on the whole preferred powerhouse strikeout displays to hidden or subtle mound craftsmanship." So Marichal likely lost votes because some writers did not appreciate his sublime finesse.

His reputation had been confused by inconsistent remarks from Alvin Dark, his manager from 1961 to 1964, who at times praised Marichal's competitiveness and at others criticized him for being "without guts." Some viewed Marichal as dominant only when he had a lead but ready to surrender when he fell behind. Games lost to odd and conventional injuries over the years seemed to complete

* In 1963, when he went 25–8 with a 2.41 ERA and 248 strikeouts, Sandy Koufax had gone 25–5 with a 1.88 ERA and 306 strikeouts. In 1964, when Marichal went 21–8 and had a 2.48 ERA and 4 shutouts, Dean Chance of the Los Angeles Angels was 20–9 with a 1.65 ERA and 11 shutouts. In 1965 Marichal was 22–13 and posted a 2.13 ERA with 10 shutouts, but Koufax was 26–8, posted a 2.04 ERA with 8 shutouts, and a record-setting 382 strikeouts. In 1966, Marichal went 25–6 with a 2.23 ERA, but Koufax again bested him with a 27–9 record and 1.73 ERA. In 1968, when Marichal won his career-high 26 games against only 9 losses and had a 2.43 ERA, Bob Gibson was 22–9 with his amazing 1.12 ERA and 13 shutouts.

the indictment against his will to win. His .631 winning percentage notwithstanding, some may have been seduced by the stereotype that Latin ballplayers did not care as much about winning, which also probably reduced his vote total.

Whether due to bias explicit or implicit, the fact remained that the members of the Baseball Writers' Association of America had not as of 1981 elected a living Latin player to the Hall of Fame. They had elected Roberto Clemente in 1973 in a special vote immediately after his death in a plane crash on a mission to aid earthquake victims in Nicaragua, but other deserving candidates such as Luis Aparicio and Orlando Cepeda had not made it on traditional votes. The Negro League Committee, formed after Ted Williams's observation in his 1966 induction speech that no Negro League players were in the Hall, did nominate Martin Dihigo, the deceased dark-skinned Cuban who had starred as a pitcher and hitter. So perhaps the threshold remained higher for the Latino who would become the first living player to be selected by the BBWAA.

All of those factors may have cast doubt about Marichal's rightful place in the Hall of Fame, but the overwhelming barrier to his induction was the Roseboro incident, the way it tarnished his reputation and threatened to permanently mar his legacy. That incident portended to reduce his remarkable career to a singular immortal moment one Sunday in August when he made a mistake as a young man that he had regretted ever since. "If the vagaries of baseball lore have established one thing, it is that a man can win 243 big league games, win over 20 games in a season six times, strike out over 200 batters in a season six times, lead the league in shutouts twice, lead in earned-run average, pitch a no-hitter—and end up being remembered most vividly for hitting another player over the head with a bat," wrote baseball historian Donald Honig.

The way the BBWAA snubbed Marichal elicited protests from players, fans, and pundits. "He was the best," said Gaylord Perry, Marichal's teammate in San Francisco from 1963 to 1971. Perry used to bet other guys in the dugout when the bases were loaded with none out that Juan would get out of the fix without allowing any runs—and won eight of ten dinner wagers that way. "He was a great competitor."

Sportswriter Leonard Koppett, who himself would be given the Hall of Fame's J. G. Taylor Spink Award in 1992, wrote in the *Sporting News,* "How anyone who did vote for Gibson could find a way to not vote for Marichal is hard to understand . . . They were contemporaries and they were equivalent by any set of standards you want to choose."

Elsewhere in the same issue of the Baseball Bible, Bill Conlin observed, "The Baseball Writers' Association of America members who did the voting didn't all do their homework." And an editorial remarked, "The results suggest that seniority doesn't assure wisdom or conscientious scrutiny of the candidates. The voters didn't show much expertise, for example, in giving Juan Marichal only 233 votes, 104 fewer than Gibson. Such a gap isn't evident in their remarkably similar records." In response to that wide gap, Jerry Kirshenbaum declared in *Sports Illustrated,* "The procedure for election to the Hall of Fame clearly needs reform. Only writers who have held association membership cards for ten years are eligible to vote, but this doesn't prevent some writers from being wrongheaded or spiteful [toward Marichal because of the Roseboro incident]."

Juan himself was surprised and stung by the results, which aroused his fears. "If that [striking Roseboro with his bat] had something to do with the voting, I would like to ask all the writers who didn't vote for me if they had ever done any wrong things in their lives," he said. "I think in my career and in my life, that is the only wrong thing I have done." Even though he had become friendly with Roseboro, the lingering memory of that moment gone wrong haunted him.

The following year, Marichal led the list of pitchers on the ballot, which again included Wilhelm, Drysdale, and Jim Bunning.

Marichal had more career victories, more career shutouts, and a vastly superior winning percentage than any of them. He came closer than he had the previous year, garnering 73.5 percent of the vote, but still fell eight votes short. Only Hank Aaron and Frank Robinson earned enough votes for induction, both in their first year of eligibility. Marichal's fight with Roseboro proved to be a larger barrier than he had anticipated. Art Rosenbaum of the *San Francisco Chronicle* said he knew of at least two other baseball writers who did not vote for Marichal because of it that year. The outcome suggested that BBWAA members considered the severity of the incident warranted more than a single year of withholding their vote. "Everyone has their own idea of what a Hall of Famer is," said Ron Rapaport, former *Los Angeles Daily News* sportswriter. "So much of it is image and reputation."

Bob August, sports editor of the *Lake County News-Herald* in Ohio, wrote that he had voted for Marichal both years but thought the pitcher's fight with Roseboro could permanently deprive him of his "deserved place" in the Hall. August also noted the sentiment against Latinos that lingered in America during the early 1980s, when states resisted educating the children of illegal aliens even though many of their parents worked in the United States: "He's from the Dominican Republic, and Latin ballplayers are always reminding us that they do not get proper recognition in this country. It's an uphill battle for Marichal."

Coming closer offered little consolation to ultimately being denied again. This time, the results angered Juan. "I hear that some writers when the Hall of Fame election is coming up, that they only write about the Roseboro incident," he said on a visit to San Francisco in March. He knew that he had more career wins than 32 of the 42 pitchers already enshrined. "I think that after everything I did in baseball, I deserve to be in there." He said he thought he would make it in the following year, but that if he didn't, he would refuse to accept his induction. In other words, he would give the BBWAA members one more chance to make things right, but if they failed him again, he would snub them as they had him.

~

Marichal had not campaigned on his own behalf. He had simply waited to see how the writers voted, but as the year 1982 wore on, he decided he might be able to influence the outcome. So he called John Roseboro at Fouch Roseboro & Associates.

Roseboro's comments at the old-timers' game seven years earlier and what he had written in his book made Juan think it might be possible for the longtime Dodgers catcher to clear Juan's name.

"Johnny, I need your help," Juan said.

Johnny knew how Juan had suffered at the hands of the press in the immediate aftermath of their fight and still now 17 years later with every article written about that day and every vote withheld by the BBWAA members. That bothered him. The guilt he felt for his part had never completely left him. Here was his chance to let Juan know he wasn't angry at him any longer. His own personal nightmare had convinced him that everybody deserved a second chance.

"Okay," he said.

They came up with the idea that Johnny would play in Juan's charity golf tournament in the Dominican Republic. The public gesture would provide opportunities for press coverage in the Caribbean and the United States. Johnny and Barbara agreed to conduct their most heartfelt public relations campaign.

In December Johnny, Barbara, and 10-year-old Nikki flew to the Dominican Republic. The Marichals welcomed them warmly to their Santo Domingo home. They served meals with food so bountiful that Nikki thought it must be Thanksgiving. The Marichal girls absorbed her into their activities, swimming in the backyard pool, hiking through the neighborhood, and visiting the island's beaches.

She bonded especially with Ursula, closest in age to her, only two years older. Day after day for a week, they splashed and explored and laughed together. "We had the best time," Nikki said.

The adults also bonded. Barbara and Alma liked one another right off. They talked about their common interests, their children, and food. Johnny and Juan, who had competed against each other and twice occupied the same clubhouse at All-Star Games, had never really talked to one another meaningfully. Over meals and poolside the two ex-ballplayers who seemed so different on the surface—one Latin, the other American; one an extrovert, the other an introvert; one a devout Catholic with six children, the other a remarried divorcé with a stepdaughter—had much in common. They shared an abiding love of baseball, competitive spirits, and an appetite for laughter. They both came from humble beginnings, had endured racism, and had experienced success. And, surprise of surprises, they enjoyed one another's company.

Johnny, who had picked up the game during his days in Los Angeles, played in Juan's golf tournament at Puerto Plata, which was a success.* They gave a press conference and posed for photos. They said that the sportswriters had made too much of their altercation in 1965, that it had simply been a game that had gone bad and that they were not enemies. Johnny pointedly said that that day should be forgotten and advocated for Marichal's election into the Hall of Fame. The Dominican papers recorded their remarks and published the photos. The message back to the United States in general and the BBWAA members in particular was clear: *We're friends now. You can't hold the past against us any longer.*

But those seven days in the Dominican Republic proved far more significant than a choreographed publicity stunt. Juan had finally delivered a personal apology to Johnny, and Johnny had deliberately

---

* Juan had also learned to golf during his playing days and became proficient at it, boasting a 5 handicap. He has twice won the Hall of Famers' annual golf tournament at the Otesaga Resort during induction weekend in Cooperstown.

forgiven Juan. Their interaction relieved both men of the weight that had burdened them for 17 years. "Johnny and his wife and daughter, they really forgave me," Juan said. "That took a big load from my body. I knew I had made a mistake, and it had been hard for me to live with that on my conscience. When Johnny forgave me, I was so happy."

While members of the BBWAA filled out their ballots in December, Juan's chances to reach the 75 percent threshold required for election into the Hall of Fame remained uncertain. Despite the PR campaign in the Dominican and the fact that Marichal remained the leading candidate among pitchers on the ballot, he could not be assured that the voting members would approve him. In late December Bob August of the *Lake County News-Herald* expressed doubt that Marichal would be able to overcome the blemish of the Roseboro incident. "I'm not sure he'll ever be enshrined," August wrote.

All that magnified the joy Juan Marichal experienced the day he received a phone call from Jack Lang, the BBWAA's national secretary. Juan was in New York at the time to film a commercial for Gillette. "Congratulations," Lang said. Marichal had received 83.6 percent of the vote. He became the first living Latin ballplayer to be elected to the National Baseball Hall of Fame. "I don't think any person on earth now is happier than I am," he said.

Juan thanked God for giving him his talent and the chance to display it during his baseball career. He was so excited he immediately called Alma back in the Dominican to tell her the news. He also called Johnny Roseboro.

"I'm going to Cooperstown," he said and choked up. "Thank you. Thank you."

Both men cried.

The National Baseball Hall of Fame officially announced on January 12, 1983, that Juan Marichal and Brooks Robinson, the Baltimore Orioles third baseman with the magical glove, had been elected by the members of the Baseball Writers' Association of America for induction into the National Baseball Hall of Fame.* The Veterans Committee also selected former Dodgers manager Walt Alston and George Kell, the strong-hitting and good-fielding third baseman, to join them in the Hall.

Juan's joy resonated throughout the Caribbean. He received congratulations from Venezuela, Mexico, and Puerto Rico, where the press and people rejoiced that a fellow Latino had been so honored. The joy was particularly acute in his homeland. "Marichal's election to the Hall of Fame, hailed as one of the great events in Dominican history, brought unconfined joy to his friends and present Dominican players,"† the *New York Times* reported. "'Somebody will go to Cooperstown one day, see Juan Marichal's plaque and wonder where he came from,' said Damaso Garcia, a second baseman for the Toronto Blue Jays [and fellow Dominican]. 'His election put us on the map.'" That statement would prove prophetic with the Dominican stars that followed the original Dominican Dandy to the major leagues in later decades.

His election also affirmed the legitimacy of the Latin players, so long dismissed and denied by organized baseball, so routinely denigrated by American society. To have the most venerable institution of the national pastime include Marichal confirmed that Latinos had established themselves. They were no longer third-class citizens in their host country; they had integrated the realm of heroes.

---

* Robinson received 92 percent of the vote in his first year of eligibility.

† They included at the time Joaquin Andujar, St. Louis Cardinals; Damaso Garcia, Toronto Blue Jays; Mario Sota, Cincinnati Reds; Pedro Guerrero, Los Angeles Dodgers; and Tony Peña, Pittsburgh Pirates.

When Juan flew home from the press conference in New York, a crowd of several thousand fans, friends, reporters, and relatives greeted his plane at the airport. They made him stop on the stairway to the tarmac so they could take pictures. He told them, "Many Latinos have written beautiful pages in major league history, and I am sure that my arrival will open the door for others." Tears of happiness underscored the emotion of his words.

President Jorge Blanco received Marichal at the Presidential Palace to offer his congratulations. The mayor of Santo Domingo recognized Marichal's accomplishment. Wherever Marichal went, his fellow Dominicans saluted him. Juan reigned that day as the Dominican Republic's favorite son.

Juan Marichal called July 31, 1983, "the greatest day of my baseball career." That was the day the National Baseball Hall of Fame hung his plaque, which read: "High-kicking right-hander from Dominican Republic won 243 games and lost only 142 over 16 seasons. Won 20 games six times and no-hit Houston in 1963. Led N.L. in complete games and shutouts twice and in ERA with 2.10 in 1969. Completed 244 games during career, striking out 2,303 and finishing with 2.89 ERA." It was significant that the plaque recognized his Dominican heritage because that became the theme of his day.

When his turn came, after "The Star-Spangled Banner" and the Dominican national anthem played, he stood at the podium on the Hall of Fame's library porch overlooking the east lawn and statue of James Fenimore Cooper. Amid the crowd of 10,000 people, he spotted the familiar *rojo, azul,* and *blanco* of the Dominican Republic flag waving among hundreds of Dominicans who had made the trip to the remote village in New York's Leatherstocking region. He smiled at Alma and the children seated in the front row. His mother was not there—she was still afraid of flying—but he knew Doña Natividad watched the national broadcast of the ceremony on Channel 7 along with hundreds of thousands more of his countrymen.

The 45-year-old Marichal looked dapper, as always, in his silver suit and striped tie, his head full of curly black hair and his thick mustache punctuating his smiling face. The day hot and humid, he felt the sweat drizzle his back. He was nervous, worse than facing Hank Aaron or Roberto Clemente. Behind him sat legends like Joe DiMaggio, Bob Feller, Cool Papa Bell, Monte Irvin, Sandy Koufax, and dozens more who had marched before him into the illustrious pantheon. He took several deep breaths, began his acceptance speech in English, then switched to Spanish and repeated, "I accept the honor conferred on me today in the name of my family; my country, the Dominican Republic; and all those who helped me make my baseball career a reality." The first inductee to speak in a language other than English, he continued in Spanish after thanking several others, "I wish to give special thanks to those who are with me here today from the Dominican Republic." He thanked them for the sacrifice they made to be there and acknowledged all of his fellow countrymen who could not make the trip: "I know that in spirit, they are here with me." The crowd applauded, perhaps none prouder than the Dominicans present.

Later, when speaking to reporters, Juan said he hoped that his selection would mean that "others from my country will make it someday." He explained in his book *My Journey from the Dominican Republic to Cooperstown*, "Although I am very proud of my country, I always felt I was representing more than just the Dominican." And indeed, so it seemed with his Spanish acceptance speech as the first living Latin American player to be enshrined in the National Baseball Hall of Fame that he had become the standard bearer for Latin American ballplayers.

The reporters inevitably asked about Roseboro. Had it delayed this day, kept him out the first two years of eligibility? He did not flinch. "Johnny and I have become friends," Juan said. "I'm just very happy, very proud, and very honored." And he thanked Johnny for his forgiveness and support. Once again, the day belonged to both of them.

CHAPTER TEN

The Man behind the Mask

YEARS PASSED. PEOPLE STILL APPROACHED JUAN IN RESTAURANTS, AT CARD SHOWS, at the ballpark, even on the streets of Cooperstown when he returned for induction days—always wanting to talk about the battle at Candlestick. Same with Johnny. Seems everywhere they went, that was the first thing people brought up. The incident stood out in the public's memory and they wanted to ask the participants about it, even though the two men had forgiven one another.

The year after Marichal was inducted into the Baseball Hall of Fame, the BBWAA elected another living Latino legend. Luis Aparicio, the base-stealing and groundball-gobbling shortstop from Venezuela,* received the most votes, 341, or 85 percent, of all

* Aparicio led the American League in stolen bases his first nine seasons, 1956–1964, and won nine Gold Gloves.

candidates and was elected along with Twins slugger Harmon Killebrew and Marichal's Dodgers nemesis, Don Drysdale. Orlando Cepeda, the pride of Puerto Rico along with Roberto Clemente, and Tony Oliva, Killebrew's Cuban teammate, also finished in the top 10, though Cepeda would have to wait until 1999 to be selected by the Veterans Committee and Oliva would run through his 15 years of eligibility without ever reaching the 75 percent threshold required for induction. Juan had opened the door to other living Latin players for inclusion in organized baseball's most exclusive club. Over the next two decades, Cepeda, Rod Carew, Tony Perez, and Roberto Alomar would follow Marichal into the Hall of Fame.

Marichal, Clemente, and Aparicio, along with the other Latin pioneers, inspired a generation of future stars. In the Dominican Republic and beyond, young boys listened to the radio broadcasts of the games Marichal pitched, watched on television his induction into the Hall of Fame, and fashioned their own dreams to play professional baseball in America. Whereas Juan's vision had been to play for the country's national team, he had stretched those boys' imaginations to see themselves starring for the Giants or the Red Sox or even the Dodgers. His desire to be the best had made them realize what was possible: not simply to get there but to be able to dominate.

That's what Pedro Martinez did when his turn came. Born in Santo Domingo too late to watch Marichal pitch, Martinez knew who he was: the nation's Hall of Famer who held the record for most major league strikeouts by a Dominican pitcher. In his 18 seasons in the majors, Martinez posted some individual season statistics even better than Marichal's—a .852 winning percentage in 1999 and 1.90 ERA in 1997, for example—and outdid Marichal's career strikeouts with 3,154 of his own. But Marichal still won more major league games, 243 to 219. Early on, Juan befriended the young pitcher, who calls him "Papa." Whether it's Martinez, Sammy Sosa, Albert Pujols, David Ortiz, Manny Ramirez, Jose Reyes, Vladimir Guerrero, Miguel Tejada, Tony Peña, or a number of other All-Star players, the generation that followed Marichal is beholden to him, not only for letting them know what was possible but for providing the opportunity by alerting Major League Baseball to the possibilities in the Dominican Republic.

Marichal's success, along with that of fellow Latin stars of the 1960s and '70s, sparked a revolution in major league scouting throughout the Caribbean. The scouts were drawn particularly to the Dominican, which presented a rich vein of talent playing the country's national obsession. Major league clubs wanted to be the first to discover the next Marichal or Alou. The rush led to Juan's next job. He had been working as president of Turideportes, a company that provided travel and broadcasting services, when he received a phone call from the Oakland Athletics in 1984. Sandy Alderson, the Oakland general manager, wanted Juan to direct the A's scouting initiative in Latin America. It wasn't the Giants calling, but it was a means back into the game. Juan accepted.

Juan spent the next 14 years working for the A's. He began by signing prospects from the Dominican Republic and soon realized that the team needed a baseball academy in the country. The Toronto Blue Jays and Los Angeles Dodgers had already built their own facilities where they were able to develop talent rather than ship the 16- and 17-year-old boys they signed to the United States. The academies allowed those boys to mature at home in their own culture, speaking their own language, and eating familiar food, rather than endure the culture shock that Marichal had experienced as a young man in a foreign country. In 1994 Marichal convinced the A's to construct their academy about an hour northeast of Santo Domingo.* Soon, just about every major league team, seeing how efficiently the academies developed players, opened its own.

Juan had a network of scouts working for him, but the competition to sign prospects had intensified. Sometimes his scouts called

* Today, the facility is named after Marichal.

upon Marichal to visit a prospect's home. The Hall of Famer in the family's living room made a significant impression. Several prospects, such as Adrian Beltre and Raul Mondesi, got away, but Juan was proud that 34 of the first 100 players he signed made it to the majors, including Miguel Tejada, Luis Polonia, Tony Batista, and Miguel Olivo. The hardest part came when he had to let a prospect know that the team did not think he had the talent to make it. Sometimes those boys pleaded for another chance or simply sobbed. He knew some of them had nothing at home and little hope for the future. "I worried about them, and it was hard to send them away," he wrote. "That's the sad part of the job."

Johnny ached to get back into baseball himself. He had worked for the Dodgers as a hitting instructor in 1977 and 1978, but after his tell-all autobiography came out, the team did not renew his contract. He worked with Barbara at Fouch Roseboro & Associates, building their agency into one of Los Angeles' premier public relations firms. The firm had become profitable, but the work wasn't his passion. "It pays the bills, and I make a good living at it, but I'm a ballplayer, you know?" he said in 1987. "When you're a ballplayer, you want to do what you do well. I like business, but I love baseball."

More than anything else, he wanted to manage a major league baseball team. "I want to get back with the Dodgers and show some of those young pitchers, those young catchers the way the game is played," he said. "I want to be in that dugout making moves during the game. That old guessing game with the guy in the other dugout, just like I used to do when I was playing the game." He was 53 years old, starting to gray at the temples, 17 years removed from the playing field, and a qualified candidate yet frustrated. "I didn't go to college, but I have a Ph.D. in baseball and I can't use it," he said.

The standard route to a major league managing post passed through the minor leagues. After 14 years directing the defense, handling pitchers, and mentally dueling batters as a catcher and another four coaching in the major leagues, Johnny felt qualified to bypass that detour to his dream. He also considered the required apprenticeship in the minors unnecessary. "Really it's a cop-out, an establishment cop-out," he said when he was still coaching with the Angels in 1974. "I don't think it is necessary to go to the minors. Major league coaches learn more than what managers can in the minors. You don't gain anything by going to the minors."

By 1987 three other African Americans—Frank Robinson, Larry Doby, and Maury Wills—had already managed in the big leagues, but none of them remained employed in that role. The number of blacks coaching in the big leagues was less than the number of teams. There were only three blacks managing in the minors (Tommie Reynolds with Oakland's Class A team in Modesto, California; Derrel Thomas with an independent Class A team in Boise, Idaho; and Jerry Manuel with Montreal's rookie team in Bradenton, Florida), the purported grooming grounds for big league managers. Minorities made up just 2 percent of baseball front office employees. An unspoken prejudice against African Americans persisted—unspoken, that is, until Los Angeles Dodgers vice president and general manager Al Campanis articulated it on national television.

The man known as "the Chief" appeared on ABC's *Nightline* in April on the 40th anniversary of Jackie Robinson breaking the color barrier on the field. Campanis, the Montreal Royals shortstop in 1946, had taught his teammate Robinson how to turn the double play at second base. But when host Ted Koppel asked why there were no black managers, no black general managers, and no black owners—"Is there still that much prejudice in baseball today?"—Campanis said, "I truly believe that they may not have some of the necessities to be, let's say, a field manager, or perhaps a general manager." He tried to justify the comment by saying that it was similar to the fact that blacks were not good swimmers "because they don't have the buoyancy."

See, there it is, laid open, the bias that's been blocking our path, many asserted. "Baseball has been hiding this ugly prejudice for years—that blacks aren't smart enough to be managers or third base coaches or part of the front office," said Frank Robinson, who had been the first African American hired and fired as a Major League Baseball manager. "There's a belief that they're fine when it comes to the physical part of the game, but if it involves brains they just can't handle it. Al Campanis made people finally understand what goes on behind closed doors: that there is racism in baseball."*

Johnny had seen racism in organized baseball and Campanis's remarks on national television confirmed it, but Johnny's Ashland upbringing may have blunted his awareness of prejudice at work. He attributed his trouble finding a job to cronyism. "The problem with baseball is no upward mobility for blacks," he told the *New York Daily News* a month after the Chief spoke out. "The mobility exists until you get to be a first base coach, then that's it. There's no bargaining power for a black man trying to move up. The game is layered with cronyism. All these white guys just keep hiring their pals as coaches. That's why I don't call what is going on racial prejudice."

Campanis may have given Johnny the opportunity he had been seeking. When Roseboro saw the Dodgers general manager speak on television, he recognized it as a watershed moment for baseball. "I felt right away it was history in the making," Johnny said. "The moment Campanis said it, I felt this might be the biggest

---

* The irony of Campanis's comments is that many did not consider him racist in attitude or practice. Not only had he played alongside Jackie Robinson in the minors, but Campanis as an executive had signed many minorities, including Roberto Clemente and Tommy Davis. He also had been willing to hire Joe Morgan, the African-American second baseman winding up his Hall of Fame career, as the Dodgers manager in 1983 when the team had reached a stalemate negotiating with Tommy Lasorda. Campanis's comments more likely reflected the 70-year-old's slipping health and tendency to blunder. Yet his *Nightline* interview became his legacy, and he never worked in a major league front office again.

breakthrough for blacks in sports since Jackie [Robinson] broke into the majors. This was a landmark. He opened a door that will change the face of baseball again."*

Within 48 hours of his remarks, the backlash coerced the Chief to resign and the Dodgers to declare that "Mr. Campanis's statements on the ABC *Nightline* show Monday night were so far removed from the beliefs of the Dodger organization that it was impossible for him to continue in his duties." As though to prove it, the organization hired Jerry Royster, an African-American infielder, to manage its Gulf Coast team after he retired as a Dodgers player in 1988. Roseboro's chance came next.

The Dodgers hired him as a roving catching instructor. He traveled to different posts in the team's organization, from Vero Beach to the Arizona Instructional League, teaching younger players the finer points of playing behind the plate. One of his trips took him to the Dominican, where he met up with Marichal to play golf at Casa de Campo, a sugar mill converted into a luxury resort.† Johnny and Juan enjoyed a round of golf on the resort's world-famous course.

Johnny had made clear to Dodgers president and owner Peter O'Malley his desire to manage. O'Malley knew Roseboro's qualifications but expressed reservations. "I don't think you have the patience with the young kids because you've been the veteran for so long," he told Johnny. But O'Malley was ready to give Johnny the chance in 1990. He offered Roseboro the managerial post with the club's affiliate in the Dominican Republic, Los Tigres del Licey.

---

* In the aftermath of Campanis's remarks, Major League Baseball commissioner Peter Ueberroth hired a consulting firm to help teams set up affirmative action procedures and appointed a special consultant to identify former players interested in field and front office jobs, but the revolution Roseboro expected did not occur. Since 1987 five teams have hired African-American general managers. Through 2013 fourteen African Americans have managed in the majors, including Cito Gaston and Ron Washington, who both led their teams to two World Series championships, and three-time Manager of the Year Dusty Baker. In the front office minorities jumped to 15 percent of employees by 1989, when Bill White became the first African-American president of the National League. But that's also when it seemed to level off.

† Casa de Campo became famous after *Sports Illustrated* shot its 1971 swimsuit issue there.

Johnny didn't really want to serve an apprenticeship in Latin America, but he had seen how that route had worked out for Frank Robinson, who managed a team in Puerto Rico before the Cleveland Indians made him the first African American hired to manage a major league team, and for Maury Wills, who managed a Mexican team before the Seattle Mariners hired him in 1980. Roseboro didn't think he needed the experience, but when he was still coaching the Angels he had expressed his willingness to manage in Latin America if that's what it took to land him the job he coveted in the big leagues. "I need a vacation," he said with a smile.

So he accepted O'Malley's offer and flew to the Dominican for the winter season. Johnny stayed in a Santo Domingo hotel near the stadium while Barbara remained with Nikki in Los Angeles, though Barbara did come to visit. Johnny was grateful to have the chance to run a ball club, especially a good one like he had with Los Tigres, which included James Brooks, Henry Rodriguez, and Juan Guzman on its roster. He was also grateful to see his friend Juan Marichal again.

When Juan came to Estadio Quisqueya, the Santo Domingo stadium that hosted Los Tigres, he sought out Johnny in the clubhouse. They chatted easily in the manager's office after games about baseball, their families, and the Dominican. Juan asked Johnny what he thought of his country. "I like it very much," Johnny said.

After playing two and a half seasons of winter ball in Venezuela, Johnny had some familiarity with Latin culture. In addition to liking the food already—there was very little food Johnny didn't like—he knew what to expect from his surroundings, which helped him acclimate. He also found the Dominican political climate a lot calmer than the revolutionary one he had fled in Venezuela. Since its civil war in 1965, the Dominican Republic had stabilized with Joaquín Balaguer still president. But the baseball games had not lost their drama, with the fans emotionally invested in the outcome and quick to let the players know it, which Roseboro loved.

Johnny also acclimated quickly to his role as skipper of Los Tigres. The Dominican press had been tough on him from the start, no doubt biased against him because of the Marichal affair, scrutinizing his every move and criticizing any mistakes they perceived. After chatting with him, Marichal had wished the new manager luck. "But he didn't need it, because he was so smart and knew the game so well," Juan said.

Johnny's acumen had Los Tigres del Licey in first place, but something went wrong one hot Sunday afternoon. Rafael Avila, the Dodgers scout, noticed when talking to Johnny in the dugout before the game that he looked ill and did not seem like himself. Avila called his wife, a nurse, to come down from the stands to have a look at him. She thought Roseboro was having a heart attack. Avila sent her with Johnny in his chauffeured car to the hospital.

Marichal was deeply concerned when he heard the news. He tried to reach Johnny by phone but couldn't get through to him at the hospital. "I was so scared because we didn't want anything to happen to him in the Dominican Republic," Juan said.

Turned out Johnny had, in fact, suffered a heart attack. He was only 57 years old. O'Malley sent his private jet to shuttle him to a Miami hospital. Johnny spent a week there. The doctors wanted him to go home to rest. "No way," he said. "If I'm winning, my team is winning, we're going to continue winning. I'm going back." He did, and the team kept winning, finishing the season in first place, taking the pennant and facing their archrival Los Leones del Escogido in the Caribbean Series. Johnny's team swept the defending champions in five games to win the Series.*

Roseboro won the satisfaction not only of his success but of proving O'Malley wrong. The Dodgers owner admitted that Johnny had surprised him, but he was still not ready to hire an African

---

* The series, for some reason, was known as Winterball I. The set was played in Miami, one of only two times the Caribbean Series by any name was staged there—unsuccessfully in terms of attendance and attracting secondary sponsors.

American to manage his major league club. He didn't have to at the time because he had Tommy Lasorda, in the middle of his managerial run from 1976 to 1996 when he won four pennants, two World Series, and two Manager of the Year awards (1983 and 1988). Nevertheless, Johnny didn't think O'Malley would ever hire an African American to manage the Dodgers, even post-Lasorda. "My success didn't change his philosophy that in certain markets a black is not going to be a manager," Johnny said.*

Fred Claire, who replaced Al Campanis as the Dodgers general manager, believed Johnny was qualified to be a major league skipper but thought circumstances rather than race kept him from getting the opportunity in Los Angeles. "I felt John had all that was needed to be a successful manager," Claire said. "Being a catcher was an asset, because you're in a position where you see the field of play. He clearly had all of the ability and background to manage in the big leagues. But we had only two managers in 45 years."†

The barrier—real or imagined—that kept him from fulfilling his dream to manage in the big leagues ate at Johnny. Typical of the man they nicknamed "Gabby," he seethed quietly, internalizing his resentments, which corroded his health. Johnny didn't return to manage another season in the Dominican. And he didn't get the chance anywhere else. His heart had begun failing him and his dreams.

Marichal's election to the Baseball Hall of Fame had elevated his status as a national hero in the Dominican Republic. Whatever animosity Dominicans had felt toward him 20 years earlier, when he

* At the time, Roseboro didn't know that O'Malley had been willing to hire Joe Morgan back in 1983.

† Forty-three years, actually, with Walt Alston skippering the team from 1954 to 1976 and Lasorda following him from 1976 to 1996.

didn't pitch in the playoffs of the winter season, had long faded. He had become a living legend, revered throughout the republic. When attorney Leonel Fernandez was elected to replace Balaguer as the country's president in 1996, he summoned Marichal to a private meeting. Juan went. The two dignitaries—one the prominent baseball hero, the other a protégé of former president Juan Bosch—greeted one another and shook hands. "I want you to become minister of sports," Fernandez said.

That surprised Juan. He had not suspected that the incoming president wanted him to be a member of his cabinet. After talking it over with his wife, Marichal accepted the offer and became the Dominican's minister of sports, physical education, and recreation. The president gave him a car, a bodyguard, and responsibility to oversee the country's athletic budget. Marichal supervised the building of parks, promoted athletics from kindergarten to the international amateur elite level, and facilitated relationships between Dominican baseball prospects and major league scouts. Remembering the days of his youth when children fashioned gloves out of cardboard and bats out of *guacima* branches, he enjoyed the chance to provide young athletes with proper equipment for baseball and other sports. During the four years of his tenure, the country sent athletes to the summer Olympic Games in 1996 and 2000, and even a couple of Nordic skiers to the Winter Olympics in Nagano. Marichal received praise for securing the Dominican Republic as host of the Pan American Games, but he was proudest of his part in starting a program to educate athletes. "Athletes now become doctors, nurses," he said. "You can only be an athlete for a short time. After that you have to prepare yourself. I'm happy we started that and the ministers of sport after me have continued it."

Like many ballplayers from his generation, who retired before the days of big money that came with free agency, Marichal also sold autographs at card shows, finding it a lucrative way to spend a few hours, particularly during the 1990s, when the demand boomed. Roseboro, too, found the card shows worthwhile. Sometimes, Marichal would have the event organizers post a sign at his table stating that he would not answer any questions about the 1965 incident. It still seemed that was all some people wanted to talk to him about, and he did not like talking about it. But other times, Juan and Johnny willingly autographed photographs of their fight. In doing so they reclaimed their legacies, taking their reputations out of the hands of the photographers who had shot the images and refashioning it, marking the event with a flourish of their Sharpies as one that they had transformed into a friendship. Bearing their signatures, the photographs no longer froze the two men as combatants but rather anointed their reconciliation.

Johnny had a *Life* magazine photo from the altercation framed in his home office, which was adorned with bats, balls, gloves, hats, and other photos commemorating his baseball career. The image of Roseboro and Marichal's fight hung behind his desk next to a photo of Johnny with Roy Campanella, his mentor who had meant so much to him and whom he had succeeded behind the plate. Johnny knew that baseball had made him and that the significant people and moments from the game had defined his place within it. He did not hide from that.

No such photograph hung on Marichal's walls. The den of his Santo Domingo home where he watched baseball on television displayed bats and balls autographed by fellow Hall of Famers, shelves lined with baseball memorabilia, framed photographs of Juan with political and baseball luminaries, and a Leroy Neiman painting of him in his famous high-kick windup. The room shrined his success; it bore no trace of his shame.

One Ohio writer thought Roseboro deserved a larger space in the country's collective memory. Steve Eighinger wondered in one of his 1986 *Mansfield News Journal* columns if Roseboro might have earned a place in the Hall of Fame. While it seemed on the surface a provincial proposition to nominate a .249 career hitter to that elite company, upon closer examination, the idea deserved some merit.

Of the 11 catchers enshrined at the time, Roseboro had hit more career home runs than five of them and played more consecutive 100-game seasons (12) than all of them except for Yankee great Bill Dickey, a testament to Johnny's durability. Most significantly, his .989 fielding percentage ranked him 14th all-time in that category and better than any of the Hall of Famers. He also ranked second all-time in career putouts (9,291), trailing only the Tigers' Bill Freehan. Some might dismiss that figure as an irrelevant and inflated statistic because catchers receive credit for the putout on a pitcher's strikeout, but many of Roseboro's pitchers credited him for the pitches he called to rack up those strikeouts. The movement for Roseboro in the Hall never gained momentum beyond one partisan writer's imagination, but it did provide a point of comparison that showed how good—and often underrated—Roseboro had been.

Johnny kept a hand in baseball in the mid-1990s by evaluating umpires. One of five Major League Baseball evaluators, he watched umps at the major league and Triple-A levels and filed his reports with the league presidents. He spent free time with people like his brother's son Tony, an attorney who appreciated his uncle's wit. "He would find humor in little things on TV or observations of people around us at a restaurant," Tony said. "He was very funny."

Johnny also spent time in his home office fiddling with some writing ideas. He loved to read, with a particular appetite for Mickey Spillane's detective stories. He tried to write some of his own but never had any of them published. He was a natural storyteller, whether talking about his glory days or relating an anecdote from the car wash. He also thrived on his second chance at fatherhood. By the mid-1990s, with the three children from his first marriage grown into adults, he had reconnected with them independent of their mother. He took pride in his son's success. Drafted by the Mets in 1986, Jaime played seven seasons of minor league ball, peaking the summer of '92 with the Tidewater Tides in Triple A. Johnny's children now had children of their own, whom he got to know and delighted in. He frequently talked to his five grandchildren on the phone and visited them when he could.

With Nikki, whom he called "a smart little son of a gun," Johnny formed a special connection. Perhaps it was because he was older, more mature, that he didn't have the tension in his marriage, that he wasn't constantly leaving on road trips, that he was able to be home and present, and that he now had only one child instead of three. For whatever reason, Johnny was able to be more of the father he wanted to be with Nikki. He indulged her when she was little, playing with her and letting her fashion barrettes in his hair. When she grew older and *The Cosby Show* became popular in the 1980s, Nikki's friends told her, "That's your dad." He told the same jokes, offered the same sort of advice, and even had some of the same mannerisms as Dr. Cliff Huxtable. Her friends sometimes came over just to hang out with Johnny. She found them downstairs in his office, chatting away. "I don't remember anyone not liking him because he was so fair, so honest, so open," Nikki said. "He was the easiest man to know and love. Never judgmental. You always knew where you stood."

She paused. "I could not have asked for a better father."

John Roseboro Sr. had moved back to Ashland in 1984. He continued to play pool, go to ball games, and hang out with his cronies. Ever in his place behind the wheel, he drove about town in his big yellow Buick. In 1995 the Cincinnati Reds honored the former Negro League player at a game. But the following spring, two months after his 91st birthday, John Sr. died of natural causes. Johnny returned to Ashland for the memorial service at Denbow-Primm-Kemery Funeral Home, the last time he visited his hometown.

John Sr.'s sons would not inherit his longevity. Johnny's younger brother, Jim, the Ohio State football star, had settled in Columbus and remained a strong presence in the community, coaching youth teams, serving on the city council, and sitting on various boards. After being diagnosed with Lou Gehrig's disease, he moved with his wife to Moreno Valley, California, in 1993, closer to Johnny and his family. The disease slowly dismantled Jim's body over five years. When Jim finally surrendered to it in December 1997, the former athlete dying at the relatively young age of 62, Johnny was with him. That was hard, to lose his younger brother.

Johnny's own health problems had announced themselves with the heart attack in the Dominican. For years before then he had not had to worry about his physical condition and, like many former athletes, even considered himself invincible. "I never thought I would be unhealthy because I was always in such good shape," he said.

His heart attack and brother's death—the reality of mortality—startled him. Johnny loved to eat, a passion that had astounded his first wife and concerned his second. His tastes did not include kale and tofu but ranged toward red meat and Coke and all those processed foods doctors tell you not to eat in bulk. He had started smoking late in his playing career and had a steady habit by the time he retired. The years of unhealthy indulgences had accumulated and hit him in his genetic Achilles' heel, his heart, a vulnerability he inherited from his mother. Barbara and Nikki had badgered, cajoled, and pleaded with Johnny to quit smoking. To eat better. To exercise. But he was stubborn and wouldn't change his habits. "I'll die with a full stomach," he told them. "And that's that."

Until the doctors informed him in 1999 that his heart couldn't take the punishment any longer. He needed a transplant. They put him on a waiting list for a new organ. He had by then battled prostate cancer, strokes, and persistent heart trouble. He had endured so many surgeries, treatments, and nights at Cedars Sinai that if the hospital awarded frequent flyer miles he could have orbited the moon with them. The fact that his heart had reached its limit finally convinced him to quit smoking and take a more active role in caring for himself. He gobbled nine pills a day for his various ailments. But then the cancer came back, which took him off the heart transplant waiting list.

The circumstances sent him into seclusion. His condition made it hard for him to get around, but really he didn't want others to see him so feeble. That's not the way a ballplayer wants to appear in public. So he sequestered himself in the basement office of his home in Bel Air, watching Dodgers games and shouting at the television set, complaining about current players being lazy. He didn't answer the phone and didn't return calls. Johnny had hit another bottom.

He could not make it to his 50th high school class reunion back in Ashland even if he had wanted to, but he did consent to taping an interview with his classmate Bonnie Sharp, who traveled out to see him. Johnny sat behind his desk in a black leather chair, absently holding a Bic pen. He wore a simple gray polo shirt. He did not look sick, just older, the hair gray on the sides of his head. For an hour he spoke about his days in Ashland, reminisced about his years in baseball, and discussed his health. "I wish I could be there with you, but unless you can come up with some spare parts, I can't make it," he told his white classmates back in Ohio. "When your heart's no good, you don't make any long-range plans."

He spoke slowly, thoughtfully, sometimes bluntly, sometimes wistfully. Toward the end he seemed to be tiring. He let Barbara, seated on the couch next to his desk, tell the story of their trip to Santo Domingo to play in Marichal's golf tournament. "We wanted to give good press to what the sportswriters had deemed an ugly, negative story," she said. "As a result of that golf tournament and our families being together, Juan was inducted into the Hall of Fame. He called to thank John. It was a very moving and tearful moment for him."

"Barbara's right," Johnny added. "Marichal and I are kissing cousins now." He laughed at his joke. But he also smiled sincerely.

The following summer, on June 13, 2002, Barbara found Johnny sitting on their bed. He couldn't speak. He had suffered another pair of strokes. She rushed him to the emergency room, the way she had 50 times already in the past 14 years. That's where the doctors discovered the two blood clots that had caused the strokes. They seemed to be the final blow to him. "I'm done," he mumbled to Barbara and Nikki.

Not yet, Barbara decided. She put out the word that Johnny seemed to have reached his end and needed some love.

Peter O'Malley called to send his good wishes. Tommy Davis called. So did Maury Wills. And Sandy Koufax. "Tell John he didn't make much sense before the stroke," Sandy joked, knowing his battery mate's sense of humor.

Juan Marichal called, too. "Please tell Johnny to hang on," he said. "Please tell him I'm praying for him." Those were heartfelt words from a man as devout as Marichal.

Perhaps the messages and prayers sustained Johnny. His condition stabilized, though he remained in the hospital.

But the inevitable only waited a short while. Two months later, on August 16, 2002, John Roseboro passed into eternity.

Every obituary—from the *Ashland Times-Gazette* to the *Los Angeles Times*—mentioned Juan Marichal. Most in the first line. Many with the photo of him flailing his bat. John Roseboro was "the target of a 1965 bat-swinging fight with San Francisco Giants pitcher Juan Marichal," the *USA Today* obit opened. *The New York Times* ran a photo with the lead, "[He] was remembered as the victim of an astonishing bat-wielding attack by the Giants' star pitcher Juan Marichal . . ."

John Roseboro—this man who was a professional ballplayer for 19 years, twice a husband, four times a father, a friend to many, a hero to others—had his memory distilled to that singular moment. His life had included so much more that it seemed somehow unfair, yet, in its own way, the incident did complete him—that is, with its full story. It revealed a determined competitor and competent ballplayer, prone like any man to making mistakes in anger, being sentenced to live with a regret, yet also a man unwilling to hold a grudge, unable to sustain enemies, willing to forgive and befriend his nemesis, capable of bestowing both with a second chance and transforming their moment of weakness into redemption. Seen that way, he had lived a good life.

Representative Diane E. Watson of California made sure the full story was recorded for posterity when she entered an account of the John Roseboro–Juan Marichal altercation into the Congressional Record, concluding, "The incident tarnished Marichal's reputation, who was only voted into baseball's Hall of Fame after Roseboro publicly stated that he thought Marichal was being unfairly kept out of the Hall of Fame. Roseboro's nobility of mind and heart defined him in his life both on and off the baseball diamond."

Juan had dreaded the phone call. Barbara reached him in the Dominican Republic. He had prayed for Johnny. Now his friend was at peace with his Creator. But the news thudded in Juan's gut.

Barbara asked him to be an honorary pallbearer.

"Yes, certainly. I would be honored."

And to deliver a eulogy. "Johnny would have wanted that."

Juan swallowed. "Of course."

Juan caught the first flight he could to Los Angeles.

Saturday morning, August 24, 2002, was a perfect summer day in Southern California, clear and sunny, temperatures in the low

80s. Juan arrived at the Forest Lawn Mortuary chapel along with a couple hundred other mourners. The Dodgers had a large presence headed by Johnny's former teammates Sandy Koufax, Don Newcombe, Tommy Davis, Lou Johnson, and Maury Wills. Other members of the Dodgers' extended family ranged from Roy Campanella's widow to former general manager Fred Claire to Tommy Lasorda, an honorary pallbearer. Fellow pallbearers included baseball dignitaries Hank Aaron, Reggie Smith, and Bill White. Former Los Angeles police chief Bernard Parks was there. So was city councilman Nate Holden and Representative Watson. Five physicians who had worked with Johnny at Cedars Sinai, along with nurses and other staff members, filled the pews alongside Johnny's friends and relatives. Johnny's children were there with their children, his treasured grandchildren. And, of course, Nikki and Barbara, who had overseen the funeral preparations. All those people were there for a service Johnny had said he didn't want, but had he seen them gathered in his memory, he certainly would have been touched.

Juan and the other mourners filed past a glass display case assembled by Barbara that included many of Johnny's personal items, such as a toiletry travel kit, one of his catcher's mitts, his spikes. Juan picked up one of the funeral programs, an eight-page, full-size handout entitled "The Man Behind the Mask" with a color photo of Johnny on the cover in his Dodgers uniform and a MacGregor catcher's mitt. Inside, beneath another color photo of Johnny with Nikki, Shelley, and one of his grandnephews, Nikki had written a tribute to her "Daddy": "Although John was undeniably great on the ball field, his greatest accomplishments lie in his legacy off the field. He was generous in his purchases for loved ones, but his best gifts were always of the non-monetary persuasion: unparalleled insight, laughs, great stories, and lots of love. Any time spent with him was guaranteed to be an unforgettable treat and its own reward."

The handout also contained the agenda of the memorial service, a biography of Johnny, and a page acknowledging "Special Friends."

But the back of the program caught Juan up short. Barbara had laid out the two-page spread from *Life* magazine of their fight. There it was again. "I wasn't thinking about seeing that," he said. "I went there to let the widow and daughter know I was sorry for the death of Johnny."

Johnny had understood. Juan was coming to. This would outlive them.

Reverend Chip Murray opened the service with a prayer, followed by a song, a scripture passage, and the silent reading of Johnny's obituary accompanied by a guitar solo. Then Juan approached the microphone, the first of a dozen speakers scheduled to share their memories. He stood for a moment in front of the hundreds gathered there who had fallen suddenly very quiet. He felt the sadness of the occasion. He was also very nervous, more so than when he had delivered his induction speech in Cooperstown. Everybody knew. This was the first time he would speak of it publicly. And in front of Johnny's family and friends and all of these people from baseball. They waited patiently and silently for Juan to compose himself.

"I'm sorry," he said, his voice succumbing to the emotion. "I wish I could've pulled back those 10 seconds."

He made it clear to Barbara and Jeri and everyone else how much he regretted that moment and how much it meant to have Johnny clear his conscience.

"Johnny's forgiving me was one of the best things that happened in my life. . . . When I became a Dodger player, Johnny told all the Dodger fans to forget what happened that day. It takes special people to forgive."

And then Marichal, the Hall of Fame pitcher who would forever be remembered alongside the man they were memorializing, concluded, "I wish I could have had John Roseboro as my catcher."

Acknowledgments

Thank you to the following for the help they provided in various ways: Freddy Berowski, John Horne, John Odell, and Tim Wiles at the National Baseball Hall of Fame; Chris Box at the Ashland County Historical Society; Morgan Fouch-Roseboro; Jaime Frias; Jack Kelley of Kelley's Collectibles in Ashland, Ohio; Mark Langill, Dodgers team historian; Yvette Marichal; Chris Nietupski; Betty Plank; Shelley Roseboro; Miranda Sarjeant at Corbis; and Roger Guenveur Smith.

A special thanks to Juan Marichal for his willingness to talk to me and his patience with my questions.

Thank you to Keith Wallman, my editor at Lyons Press, for his early belief in this book and his willingness to consider my ideas—even as they changed. Thanks to Bret Kerr for his persistence and patience in designing a great cover.

Thank you to Lukas Ortiz at the Philip G. Spitzer Literary Agency for his diligence in finding a home for this story.

A final thank you to my family—Maria, Alison, and Brendan—for their support while I researched and wrote this book. Our trip to Cooperstown will long remain a happy memory.

Sources

Prologue: A Moment of Madness

ix. *camera trained on the mound.: San Francisco Chronicle,* September 4, 1965.

Chapter One: El Rey de Ponche

2. *world Juan was born into.:* www.npr.org; www.csmonitor.com; Turtis, "A World Destroyed," 590.

2. letrina, *or outhouse, in the back.: Time,* June 10, 1966; Marichal, *My Journey,* 11–14; Marichal, *A Pitcher's Story,* 36; Kaplan, *Greatest Game,* 17.

2. *day," he told her frequently.:* Marichal, *A Pitcher's Story*, 27; Marichal interview with Markusen; Marichal, *My Journey*, 14–16.

3. *explains in* Nota Acerca del Beisbol.: Kaplan, *Greatest Game,* 13–14; Klein, *Sugarball,* 1.

3. *pitched," Marichal recounted years later.:* Kaplan, *Greatest Game,* 21; Marichal, *My Journey,* 19.

3. and the Pitching Duel of the Century.: Kaplan, *Greatest Game,* 13.

4. *has remained firm ever since.:* Marichal, *My Journey,* 21–23.

4. *he pitched the team to victory.:* Kaplan, *Greatest Game*, 22; Ruck, *Tropic of Baseball,* 66–67.

4. *Dominican Aviacion (Air Force) team.:* Marichal, *My Journey,* 23–24; Kaplan, *Greatest Game,* 22; Regalado, *Viva Baseball,* 127; *Time,* June 10, 1966.

5. *United Fruit team with a 2–1 performance.:* Ruck, *Tropic of Baseball,* 32, 73; Kaplan, *Greatest Game,* 24.

5. *he volunteered for service.:* Marichal, *My Journey*, 24–25.

5. *escape Mexico without injury.:* Marichal interview with Markusen; Kaplan, *Greatest Game,* 22–23; Ruck, *Tropic of Baseball,* 70–71.

6. *lose a doubleheader," Marichal said.:* Marichal, *A Pitcher's Story,* 24; Marichal, *My Journey,* 26–27; *Studio 42 with Bob Costas,* November 24, 2009; Ruck, *Tropic of Baseball,* 73; *Time,* June 10, 1966.

6. *Marichal lost only three games.:* Marichal, *A Pitcher's Story,* 30–31; Marichal, *My Journey,* 26–27; Ruck, *Tropic of Baseball,* 72–73; Kaplan, *Greatest Game,* 24.

6. *want to pitch in the major leagues, you can.":* Marichal, *A Pitcher's Story,* 30–31; Ruck, *Tropic of Baseball,* 72–73.

7. *give Escogido's rival his top pitcher.: New York Times*, October 21, 1962; Ruck, *Tropic of Baseball,* 74; Kaplan, *Greatest Game,* 25; *Sports Illustrated,* August 9, 1965.

7. (fn.) *making Marichal a Giant.:* Author interview with Marichal, March 26, 2013.

7. *new clothes with his signing bonus.:* Marichal, *My Journey,* 29–34; Kaplan, *Greatest Game,* 25–26; Ruck, *Tropic of Cancer,* 75.

8. *in love with a white girl.": Sport,* September 1964; Kaplan, *Greatest Game,* 43; *Sports Illustrated,* August 9, 1965.

8. *I'd never experienced that.": Sport,* September 1964; *APF Reporter* 18, no. 1 (1966); Regalado, *Viva Baseball,* 71–72; Marichal, *My Journey,* 34; *Studio 42 with Bob Costas,* November 24, 2009.

9. *It was a long trip.:* Marichal, *My Journey,* 35.

9. *run the two out of the league.:* Kaplan, *Greatest Game,* 43; *La Voz Hispana de Colorado,* June 12, 2002; Regalado, *Viva Baseball,* 78–79; *Sport,* November 1963.

10. *country is this?" Power asked.:* Regalado, *Viva Baseball,* 66–67, 74.

10. *had the award been introduced prior to 1958.:* Regalado, *Viva Baseball!,* 74; Kaplan, *Greatest Game,* 19.

10. *Your dream didn't come true.'":* Wendel and Villegas, *Far from Home,* 39; Marichal interview with Markusen.

11. *the Midwest League's Most Valuable Player honors.:* Kaplan, *Greatest Game,* 44; *News Dispatch,* July 26, 1998.

11. *prayed for the strength to persevere.:* Author interview with Marichal, March 26, 2013; Marichal, *My Journey,* 36; *Boston Globe,* March 13, 2000; *Studio 42 with Bob Costas,* November 24, 2009.

12. *three Dominicans shared an apartment in Springfield.:* Ruck, *Tropic of Baseball,* 75; Kaplan, *Greatest Game,* 45.

12. *stereotype of laid-back Latinos.:* Griggs scouting report, http://scouts.baseballhall.org/report?reportid=00195&playerid=maricju01.

12. *told me I could get anybody out.":* Marichal, *A Pitcher's Story,* 98; Kaplan, *Greatest Game,* 45.

13. *possible to learn," Juan said.:* Marichal, *A Pitcher's Story,* 98.

13. *thought I would be more effective.":* Marichal, *A Pitcher's Story,* 98–99; Marichal, *My Journey,* 40.

14. *he could not pitch for a month.:* Marichal, *My Journey,* 41–42; Kaplan, *Greatest Game,* 47.

14. *until he gets to the big leagues.":* Kaplan, *Greatest Game,* 46.

14. *cared about you as a human being.":* Marichal, *My Journey,* 42.

14. *drove him from Sacramento to San Francisco.:* Kaplan, *Greatest Game,* 46; Marichal interview with Markusen.

15. *going to be a baseball player," he said.:* Kaplan, *Greatest Game,* 73; Marichal interview with Markusen; author interview with Marichal, March 26, 2013.

16. *a handicap he can't outgrow.":* Kurlansky, *Eastern Stars,* 59; Kaplan, *Greatest Game,* 18; baseballhall.org.

16. *was called a "Cuban nigger.":* Bjarkman, *Latin Beat,* 323; *La Voz Hispana de Colorado,* May 22, 2002; *Black Sports,* April 1978.

17. *He finally had his chance.:* Wendel and Villegas, *Far from Home,* 35; Kaplan, *Greatest Game,* 18; Bjarkman, *National Pastime*; Kurlansky, *Eastern Stars,* 73–75.

Chapter Two: My Own Little Bailiwick

19. *translate into cultural sensitivity.:* Author interview with Joe Mason, November 23, 2012.

20. *acutely aware of his otherness.:* Roseboro, *Glory Days,* 20–21.

20. *His mother was 15.:* Roseboro, *Glory Days,* 14–15; *Ashland Times-Gazette,* May 28, 1996; *News Journal,* September 24, 1995; author interview with Betty Plank, November 13, 2012; author interview with Tony Roseboro, November 15, 2012.

21. *waiting on them at J. C. Penney.":* Roseboro, *Glory Days,* 15–16; author interview with Betty Plank, November 13, 2012.

21. *That's how the kid got it.":* Roseboro, *Glory Days,* 16; author interview with Ted Jacobs, November 28, 2012.

21. *Johnny got serious about baseball.:* Roseboro, *Glory Days,* 35–36; Sharp eulogy for Roseboro; author interview with Shelley Roseboro, July 26, 2013.

22. *as a professional ballplayer.:* Roseboro, *Glory Days,* 17–19, 22–24.

22. *social failures of my youth.":* Ibid., 27–28.

22. *the hell with the rest of them.":* Author interview with Betty Plank, November 13, 2012; author interview with Joe Mason, November 23, 2012.

23. *style he later tried to copy.:* Roseboro, *Glory Days,* 34–35.

23. *liked it," Johnny wrote. "Who wouldn't?":* Roseboro, *Glory Days,* 20, 37–40; Ashland High School yearbook, 1951.

24. *until I coached for Ted Williams.":* Roseboro, *Glory Days,* 36.

24. *stealing bases without the sign.":* Roseboro, *Glory Days,* 36–37; author interview with Betty Plank, November 13, 2012.

24. *football scholarship at the last minute.:* Ashland High School yearbook, 1951; Roseboro video interview with Sharp; Hochsteller e-mail to Sharp.

25. *as a catcher, blocking the plate.":* Roseboro, *Glory Days,* 48–50.

25. *he happily accepted the invitation.:* Roseboro, *Glory Days,* 51; *Atlanta Journal,* October 4, 1966.

25. the life for me, *Johnny thought.:* Roseboro, *Glory Days,* 51; Roseboro video interview with Sharp.

26. *have signed for nothing," he wrote.:* Roseboro, *Glory Days,* 52; Roseboro video interview with Sharp.

26. *racism as a young African American.:* Roseboro, *Glory Days,* 21; *Los Angeles Times,* March 12, 1967.

26. *nigger!" Johnny decided to focus on the field.:* Roseboro, *Glory Days,* 54–55.

27. *his debut season in pro ball.:* Roseboro, *Glory Days,* 56–57; *Ashland Times-Gazette,* undated.

28. *good place for me. I hated it.":* Roseboro, *Glory Days,* 110–14; Roseboro video interview with Sharp.

28. *finished the season at Fort Knox.:* Roseboro, *Glory Days,* 57–59.

29. *Class A team in the Western League.:* Ibid., 61–71.

29. *reaction to an incident in Salt Lake.:* Ibid., 71–72.

29. *what to do about the bigotry.":* Roseboro, *Glory Days,* 72; *Los Angeles Times,* March 12, 1967.

29. *experienced a little death inside.:* Roseboro, *Glory Days,* 73.

30. *gained more confidence in his defense.:* Roseboro, *Glory Days,* 74–76; Roseboro video interview with Sharp.

30. *to play winter ball in Venezuela.:* Roseboro, *Glory Days,* 79–80.

30. *Bryant's resistance until years later.:* Roseboro, *Glory Days,* 85–86; Roseboro video interview with Sharp.

31. *He was 22 and moving up.*: Roseboro, *Glory Days,* 85–87.

31. *anxiously and with anticipation."*: *Ashland Times-Gazette,* date unknown.

32. *did not know one another very well.*: Roseboro, *Glory Days,* 80–83.

32. *left-handed hitting catcher with power."*: Roseboro, *Glory Days,* 87; *Ashland Times-Gazette,* February 15, 1957.

32. *but his catching could be better."*: *Ashland Times-Gazette,* February 15, 1957; *Los Angeles Examiner,* February 10, 1958.

33. *to force feed him with savvy."*: Roseboro, *Glory Days,* 94–5; *New York Daily News,* June 18, 1957.

33. *emptied his nerves in a bathroom stall.*: Roseboro, *Glory Days,* 102–3.

34. *and he'll bring it to you."*: Ibid., 122.

34. *him, 12 years his senior, a second father.*: Roseboro, *Glory Days,* 107–9; *Dodger Blue,* June 15, 1983; *Sport*, September 1964.

34. *heir apparent to the future Hall of Famer.*: Roseboro, *Glory Days,* 108–9; Swaine, SABR bio project on Roy Campanella.

35. *down, not even when scared.*: Roseboro, *Glory Days,* 105–6.

35. *though sorry to leave so soon.*: Ibid., 96–109.

36. *by the gunfire in the streets outside.*: Ibid., 87–89.

36. *And now he had to do his job.:* Roseboro, *Glory Days,* 109; *Sport,* September 1964.

Chapter Three: The Pride of the Dominican

38. *any pitcher I've seen this year.":* Marichal, *A Pitcher's Story,* 100; Marichal, *My Journey,* 2–7; Kaplan, *Greatest Game,* 73.

38. *go back to the minor leagues.":* Marichal, *My Journey,* 7–8.

38. *was "faster than Walter Johnson.":* *New York Sun,* July 20, 1960; *Sport,* June 1960; *San Francisco Chronicle,* July 24, 1960.

39. *a long devotion to Marichal.:* *San Francisco Chronicle,* July 24, 1960.

39. *Hispanic pronunciations of English words.:* *Philadelphia Evening Bulletin,* August 3, 1960; Regalado, *Viva Baseball,* 68; *All-Star Sports,* date unknown.

39. *so often expressed toward Latin culture.:* Brosnan, *Pennant Race,* 17.

40. *America, let 'em talk American.":* *APF Reporter* 18, no. 1 (1966); *New York Post,* June 27, 1961.

40. *managed in the bigs another 14.:* Kaplan, *Greatest Game,* 19; *Los Angeles Times,* June 21, 1979; Klein, *Sugarball,* 151; McKenna, SABR bio project on Cambria.

41. *hit the home run that won the Series.:* Wendel and Villegas, *Far from Home,* 44.

41. *"We are like some stray dog.":* Regalado, *Viva Baseball,* 3, 136; *Americas,* date unknown; *APF Reporter* 18, no. 1 (1966).

42. *opportunities, I think, as we should.":* *APF Reporter* 18, no. 1 (1966); *Sport,* September 1964.

42. *to learn to dreenk apple juice.":* *Sport,* September 1964.

42. *conclude,* That's just the way they are.: *Elysian Fields Quarterly,* Winter 1998.

43. *excitement that makes you act like that.":* Bjarkman, *Latin Beat,* 331; *Elysian Fields Quarterly,* Winter 1998; Regalado, *Viva Baseball,* 137; Ruck, *Tropic of Baseball,* 82.

43. (fn.) *Mays decked Gomez with a right.:* *New York Times,* August 23, 1965.

44. *would be as sympathetic as Sheehan.:* Marichal, *A Pitcher's Story,* 55–56.

44. *turbulent over the next three years.:* Marichal, *My Journey,* 62; *Sport,* June 1963; Kaplan, *Greatest Game,* 80.

45. *and improved his English slowly.:* Marichal, *My Journey,* 57–58; Marichal, *A Pitcher's Story,* 101; *Sport,* September 1964.

45. *Juan took comfort in the familiar food.:* Marichal, *A Pitcher's Story,* 101; *Boston Globe,* March 13, 2000.

45. (fn.) *other prisoners waiting their turn.":* *Time,* May 7, 1965.

46. *That's where the CIA came in.:* Ruck, *Tropic of Baseball,* 78; www.spartacus.schoolnet.co.uk; "Dominican Republic: The Era of Trujillo," Country Studies, Library of Congress, http://countrystudies.us/dominican-republic/11.htm; Marichal, *My Journey,* 56; *Time,* May 7, 1965.

46. (fn.) *of the first modern kleptocracy.":* Díaz, *Brief Wondrous Life,* 3.

46. *Dominican Republic's undesirable dictator.:* www.spartacus.schoolnet.co.uk; "Dominican Republic: Occupation by the United States 1916–24," Country Studies, Library of Congress, http://countrystudies.us/dominican-republic/10.htm); *Time,* May 7, 1965.

46. *take out Fidel Castro's neighbor.:* www.spartacus.schoolnet.co.uk; www.bbc.co.uk; "Dominican Republic: The Era of Trujillo," Country Studies, Library of Congress, http://countrystudies.us/dominican-republic/11.htm.

47. *sometimes it's impossible," he said.:* www.spartacus.schoolnet.co.uk; "Dominican Republic: The Post-Trujillo Era," Country Studies, Library of Congress, http://countrystudies.us/dominican-republic/12.htm; author interview with Marichal, March 26, 2013.

47. *he called Papa Jose and Doña Polonia.:* Marichal, *A Pitcher's Story,* 137–39; Marichal, *My Journey,* 52–54; Ruck, *Tropic of Baseball,* 78.

48. *can kiss her," El General said, smiling.:* Marichal, *A Pitcher's Story,* 137–39; Marichal, *My Journey,* 52–54.

48. *safety from afar in Arizona.:* Marichal, *A Pitcher's Story,* 139; Marichal, *My Journey,* 54; "Dominican Republic: The Post-Trujillo Era," Country Studies, Library of Congress, http://countrystudies.us/dominican-republic/12.htm; *Sport,* September 1964.

48. *political situation for Marichal and his country.:* Marichal, *A Pitcher's Story,* 139; Marichal, *My Journey,* 54; *San Francisco Examiner,* March 8, 1962.

49. *drove in two runs in the 6–0 victory.: Sport,* September 1964; Ruck, *Tropic of Baseball,* 78.

49. *in his first three games of 1960.:* Kaplan, *Greatest Game,* 81.

49. *play in that All-Star Game," Juan said.:* Author interview with Marichal, March 26, 2013.

50. *pitch as much as* what *you want to.":* Marichal, *A Pitcher's Story,* 134; Marichal, *My Journey,* 83; Kaplan, *Greatest Game,* 81.

50. *and dangerous farm implement.": Atlanta Journal,* April 14, 1967; Marichal, *A Pitcher's Story,* 126; *Philadelphia Evening Bulletin,* July 12, 1963; Kaplan, *Greatest Game,* 6.

50. *control were what set him apart.":* Marichal, *My Journey,* 79.

51. *well-placed firecracker under his chair.:* Marichal, *My Journey,* 136; *Saturday Evening Post,* July 29, 1967.

51. *and prescribed complete rest.:* Marichal, *A Pitcher's Story,* 53–55.

52. *accused the manager with angry looks.: Sport,* September 1964; Marichal, *A Pitcher's Story,* 141–42; Plaut, *Chasing October,* 167.

52. *the first involuntary volunteer.:* Marichal, *A Pitcher's Story,* 141.

53. *a gesture rife with symbolism.:* Marichal, *A Pitcher's Story,* 62–63; Marichal, *My Journey,* 69; Regalado, *Viva Baseball,* 85; *San Francisco Chronicle,* January 9, 2012.

53. *God's will," Marichal said matter-of-factly.:* Kaplan, *Greatest Game,* 82.

53. *World Series debut ended abruptly.:* Marichal, *My Journey,* 65–66; Kaplan, *Greatest Game,* 83; *Sport,* June 1963.

54. *stereotype that Latins quit when behind.:* Marichal, *My Journey,* 150.

55. *to play the '63 season in the United States.: Sport,* November 1963; Regalado, *Viva Baseball,* 143–44.

55. (fn.) *the position was abolished.:* Regalado, *Viva Baseball,* 144–45.

56. *that deposed Bosch in September.:* countrystudies.us/dominican-republic; Kurlansky, *Eastern Stars,* 29–31.

56. *the first Latino to pitch a no-hitter.:* Marichal, *A Pitcher's Story,* 157; Kaplan, *Greatest Game,* 85; *Sport,* September 1964.

57. *bottom half of the 16th out of the park.:* Marichal, *My Journey,* 96–98; Kaplan, *Greatest Game,* 60–132.

57. *wouldn't want to go back and hit.":* Marichal, *My Journey,* 64.

57. Chronicle's *beat writer for the Giants.: San Francisco Chronicle,* August 1, 1983.

58. *to keep him from being ejected.: Sport,* September 1964; Kaplan, *Greatest Game,* 163; Marichal, *My Journey,* 149.

58. *Nuxhall after he threw at a Giants batter.:* Kaplan, *Greatest Game,* 163.

58. *not the guy who tried to hit Willie.": Sport,* September 1964.

60. *in Phoenix, Arizona, in prime condition.":* Marichal, *A Pitcher's Story,* 169–72; *Sport,* September 1964; *Sports Illustrated,* March 16, 1964; *San Francisco Examiner,* January 7, 1964, and March 12, 1964.

61. *family he had started with Alma.:* Marichal, *A Pitcher's Story,* 172; *Sport,* September 1964.

61. *be closer to that of his peers.:* Marichal, *A Pitcher's Story,* 172; *Sport,* September 1964; www.baseball-reference.com.

61. *a Latin person in another city," Marichal wrote.:* Marichal, *My Journey,* 113–17.

62. *beat them despite Dark's intervention.:* Marichal, *A Pitcher's Story,* 173; Kaplan, *Greatest Game,* 78–79.

63. *for slandering minorities at the time.:* Marichal, *A Pitcher's Story,* 174; Kaplan, *Greatest Game,* 78–79; Dark and Underwood, *When in Doubt,* 93–98.

63. *Juan desired the same for his troubled back.:* Marichal, *A Pitcher's Story,* 59–60.

64. *widespread attention," a newspaper reported.:* Unidentified newspaper clipping from Giamatti Research Center.

64. *revolution in Santo Domingo's streets.:* "Dominican Republic: Civil War and United States Intervention, 1965," Country Studies, Library of Congress, http://countrystudies.us/dominican-republic/13.htm.

Chapter Four: Filling Campy's Shoes

65. *like a lady warding off a mouse.":* Roseboro, *Glory Days,* 121; Laughlin and Theobold, *Meet the Dodger Family.*

66. *Cannon sniped in the* New York Journal-American.: *New York Journal-American,* September 29, 1959.

66. *to look good when he did go out.:* Roseboro, *Glory Days,* 129, 136–39.

67. *how to handle pitchers.:* Laughlin and Theobold, *Meet the Dodger Family; Atlanta Journal,* October 4, 1966; Lanctot, *Campy,* 390.

67. *Campanella could do any better.":* United Press International, September 29, 1959; *New York Journal-American,* September 29, 1959; Laughlin and Theobold, *Meet the Dodger Family; Los Angeles Times,* August 20, 2002.

67. *but he'll cut them down.":* Roseboro, *Glory Days,* 134.

68. *would define his big league career.:* Roseboro, *Glory Days,* 134–35; Laughlin and Theobold, *Meet the Dodger Family.*

68. *watch her fall asleep on his chest.:* Roseboro, *Glory Days,* 139–40.

68. *and the resentments smoldered.:* Ibid., 139–42.

69. (fn.) *with dubbing him "Gabby.":* Roger Craig letter to Jack Kelley; Roseboro, *Glory Days,* 129.

69. *playing Robinson a little too close.": Los Angeles Times,* September 6, 1962; *Sport,* September 1964; Larry Miller letter to Jack Kelley.

69. *Allen grounded out to third.:* Dick Egan letter to Jack Kelley.

70. *not sportsmanship trophies for fair play.":* Stan Williams letter to Jack Kelley; Ken McMullen letter to Jack Kelley; Roseboro, *Glory Days,* 101.

70. *buffs them between innings.":* Plaut, *Chasing October,* 52, 66; *Los Angeles Times,* September 6, 1962.

71. *but overriding sense of unity.:* Wills and Celizic, *On the Run,* 207–8; Stan Williams letter to Jack Kelley.

71. *say the same about himself.:* Roseboro, *Glory Days,* 114–15.

72. *but I know where it's at.":* Topps baseball cards 1959–68; Roseboro, *Glory Days,* 145; author interview with Jeri Roseboro, July 29, 2013.

73. *any more of these goddam parties.":* "The Man Behind the Mask," handout at John Roseboro funeral, August 24, 2002; www.imdb.com; Roseboro, *Glory Days,* 128–29; author interview with Jeri Roseboro, August 28, 2013.

73. *explain what happened to us," Roseboro wrote.:* Roseboro, *Glory Days,* 205–6.

74. *to take some of the pressure off.":* Plaut, *Chasing October,* 60; Roger Craig letter to Jack Kelley,; Leavy, *Sandy Koufax,* 2; *Los Angeles Times,* June 30, 2002.

75. *was more than that this time.":* Roseboro, *Glory Days,* 207–8.

75. *an unsung hero of the club.": Los Angeles Herald-Examiner,* March 18, 1964; Roseboro, *Glory Days,* 207–8.

75. *receiving that check after the World Series.": Los Angeles Herald-Examiner,* March 18, 1964.

75. *He's coming into his own.":* Ibid.

76. *how he takes the beating he does.": Los Angeles Herald-Examiner,* June 13, 1964, and February 15, 1964; Roseboro, *Glory Days,* 185.

76. *covered in blood then return the next inning.: Los Angeles Herald-Examiner,* June 13, 1964; Joe Moeller letter to Jack Kelley.

77. *durability has become almost a legend.":* Unidentified newspaper clipping, August 1, 1964; unidentified newspaper clipping, January 23, 1965.

77. *He was the Rock of Gibraltar.":* Plaut, *Chasing October,* 60.

77. *with a hell of a jolt," Roseboro recalled.:* Markusen, *The Orlando Cepeda Story,* 46; Roseboro, *Glory Days,* 186–88.

77. *his head suddenly hit his shoulders.": Los Angeles Times,* September 6, 1962.

78. *was the ideal situation for me.":* Unidentified newspaper clipping, date unknown; Roseboro, *Glory Days,* 186.

78. *John behind the plate," Moeller said.:* Jim Moeller letter to Jack Kelley.

78. *he could hurt anybody," Jeri said.:* Author interview with Jeri Roseboro, August 28, 2013.

Chapter Five: Summer of Fury

82. *tension was always there.":* Plaut, *Chasing October,* 13–15.

82. *anger in that first series of 1965.: Sporting News,* May 22, 1965.

83. *the intensity the rivalry inspired.: San Francisco Examiner,* August 23, 1965; thatsbaseball1.tripod.com; *New York Times,* January 22, 1989.

84. *the rumblings of revolution:* Marichal, *A Pitcher's Story,* 176–77.

85. *he could not suppress his worries.: Time,* September 5, 1960, and May 7, 1965; author interviews with Marichal, March 26, 2013, and July 19, 2013.

85. *didn't hesitate to call for an inside pitch.:* Roseboro, *Glory Days,* 178.

86. *most intense competitor I ever saw.":* Roseboro, *Glory Days,* 185; Ruck, *Tropic of Baseball,* 80.

86. *grounded out harmlessly to third base.:* Roseboro, *Glory Days,* 178.

86. *clobbered a female Giants fan over the head with her shoe.:* Wills and Celizic, *On the Run,* 177.

86. *grip the rivalry had on those it possessed.:* www.youtube.com/watch?v=lL4jLzPhYV8, published March 10, 2012, by Carl Neisser.

87. *the ridicule directed at his Dodgers.:* Golenbock, "The Dodgers vs. Giants, 1951," http://thatsbaseball1.tripod.com/id174.htm.

87. *automatic disdain so close at hand.":* Plaut, *Chasing October,* 12; *Sports Illustrated,* August 7, 1978.

88. *prefer Los Angeles to San Francisco live there?":* Plaut, *Chasing October,* 12.

88. *more than in San Francisco and Los Angeles.":* Plaut, *Chasing October,* 12–13.

89. *indignities inflicted on Sam Jones' no-hitter.":* *Sports Illustrated,* August 7, 1978.

89. (fn.) *second nickname was "Sad Sam.":* Costello, SABR bio project on Sam Jones.

89. *for his contribution to their success.:* *Sports Illustrated,* August 7, 1978.

90. *was like a war all the time.":* *Time,* September 3, 1965; Wills and Celizic, *On the Run,* 173.

90. *just hated the uniform.":* Plaut, *Chasing October,* 13; www.youtube.com/watch?v=lL4jLzPhYV8, March 10, 2012; www.baseball-almanac.com.

90. *get hit. And real good, too.": Sporting News,* May 15, 1965; Hano, "Can He Forget?" 98.

91. *assessed a $1,000 fine.:* Marichal, *A Pitcher's Story,* 178.

91. (fn.) *made $18,250,000 in 2012.:* "MLB's 25 Highest-Paid Players in 2012," *USA Today,* http://mediagallery.usatoday.com/G3650.

91. *don't mean those .220 hitters, either.": Sporting News,* July 17, 1965.

91. *in recent Latin American history.": Time,* May 7, 1965.

92. *any semblance of sanity,"* Time *reported.:* Ibid.

92. *substituted Gaylord Perry for Marichal.:* Marichal, *My Journey,* 172; *Sporting News,* May 22, 1965; *Time,* May 28, 1965; Marichal, *A Pitcher's Story,* 176.

94. *revolution in his native Dominican Republic.": Time,* May 14, 1965, May 21, 1965, and May 28, 1965.

94. *pull over his car until they passed.:* Author interview with Marichal, March 26, 2013; *Sporting News,* June 12, 1965.

95. *whittled the gap to two and a half games.: Sporting News,* May 22, 1965; *New York Times,* June 28, 1965.

96. *1965, both had won 91 games.: Time,* June 10, 1966; *Elysian Fields Quarterly,* Winter 1998.

96. *August—with everlasting consequences.: Elysian Fields Quarterly,* Winter 1998.

97. *reporter's heart rate eventually stabilized.: Sports Illustrated,* August 9, 1965.

97. *each other,"* Time *reported in August.: Time,* August 13, 1965, and August 20, 1965.

97. *not so sure about him [Koufax].": Sporting News,* July 31, 1965.

99. *woman that would end their marriage.:* Roseboro, *Glory Days,* 141–50; *Sporting News,* July 24, 1965.

99. *couple of games the final week of July.: Sporting News,* August 7, 1965.

100. *remained taut throughout the nation.: Time,* August 13, 1965.

100. *so hard and with such accuracy.":* Roseboro, *Glory Days,* 194.

101. *The Watts riot had begun.:* Cohen and Murphy, *Burn, Baby, Burn,* 1–64.

102. *we are going to get kicked.":* Regalado, *Viva Baseball,* 137; *Time,* August 20, 1965, and August 27, 1965.

103. *'Why are they playing games?'":* Leavy, *Sandy Koufax,* 18; *Sport,* October 1967.

103. *the children some temporary relief.:* Roseboro, *Glory Days,* 265; Cohen and Murphy, *Burn, Baby, Burn,* 117–20; *Time,* August 27, 1965; Wally Moon letter to Jack Kelley; author interview with Jeri Roseboro, July 29, 2013.

104. *reflected the violence in society.: Sport,* October 1967.

104. *safe in the summer of fury.:* Kaplan, *Greatest Game,* 159; Associated Press, May 17, 1965.

104. *and see our loved ones," Juan said.:* Author interview with Marichal, March 26, 2013.

105. *fear and anger, and holding it inside.": New York Times,* August 22, 2005; Kaplan, *Greatest Game,* 157.

Chapter Six: Bloody Sunday

117. *He flashed them the finger.:* Marichal, *A Pitcher's Story,* 181–82; Marichal, *My Journey,* 119–29; Roseboro, *Glory Days,* 3–13; Kaplan, *Greatest Game,* 157–58; Wills and Celizic, *On the Run,* 165–69; *Los Angeles Herald-Examiner,* August 23, 1965; *Herald-Examiner,* August 23, 1965; *New York Times,* August 23, 1965; *New York Post,* August 23, 1965; Associated Press, August 22, 1965; *Time,* September 3, 1965; *Sport,* December 1965; *Sports Illustrated,* August 30, 1965; *San Francisco Examiner,* September 8, 1965; *New York World-Telegram and Sun,* August 23, 1965; *Sporting News,* September 11, 1965; Crawford interview with Gerlach, tape 1; photographs from *San Francisco Examiner, Life, Sports Illustrated.*

117. *dozen policemen guarding each entrance.: Los Angeles Herald-Examiner,* August 23, 1965.

118. *and listened to the game on the radio.: New York Post,* August 23, 1965.

118. *We don't want a riot here.":* Crawford interview with Gerlach.

118. *cannibals roam in Candlestick these days?": Los Angeles Herald-Examiner,* August 23, 1965.

118. *491st of his career put the Giants up 4–2.: New York Times,* August 23, 1965.

Chapter Seven: This Ain't Over

122. *"Burn, baby, burn," he chanted.:* Author interview with Roger Guenveur Smith, May 26, 2011.

122. *tape wouldn't be good for baseball.": Chronicle Sports,* September 4, 1965.

123. *heard he still had his famous appetite.:* author interview with Jeri Roseboro, July 29, 2013.

123. *when somebody splits your head open.": New York Post,* August 23, 1965.

123. *looking for him or anything like that.": New York World-Telegram and Sun,* August 23, 1965; *New York Times,* August 24, 1965.

124. *"But she'll get over it.": Studio 42 with Bob Costas,* November 24, 2009.

124. *in a room together for about ten minutes.": Los Angeles Times,* August 23, 1965.

124. *"Nothing was there," he joked.: New York World-Telegram and Sun,* August 25, 1965.

124. *to Pittsburgh and napped fitfully.: Sport,* June 1966.

124. *how Giles should deal with Marichal.: Los Angeles Times,* August 26, 1965.

124. *good guy he was, and we gave him that.":* Regalado, *Viva Baseball,* 139.

125. *flail another on the skull with a bat.": Los Angeles Times,* August 25, 1965; *Los Angeles Herald-Examiner,* August 23, 1965; *New York World-Telegram and Sun,* August 24, 1965; *New York Times,* August 25, 1965.

125. *be paid prior to his reinstatement.: New York Times,* August 24, 1965.

126. *pitcher's suspension would hurt his team.:* Kaplan, *Greatest Game,* 160–61; *New York Times,* August 24, 1965.

127. *he should keep his mouth shut.": Los Angeles Times,* August 29, 1965.

127. *is as big as your baseball talent.": Sporting News,* September 11, 1965.

127. *money to pay Marichal's fine.: Los Angeles Times,* August 26, 1965.

127. *some of those whiners really deserve it.":* Ibid.

128. *were both involved, both liable.":* Author interview with Lon Simmons, 2007.

128. *should have been much more severe.": Philadelphia Evening Bulletin,* August 24, 1965.

128. *shortstop had sidestepped the challenge.: New York World-Telegram and Sun,* August 23, 1965.

128. *but you also want to be fair.": New York World-Telegram and Sun,* August 24, 1965.

129. *the misdemeanor of a single player.": Pittsburgh Press,* date unknown.

129. *would have been suspended for thirty days.": Sporting News,* September 11, 1965; *Herald-Examiner,* August 25, 1965.

130. *through the lens of this widespread attitude.: Sports Illustrated,* August 9, 1965.

131. *"Especially if you're a fiery Dominican.":* Kaplan, *Greatest Game,* 159; *St. Louis Post-Dispatch,* September 4, 1965.

131. *Frank Thomas's head or calling him a savage.": New York Daily News,* August 25, 1965.

132. *a white man born in Pennsylvania.:* Kaplan, *Greatest Game,* 159.

132. *he later wrote in his autobiography.:* Roseboro, *Glory Days,* 210.

133. *and justify his outrageous conduct.": New York World-Telegram and Sun,* September 2, 1965.

133. *heard the journalistic chorus condemning him.: San Francisco Chronicle,* September 18, 1965; *Sports Illustrated,* September 13, 1965.

133. *for playing in his own country.:* United Press International, August 26, 1965; *New York World-Telegram and Sun,* August 24, 1965.

134. *and that is the real punishment.": New York World-Telegram and Sun,* August 24, 1965.

134. *in the days and years to come? Daley asked.": New York Times,* August 25, 1965.

134. *until September 2 and covered ten games.: New York Times,* September 3, 1965.

135. *Matty Alou to pitch two innings.:* Bjarkman, *Elysian Fields Quarterly,* Winter 1968; *Philadelphia Evening Bulletin,* August 24, 1965.

135. *I will pitch the second game, too.":* Hano, "Can He Forget?" 99.

135. *quarter that much, but I don't.": New York World-Telegram and Sun,* September 2, 1965; *Los Angeles Times,* September 3, 1965.

136. *And Juan wept inside.: New York World-Telegram and Sun,* September 3, 1965; *New York Times,* September 3, 1965; *Sport,* June 1966.

136. *remain one game behind the Dodgers.: Los Angeles Times,* September 3, 1965.

136. *he could be with his family again.: Time,* September 20, 1965.

137. *that Sunday to defeat the Cubs 4–2.: New York Times,* September 3, 1965; *San Francisco Chronicle,* September 18, 1965; United Press International, September 4, 1965.

137. *probably made Giles seem prudent.: Los Angeles Times,* September 3, 1965; *San Francisco Examiner,* September 8, 1965.

138. *heard the applause from the crowd!":* Marichal, *A Pitcher's Story,* 187.

139. *"He gave us confidence.":* Roseboro, *Glory Days,* 213.

139. *to contemplate through the long nights.":* Kaplan, *Greatest Game,* 161; Ellison, "After the Incident," 89–90.

140. *before he could seriously harm Sherry.:* Kurlansky, *Eastern Stars,* 83–85; *Wilmington Star-News,* September 21, 1965; *Tri-City Herald,* September 21, 1965.

140. *will punish fighting of any kind.": Wilmington Star-News,* September 21, 1965.

141. *if they were from the same background.":* Kaplan, *Greatest Game,* 162.

141. *especially satisfying series," he wrote.:* Roseboro, *Glory Days,* 214.

Chapter Eight: That's Not How the Story Goes

144. *killed, but if it's going to happen . . .": Sport,* June 1966.

144. *be about the fight with Marichal.: Sporting News,* January 22, 1966; *Wall Street Journal,* February 15, 1966.

145. *with a weapon. But I lost my head.": Los Angeles Herald-Examiner,* March 3, 1966; Associated Press, April 18, 1975.

146. *He withdrew, became sullen.:* Marichal, *A Pitcher's Story,* 197–99; Devaney, *Mr. Strike,* 132–34.

147. *the feeling I had at the moment.": Sport,* June 1966.

147. *if he struck a batter with a pitch.:* Marichal, *A Pitcher's Story,* 16–18; Hirsch, *Willie Mays,* 347.

148. *drew an* X *across his heart.:* Devaney, *Mr. Strike,* 134–37.

148. *for money but for appreciation.":* *Saturday Evening Post,* July 29, 1967.

149. *doesn't have the pitches Marichal does.":* *San Francisco Examiner,* May 23, 1966.

149. *once again, a complete pitcher.:* Marichal, *A Pitcher's Story,* 190–91.

150. *disturbance, provided some measure of relief.:* *Sport,* June 1966; *Sports Illustrated,* June 13, 1966; *Time,* June 10, 1966.

151. *Drysdale watched for strike three.:* Marichal, *A Pitcher's Story,* 65–81.

151. *I can still pitch," he wrote.:* Ibid., 81.

151. *know where my vote would go.":* *Los Angeles Times,* September 4, 1966.

152. *"turned into a wake," Roseboro wrote.:* Roseboro, *Glory Days,* 218.

153. *rejected. He cried at the news.:* Ibid., 218–22.

153. *Juan's hero status in his native country.:* Author interview with Marichal, July 19, 2013.

153. *didn't even make the Baseball Guide?":* www.baseball-reference.com; *Atlanta Journal,* April 16, 1967.

154. *victims of a subtly functioning prejudice.": Saturday Evening Post,* July 29, 1967.

154. *sting of prejudice and resented it.: Sporting News,* August 5, 1967.

155. *Giants might trade him after the season.: San Francisco Examiner,* March 27, 1967; *Sporting News,* November 11, 1967; unidentified newspaper clipping, November 7, 1967.

155. *seven seasons of professional baseball.:* Roseboro, *Glory Days,* 140–41; Roseboro video interview with Sharp.

155. *The trade spoiled all that.:* Author interview with Shelley Roseboro, July 26, 2013; *Ashland-Times Gazette,* February 5, 1970.

156. *a chant it'll scare you to death.":* Roseboro, *Glory Days,* 229–32; *Minneapolis Star Tribune,* October 1, 1978.

156. *Take this, or you'll never work again.": New York Daily News,* May 6, 1987; *Sporting News,* July 5, 1969.

157. *best thing that ever happened to me.": Sporting News,* January 10, 1970; Roseboro, *Glory Days,* 234–40; Roseboro video interview with Sharp.

158. *comeback from his subpar '67 season.:* Author interview with Marichal, March 26, 2013; *Houston Chronicle,* July 29, 1968; Marichal, *My Journey,* 174–76.

159. *is about 25 games each year.": Sporting News,* January 8, 1972; Associated Press, May 10, 1969; United Press International, September 14, 1969; scouts.baseballhall.org.

159. *not ready to ask forgiveness himself.:* Author interview with Marichal, March 26, 2013; Roseboro, *Glory Days,* 1–13.

160. *became the ordeal I dreaded," he wrote.:* Roseboro, *Glory Days,* 30–32; Roseboro video interview with Sharp.

162. *course, no one gets that chance.:* Roseboro, *Glory Days,* 241–46.

163. *critics considered it a telltale mark.:* Kaplan, *Greatest Game,* 153; *Sporting News,* September 12, 1970, and January 2, 1971.

163. *indicative of his immediate effectiveness.: Sporting News,* January 2, 1971, August 28, 1971, and January 8, 1972; *All-Star Sports,* date unknown.

164. *the Dodgers despise him in a game.": Los Angeles Herald-Examiner,* September 15, 1971; *Sporting News,* October 2, 1971.

164. *but he had made his feelings clear.: Los Angeles Herald-Examiner,* March 12, 1975.

164. *he looked like a has-been.:* United Press International, February 29, 1972.

165. *I was never back to my old self.":* Marichal, *A Pitcher's Story,* 182–83.

165. *Koufax as the best pitcher in the game.: Sporting News,* April 28, 1973.

165. *across the country to a different league.:* Marichal, *My Journey,* 181.

165. *suspicions, releasing him in October 1974.:* Associated Press, June 12, 1974.

166. *Both men smiled broadly.:* Marichal, *My Journey,* 184; author interview with Rafael Avila, August 26, 2013; *Los Angeles Herald-Examiner,* March 15, 1975; United Press International photograph, March 17, 1975.

166. *forget old wars," Durslag rationalized.: Long Beach Press-Telegram,* March 1975; *Los Angeles Herald-Examiner,* March 14, 1975.

167. *he could redeem himself.: Long Beach Press-Telegram,* March 1975; *Los Angeles Times,* March 1975; *Studio 42 with Bob Costas,* November 24, 2009.

168. *and returned to his family.: Los Angeles Herald-Examiner,* April 18, 1975; Marichal, *My Journey,* 184–85; author interview with Fred Claire, 2007; author interview with Rafael Avila, August 26, 2013.

168. *would have solved a lot of problems.":* Associated Press, April 18, 1975.

Chapter Nine: Johnny, I Need Your Help

170. *"Baseball gets in your blood," he said.:* Unidentified newspaper article by Dick Miller, February 5, 1972; Roseboro, *Glory Days,* 267; Roseboro video interview with Sharp.

171. *baseball, he was willing to do so.:* Roseboro, *Glory Days,* 247.

171. *when you're just an ex-ballplayer.":* Ibid., 257.

171. *Young's column validated Roseboro's aspirations.: New York Daily News,* March 25, 1970.

172. *in the staunchly conservative Orange County.":* Unidentified newspaper clipping by Dick Miller, November 18, 1972.

172. *none of them on the third base side.:* Unidentified newspaper clippings by Dick Miller, November 18, 1972, and June 8, 1974.

172. *finishing 15 games back in the American League West.:* Roseboro, *Glory Days,* 250–51.

173. *was not an amicable divorce.:* Author interview with Jeri Roseboro, July 29, 2013; Roseboro, *Glory Days,* 280–86.

173. *Johnny was out of baseball, again.:* Roseboro, *Glory Days,* 254–57.

174. *bum partners blowing Roseboro's money.:* Roseboro, *Glory Days,* 259–65.

175. *plugging a bullet though his brain.:* Roseboro, *Glory Days,* 259–87; *Sporting News,* September 11, 1976; Roseboro video interview with Sharp.

175. *proved to be the tonic he needed.:* Roseboro, *Glory Days,* 288–89.

176. *He didn't resent Marichal.:* Author interview with Shelley Roseboro, July 26, 2013; *Los Angeles Times,* August 25, 1975; Roseboro, *Glory Days,* 11, 296.

176. *a larger office down Sunset Boulevard.:* Roseboro, *Glory Days,* 290–91; author interview with Morgan Fouch-Roseboro, August 1, 2013.

177. *a troubling presence between them.:* Roseboro, *Glory Days,* 292; author interview with Shelley Roseboro, July 16, 2013; author interview with Jeri Roseboro, July 29, 2013.

177. *and he hit me with his bat.":* Roseboro, *Glory Days,* 3–7.

178. *he suffered, too," Barbara said.:* Author interview with Barbara Fouch-Roseboro, September 8, 2006.

178. *became their family's home.:* Marichal, *A Pitcher's Story,* 186–88.

179. *with that on my conscience," he said.:* Author interview with Marichal, March 26, 2013.

179. *his 16 seasons in the big leagues.:* Kaplan, *Greatest Game,* 45.

179. *greatest pitcher I ever saw," Gibson said.:* Ottoway News Service, July 30, 1983; Ruck, *Tropic of Baseball,* 85.

180. *not appreciate his sublime finesse.: San Francisco Chronicle,* August 1, 1983; *Elysian Fields Quarterly,* Winter 1998.

181. *which also probably reduced his vote total.: Elysian Fields Quarterly,* Winter 1998.

181. *first living player to be selected by the BBWAA.: Americas,* date unknown.

181. *with a bat," wrote baseball historian Donald Honig.: Elysian Fields Quarterly,* Winter 1998.

182. *because of the Roseboro incident].":* Ottoway News Service, July 30, 1983; *Sporting News,* February 7, 1981; *Sports Illustrated,* January 26, 1981.

182. *moment gone wrong haunted him.: Sporting News,* February 7, 1981.

183. *"So much of it is image and reputation.": San Francisco Chronicle,* January 5, 1983; author interview with Ron Rapaport, August 9, 2013.

183. *It's an uphill battle for Marichal.": Lake County News-Herald,* December 28, 1982.

184. *he would snub them as they had him.: New York Post,* March 17, 1982.

184. *most heartfelt public relations campaign.:* Author interview with Barbara Fouch-Roseboro, September 8, 2006; *Los Angeles Times,* June 30, 2002.

185. (fn.) *during induction weekend in Cooperstown.:* Marichal, *My Journey,* 242.

185. hold the past against us any longer.: Author interview with Barbara Fouch-Roseboro, September 8, 2006; author interview with Marichal, March 26, 2013; author interview with Morgan Fouch-Roseboro, August 1, 2013; Ruck, *Tropic of Baseball,* 85; *Dodger Blue,* June 15, 1983; *Syracuse Post Standard,* January 13, 1983; *Twin Falls Times News,* January 13, 1983.

186. *Johnny forgave me, I was so happy.":* Author interview with Barbara Fouch-Roseboro, September 8, 2006; author interview with Marichal, March 26, 2013.

186. *now is happier than I am," he said.:* Marichal, *My Journey,* 192–93; Associated Press, January 13, 1983.

186. *Both men cried.:* Marichal, *My Journey,* 193; Kaplan, *Greatest Game,* 165; author interview with Barbara Fouch-Roseboro, September 8, 2006.

187. *to the major leagues in later decades.: New York Times,* January 24, 1983; Ruck, *Tropic of Baseball,* 85.

188. *underscored the emotion of his words.: New York Times,* January 24, 1983; Associated Press, August 2, 1983; Marichal, *My Journey,* 197.

188. *the Dominican Republic's favorite son.:* Marichal, *My Journey,* 198.

188. *that became the theme of his day.:* Marichal, *My Journey,* 195.

189. *none prouder than the Dominicans present.:* Marichal, Hall of Fame induction speech; Kaplan, *Greatest Game,* 166; *San Francisco Chronicle,* August 1, 1963; Associated Press, August 2, 1983.

189. *standard bearer for Latin American ballplayers.:* Associated Press, August 2, 1983, Marichal, *My Journey,* 194.

Chapter Ten: The Man behind the Mask

193. *to the possibilities in the Dominican Republic.:* Marichal, *My Journey,* 232.

193. *back into the game. Juan accepted.:* Associated Press, May 17, 1983; Marichal, *My Journey,* 204.

193. *developed players, opened its own.:* Marichal, *My Journey,* 204–5.

194. *"That's the sad part of the job.":* Ibid., 205–9.

194. *business, but I love baseball.": New York Daily News,* May 6, 1987; author interview with Barbara Fouch-Roseboro, September 8, 2006.

194. *Ph.D. in baseball and I can't use it," he said.: New York Daily News,* May 6, 1987.

195. *anything by going to the minors.":* Unidentified newspaper clipping, June 8, 1974.

196. *they don't have the buoyancy.": Los Angeles Times,* August 5, 2008; *Nightline,* April 6, 1987; *New York Daily News,* May 6, 1987; Associated Press, June 21, 1998; author interview with Charlie Blaney, August 21, 2013.

196. *that there is racism in baseball.": Nation,* April 16, 2012.

196. (fn.) *in a major league front office again.:* June 21, 1998; http://espn.go.com/espn/otl/story/_/id/7751398/how-al-campanis-controversial-racial-remarks-cost-career-highlighted-mlb-hiring-practices, March 30, 2012; author interview with Fred Claire, August 21, 2013.

196. *what is going on racial prejudice.":* Roseboro video interview with Sharp; author interview with Shelley Roseboro, July 26, 2013; *New York Daily News,* May 6, 1987.

197. *will change the face of baseball again.": New York Daily News,* May 6, 1987.

197. (fn.) *also when it seemed to level off.: Pacific Stars and Stripes,* August 12, 1990; *Nation,* April 16, 2012; Associated Press, June 21, 1998.

197. *Roseboro's chance came next.:* http://espn.go.com/espn/otl/story/_/id/7751398/how-al-campanis-controversial-racial-remarks-cost-career-highlighted-mlb-hiring-practices, March 30, 2012.

197. *on the resort's world-famous course.:* Author interview with Rafael Avila, August 26, 2013.

197. *the Dominican Republic, Los Tigres del Licey.*: Roseboro video interview with Sharp.

198. *need a vacation," he said with a smile.:* Unidentified newspaper clipping, June 8, 1974.

198. *players know it, which Roseboro loved.:* Author interview with Shelley Roseboro, July 26, 2013.

199. *knew the game so well," Juan said.:* Author interview with Marichal, March 26, 2013.

199. *chauffeured car to the hospital.:* Author interview with Rafael Avila, August 26, 2013.

199. *to him in the Dominican Republic," Juan said.:* Author interviews with Juan Marichal, March 26, 2013, and July 19, 2013.

199. *in five games to win the Series.:* Roseboro video interview with Sharp.

200. *not going to be a manager," Johnny said.:* Ibid.

200. (fn.) *to hire Joe Morgan back in 1983.:* Author interview with Fred Claire, August 21, 2013.

200. *only two managers in 45 years.":* Ibid.

201. *sport after me have continued it.":* Marichal, *My Journey,* 213–20; *Sports Illustrated,* September 15, 1997; Kaplan, *Greatest Game,* 168.

202. *rather anointed their reconciliation.:* Author interview with Roger Guenveur Smith, November 21, 2012.

202. *He did not hide from that.:* Roseboro video interview with Sharp.

202. *it bore no trace of his shame.:* Marichal, *My Journey,* xv.

203. *often underrated—Roseboro had been.: Mansfield (OH) News Journal,* July 6, 1986.

203. *Tony said. "He was very funny.":* Author interview with Tony Roseboro, November 15, 2012.

204. *and visited them when he could.:* Author interview with Morgan Fouch-Roseboro, August 1, 2013; "The Man behind the Mask," handout at John Roseboro funeral, August 24, 2002; author interview with Shelley Roseboro, July 26, 2013.

204. *not have asked for a better father.":* Author interview with Morgan Fouch-Roseboro, August 1, 2013.

204. *last time he visited his hometown.: Ashland Times-Gazette,* May 28, 1996; author interview with Joe Mason, November 23, 2012.

205. *hard, to lose his younger brother.:* Roseboro video interview with Sharp; *Ashland Times-Gazette,* December 16, 1997; Associated Press, December 15, 1997.

205. *I was always in such good shape," he said.:* Roseboro video interview with Sharp.

205. *he told them. "And that's that.":* Roseboro, *Glory Days,* 30; Roseboro video interview with Sharp; "The Man behind the Mask," handout at John Roseboro funeral, August 24, 2002.

206. *off the heart transplant waiting list.: Mansfield (OH) News Journal,* August 20, 2002; *Los Angeles Times,* June 30, 2002; Roseboro video interview with Sharp.

206. *Johnny had hit another bottom.: Los Angeles Times,* June 30, 2002.

206. *you don't make any long-range plans.":* Roseboro video interview with Sharp.

206. *But he also smiled sincerely.:* Ibid.

207. *though he remained in the hospital.: Los Angeles Times,* June 30, 2002.

207. *by the Giants' star pitcher Juan Marichal . . .": Ashland Times-Gazette,* August 20, 2002; *Los Angeles Times,* August 20, 2002; *USA Today,* August 16, 2002; *New York Times,* August 20, 2002.

208. *on and off the baseball diamond.":* Congressional Record, US House of Representatives, September 10, 2002.

208. *first flight he could to Los Angeles.: 108 Magazine,* Summer 2007.

210. *I could have had John Roseboro as my catcher.":* MLB.com, August 27, 2002; author interview with Barbara Fouch-Roseboro, September 8, 2006; author interview with Mark Langill, November 15, 2012; author interview with Marichal, July 19, 2013; author interview with Tony Roseboro, November 15, 2012; author interview with Shelley Roseboro, July 26, 2013; "The Man behind the Mask," handout at John Roseboro funeral, August 24, 2002; author interview with Morgan Fouch-Roseboro, August 1, 2013; author interview with Jeri Roseboro, August 28, 2013.

Bibliography

A note about sources: Game accounts are re-created from box scores, MLB daily logs, and Baseball-Reference.com play-by-plays. Player statistics are derived from MLB daily logs and Baseball-Reference.com.

Articles and Pamphlets

Bjarkman, Peter C. "Dandy, Sandy and the Summer of '65." *Elysian Fields Quarterly*, Winter 1998.

Laughlin, Bob, with Budd Theobald. *Meet the Dodger Family: John Roseboro, the Boy Who Took Over for Campy.* Los Angeles: Union Oil Company, 1960.

———. *The Dodger Family: John Roseboro, Hard-working Dodger Backstop.* Los Angeles: Union Oil Company, 1961.

Regalado, Samuel J. "Latinos within Baseball Purgatory: The Latin Experience in the Minor Leagues, 1950–1968." Paper delivered to North American Society for Sport History conference at University of Louisville, 1984.

Turtis, Richard Lee. "A World Destroyed, a Nation Imposed: The 1937 Haitian Massacre in the Dominican Republic." *Hispanic American Historical Review* 82, no. 3 (2002): 589–635.

Audiovisual Materials

Interview with Shag Crawford by Larry Gerlach. Sound recording, three cassettes.

Interview with John Roseboro by Bonnie Bender Sharp. Video recording. Ashland High School 50th Reunion, Class of 1951. Los Angeles, 2001.

Nightline. ABC News. New York: April 6, 1987. Viewed on youtube.com.

Studio 42 with Bob Costas. MLB Network. Secaucus, NJ: MLB Productions, November 24, 2009.

This Week in Baseball. MLB Network. Secaucus, NJ: MLB Productions, June 1987.

Books

Adelman, Tom. *Black and Blue: The Golden Arm, the Robinson Boys, and the 1966 World Series That Stunned America.* New York: Little, Brown and Co., 2006.

Alston, Walter, with Jack Tobin. *A Year at a Time.* Waco, TX: Word Books, 1976.

Bjarkman, Peter C. *Baseball with a Latin Beat.* Jefferson, NC: McFarland & Company, 1994.

Brosnan, Jim. *The Long Season.* Chicago: Ivan R. Dee, 2002.

———. *Pennant Race.* Chicago: Ivan R. Dee, 2004.

Claire, Fred. *My 30 Years in Dodger Blue.* Champaign, IL: Sports Publishing, 2004.

Cohen, Jerry, and William S. Murphy. *Burn, Baby, Burn! The Los Angeles Race Riot, August 1965.* New York: Dutton & Co., 1966.

Cordova, Cuqui. *Juan Marichal: El Monstruo de Laguna Verde.* Santo Domingo: Omnimedia, 2005.

Dark, Alvin, and John Underwood. *When in Doubt, Fire the Manager: My Life and Times in Baseball.* New York: Dutton, 1980.

Devaney, John. *Juan Marichal: Mr. Strike.* New York: Putnam, 1970.

Díaz, Junot. *The Brief Wondrous Life of Oscar Wao.* New York: Riverhead, 2007.

Ellison, Jim. "Juan Marichal: After the Incident." In *Baseball Stars of 1967,* edited by Ray Robinson, New York: Pyramid, 1965.

Gerlach, Larry R. *The Men in Blue: Conversations with Umpires.* New York: Viking, 1980.

Hano, Arnold. "Juan Marichal: Can He Forget?" In *Baseball Stars of 1966,* edited by Ray Robinson. New York: Pyramid, 1965.

Hirsch, James. *Willie Mays: The Life, the Legend.* New York: Scribner, 2010.

Kaplan, Jim. *The Greatest Game Ever Pitched: Juan Marichal, Warren Spahn, and the Pitching Duel of the Century.* Chicago: Triumph, 2011.

Klein, Alan M. *Sugarball: The American Game, the Dominican Dream.* New Haven, CT: Yale, 1991.

Knapp, H. S. *A History of the Pioneer and Modern Times of Ashland County*. Philadelphia: Lippincott, 1863.

Kurlansky, Mark. *The Eastern Stars: How Baseball Changed the Dominican Town of San Pedro de Macoris*. New York: Riverhead, 2010.

Lanctot, Neil. *Campy: The Two Lives of Roy Campanella*. New York: Simon and Schuster, 2011.

Leavy, Jane. *Sandy Koufax: A Lefty's Legacy*. New York: HarperCollins, 2002.

Marichal, Juan, with Charles Einstein. *A Pitcher's Story: The Greatest Pitcher in the Major Leagues Tells the Inside Story of His Rise to the Top*. New York: Doubleday, 1967.

Marichal, Juan, and Lew Freedman. *Juan Marichal: My Journey from the Dominican Republic to Cooperstown*. Minneapolis: MVP Books, 2011.

Markusen, Bruce. *The Orlando Cepeda Story*. Houston: Piñata, 2001.

Murray, Jim. *The Best of Jim Murray*. New York: Doubleday, 1965.

———. *The Sporting World of Jim Murray*. New York: Doubleday, 1968.

Plaut, David. *Chasing October: The Dodgers-Giants Pennant Race of 1962*. South Bend, IN: Diamond Communications, 1994.

Regalado, Samuel O. *Viva Baseball! Latin Major Leaguers and Their Special Hunger*. Urbana: University of Illinois, 1998.

Roseboro, John, with Bill Libby. *Glory Days with the Dodgers and Other Days with Others*. New York: Atheneum, 1978.

Ruck, Rob. *The Tropic of Baseball: Baseball in the Dominican Republic.* Lincoln: University of Nebraska, 1991.

Shiner, David. *Baseball's Greatest Players: The Saga Continues.* Bridgewater, NJ: Bridgewater Books, 2001.

Tygiel, Jules. *Baseball's Great Experiment: Jackie Robinson and His Legacy.* New York: Oxford University Press, 1983.

Wendel, Tim, and Jose Luis Villegas. *Far from Home: Latino Baseball Players in America.* Washington, DC: National Geographic, 2008.

Wills, Maury, and Mike Celizic. *On the Run: The Never Dull and Often Shocking Life of Maury Wills.* New York: Carroll & Graf, 1991.

Interviews Conducted by Author

Rafael Avila, Charlie Blaney, Chris Box, Fred Claire, Gordon Conrad, Cuqui Cordova, Barbara Fouch-Roseboro, Morgan Fouch-Roseboro, Ted Jacobs, Jack Kelley, Mark Langill, Bruce Macgowan, Juan Marichal, Joe Mason, Roy McHugh, Ross Newhan, John Odell, Jim Perry, Betty Plank, Ron Rapaport, Marc Risman, Jeri Roseboro, Shelley Roseboro, Tony Roseboro, Rob Ruck, Lon Simmons, Roger Guenveur Smith, Gordon Verrell

Journals and Magazines

108 Magazine
All-Star Sports
Americas
APF Reporter
Black Sports
Elysian Fields Quarterly
Life

The Nation
Newsweek
Primera Fila
SABR: The National Pastime
Saturday Evening Post
Sport
Sports Collectors Digest
Sports Illustrated
Time

Miscellaneous

Armour, Mark. Society for American Baseball Research biography project on Jim Brosnan. http://sabr.org/bioproj/person/b15e9d74.

Ashland (OH) High School yearbook, 1951.

Congressional Record, US House of Representatives, September 10, 2002.

Costello, Rory. Society for American Baseball Research biography project on Sam Jones. http://sabr.org/bioproj/person/b2f99b7e.

Los Angeles Dodgers 1959 souvenir yearbook.

Los Angeles Dodgers 1964 official yearbook.

Marichal, Juan. Induction speech, National Baseball Hall of Fame, Cooperstown, NY, July 31, 1983.

Marichal, Juan. Interview with Bruce Markusen, English transcript. Viva Beisbol program, National Baseball Hall of Fame, Cooperstown, NY, November 12, 2008.

Marichal, Juan. MLB daily log, pitching, 1960–75. A. Bartlett Giamatti Research Center, National Baseball Hall of Fame, Cooperstown, NY.

Marichal, Juan. Transaction records, 1957–75. A. Bartlett Giamatti Research Center, National Baseball Hall of Fame, Cooperstown, NY.

McKenna, Brian. Society for American Baseball Research biography project on Joe Cambria. http://sabr.org/bioproj/person/4e7d25a0.

Roseboro, John. Birth certificate. Department of Health, State of Ohio, June 10, 1933.

Roseboro, John. MLB daily log, batting, 1957–70. A. Bartlett Giamatti Research Center, National Baseball Hall of Fame, Cooperstown, NY.

Roseboro, John. Transaction records, 1952–77. A. Bartlett Giamatti Research Center, National Baseball Hall of Fame, Cooperstown, NY.

Sharp, Bonnie. Eulogy at John Roseboro memorial service, August 24, 2002.

Swaine, Rick. Society for American Baseball Research biography project on Roy Campanella. http://sabr.org/bioproj/person/a52ccbb5.

Topps baseball cards, 1958–1975.

E-mails

Bohachel, Ann Shoenagel. E-mail to Bonnie Sharp, August 22, 2002.

Boyer, Harry. E-mail to Bonnie Sharp, August 23, 2002.

Hochsteller, Paul. E-mail to Bonnie Sharp, August 22, 2002.

Schneider, Rolinda Barnett. E-mail to Bonnie Sharp, August 22, 2002.

Letters

Calmus, Dick. Letter to Jack Kelley, September 30, 2011.

Campanis, Jim. Letter to Jack Kelley, October 20, 2011.

Craig, Roger. Letter to Jack Kelley, October 9, 2011.

Demeter, Don. Letter to Jack Kelley, October 11, 2011.

Duffie, John. Letter to Jack Kelley, September 28, 2011.

Egan, Dick. Letter to Jack Kelley, October 17, 2011.

Gray, Dick. Letter to Jack Kelley, October 27, 2011.

Harkness, Tim. Letter to Jack Kelley, October 17, 2011.

Kipp, Fred. Letter to Jack Kelley, September 26, 2011.

McMullen, Ken. Letter to Jack Kelley, November 17, 2011.

Miller, Larry. Letter to Jack Kelley, October 26, 2011.

Moeller, Joe. Letter to Jack Kelley, October 13, 2011.

Moon, Wally. Letter to Jack Kelley, September 26, 2011.

Osteen, Claude. Letter to Jack Kelley, October 25, 2011.

Peranowski, Ron. Letter to Jack Kelley, December 12, 2011.

Pignatano, Joe. Letter to Jack Kelley, September 26, 2011.

Singer, Bill. Letter to Jack Kelley, October 28, 2011.

Torborg, Jeff. Letter to Jack Kelley, October 7, 2011.

Trazewski, Dick. Letter to Jack Kelley, October 19, 2011.

Warwick, Carl. Letter to Jack Kelley, November 13, 2011.

Williams, Stan. Letter to Jack Kelley, September 19, 2011.

Worthington, Al. Letter to Jack Kelley, September 26, 2011.

Zimmer, Don. Letter to Jack Kelley, October 27, 2011.

Newspapers and News Organizations

Albany Times-Union

Ashland Times-Gazette

Associated Press

Atlanta Journal

Baltimore Sun

Boston Globe

Boston Herald American

Houston Chronicle

Kansas City Star

Lake County (OH) News-Herald

Long Beach Press-Telegram

Los Angeles Herald-Examiner

Los Angeles Times

Mansfield (OH) News Journal

Milwaukee Sentinel

Minneapolis Star Tribune

Newark Star-Ledger

News Dispatch

Newspaper Enterprise Association

New York Daily News

New York Journal-American

New York Post

New York Sun

New York Times

New York World-Telegram and Sun

Ottoway News Service

Pacific Stars and Stripes

Philadelphia Evening Bulletin

San Francisco Chronicle

San Francisco Examiner

Sporting News

St. Louis Post-Dispatch

Syracuse Herald American

Syracuse Post Standard

Toledo Blade

Tri-City (WA) Herald

Twin Falls (ID) Times-News

United Press International

USA Today

La Voz Hispana de Colorado

La Voz Nueva de Colorado

Wall Street Journal

Washington Post

Wilmington (NC) Star-News

Websites

ashlandohiogenealogy.org

baseballalmanac.com

baseballhall.org

baseballlibrary.com

baseball-reference.com

bbc.co.uk

countrystudies.us/dominican-republic

csmonitor.com

dodgers-giants.com

ESPN.com

foxsportswest.com

hardballtimes.com

imdb.com

mlb.com

npr.org

scouts.baseball.org

spartacus.schoolnet.co.uk

sportsillustrated.cnn.com

thatsbaseball1.tripod.com

youtube.com

Index

C

S

About the Author

John Rosengren is the award-winning author of seven previous books. His most recent is *Hank Greenberg: The Hero of Heroes,* the definitive biography of the Hall of Fame baseball player and America's first Jewish superstar. Prior to that, he wrote *Hammerin' Hank, George Almighty and the Say Hey Kid: The Year That Changed Baseball Forever,* which chronicles the 1973 MLB season. His other books include *Blades of Glory: The True Story of a Young Team Bred to Win* and a collaboration with Esera Tuaolo, *Alone in the Trenches: My Life as a Gay Man in the NFL.* Rosengren's articles have appeared in *Men's Journal, Reader's Digest, Runner's World, Sports Illustrated, Tennis,* and *Utne Reader,* among other publications. He is a member of the Society for American Baseball Research and the American Society of Journalists and Authors. Rosengren lives with his wife, Maria, and their two children in Minneapolis. He plays catcher for the Richfield Rockets in the Federal League.

www.fightoftheirlives.net
www.johnrosengren.net
@johnrosengren
facebook.com/john.rosengren.3